Philosophy for Linguists

... a much needed resource, boiling down the daunting mass of philosophical writings on language to a clear and readable introduction to who said what and why.

Catriona McPherson, University of Leeds

Philosophy for Linguists provides students with a clear, concise introduction to the main topics in the philosophy of language.

Focusing on what linguists need to know and how philosophy relates to modern linguistics, the book is structured around key branches of linguistics, including semantics, pragmatics and language acquisition. Assuming no prior knowledge of philosophy, Siobhan Chapman traces the history and development of ideas in the philosophy of language, and outlines the contributions of specific philosophers. The book is highly accessible and student-oriented, and includes:

- a general introduction and introductions to each chapter
- numerous examples and quotations
- comprehensive suggestions for further reading
- an extensive glossary of philosophical terms

Siobhan Chapman is a lecturer in the Department of English Language and Literature at the University of Liverpool.

Philosophy for Linguists

An introduction

Siobhan Chapman

London and New York

First published 2000
by Routledge
11 New Fetter Lane, London EC4P 4EE

Simultaneously published in the USA and Canada
by Routledge
29 West 35th Street, New York, NY 10001

Routledge is an imprint of the Taylor & Francis Group

© 2000 Siobhan Chapman

Typeset in Sabon by Taylor & Francis Books Ltd
Printed and bound in Great Britain by St Edmundsbury Press,
Bury St Edmunds, Suffolk

British Library Cataloguing in Publication Data
A catalogue record for this book is available from the British Library

Library of Congress Cataloging in Publication Data
Chapman, Siobhan, 1968–
Philosophy for linguists: an introduction / Siobhan Chapman
Includes bibliographical references and index.
1. Language and languages – Philosophy. I. Title.

P106 .C513 2000
401–dc21   99–462292

ISBN 0–415–20658–8 (hbk)
ISBN 0–415–20659–6 (pbk)

For Chris

Acknowledgements

The idea for this book arose when I was teaching linguistics and English language at the University of Kent at Canterbury. Some of my students were understandably dismayed by the occasional references to philosophy I was making, and asked if I could suggest something which would explain these in more detail. When I found that I couldn't really recommend a book to suit their exact needs, I decided I would just have to write one myself. I am therefore grateful to my students at Kent for, in effect, coming up with the idea, and also to Tony Bex, my colleague at the time, for convincing me that it was a good one, and encouraging me to get it published.

I would also like to thank the linguistics team at Routledge, who have seen this project through from initial idea to finished product with efficiency, cheerfulness and, where necessary, patience.

Finally but most importantly, my thanks to Christopher Routledge and Catriona McPherson, who read the first and second drafts, respectively, and commented on them in detail. Their suggestions, both specific and more general, were invariably insightful. All the faults and any errors which remain are, of course, my own, but without their help there would undoubtedly have been many more.

Introduction

Anyone who studies linguistics will, sooner or later, come across references to philosophy. These may be to general philosophical themes and concepts, or to the ideas of individual philosophers and schools of thought. Either way, students of linguistics will probably find themselves looking for some guidance in understanding how the philosophy referred to relates to their interest in language. But even if they know where to start, they are likely to end up grappling with complex philosophical works, or with introductions to them which don't make any mention of linguistics. This book is intended for just these people. Its aim is to introduce some topics from the history of philosophy, and to explain their relevance for present-day linguists.

It's not surprising that there is so much philosophy in linguistics. Linguistics itself is a fairly recent academic discipline, but much of our current thinking about language has developed from ideas which date from the decades and centuries before it came into being. Many of these were originally put forward by philosophers. So some areas of the study of language can be seen, at least in part, as originating within philosophy and only later becoming a focus of the new discipline of linguistics. And all areas have benefited from discussions of the nature of language, and particularly the nature of meaning, which are to be found in philosophy. As we will see, these discussions are relevant even to those who see themselves as primarily concerned with language as a means of communication, or a type of human behaviour, and may therefore be tempted to question the importance of detailed philosophical analysis to their interests.

Throughout this book, no prior knowledge of philosophy is assumed; philosophers and their ideas are introduced from scratch as they are needed. However, because the book is primarily intended for those following specialist courses in language, or those who already have a general interest in the subject, there isn't much detailed explanation of the ideas and theories of present-day linguistics. Some of these are mentioned later in this introduction, and can be followed up in the books recommended in the 'further reading' section at the end of it. But we will begin by looking at the branch of philosophy we will be concerned with, and the reasons why we will chiefly be limiting ourselves to this area.

The philosophy

Philosophy has been practised, in various forms, for thousands of years and in all parts of the world. In this book, however, we will be concentrating chiefly on work from twentieth-century Britain and America. This is certainly not intended to suggest that the works we will be looking at are the only ones of interest to linguists, or that highly important work on language hasn't been produced at other times and in other places. But twentieth-century philosophy in English, particularly of the tradition which has become known as *analytic philosophy*, has had the most obvious and direct influence on the development of linguistics as an academic discipline. This is perhaps some excuse for such a narrow focus; the references to philosophy which students of linguistics come across are most likely to be to analytic philosophy. Twentieth-century philosophy didn't, of course, emerge from a vacuum, and we will be looking at some of the work which influenced its development, particularly work from Ancient Greece, and from seventeenth- and eighteenth-century Europe. But we won't be looking at important work on language from other periods, such as medieval philosophy, or from non-Western traditions, such as Indian and Chinese philosophies.

Analytic philosophy, as its name suggests, is an approach to the subjects and problems of philosophy which relies on detailed analysis. In particular, complex notions and problems are analysed, or 'broken down' into smaller components so that they can be better understood, or perhaps even shown not to be problems at all. Early analytic philosophy was concerned with the logical relationships between individual concepts and propositions. It can arguably be seen as originating in the work of the German philosopher Gotlob Frege at the end of the nineteenth century, and being exemplified in England by the work of philosophers such as Bertrand Russell. During the early twentieth century, this branch of philosophy took what is sometimes described as a 'linguistic turn', the emphasis switching to the language in which philosophy was expressed, and hence to language itself as a legitimate topic of serious philosophical investigation. This type of analytic philosophy also became known as 'linguistic philosophy', a term which is applied in particular to the work of the philosophers of the British school of 'ordinary language philosophy' such as Peter Strawson and John Austin. We will be looking at some of the work of the philosophers mentioned in this paragraph, and many others, in the course of this book.

The other major development in twentieth century philosophy in which language has played a central part, and one which is often contrasted with analytic philosophy, is *continental philosophy*. This term is applied to a type of philosophy produced in continental Europe, and is closely associated with names such as Foucault, Lyotard and Derrida. The philosophical method of this school, which is often reflected in the style of writing used, is based on rhetoric and argument. It rejects the idea of fixed, certain meaning, and therefore the possibility of reaching understanding by rigorous analysis of the language in which philosophical problems are expressed; the language itself is open to interpretation and negotiation. This philosophical tradition has proved very important in the development of critical theory.

Continental philosophy, then, is highly relevant to any discussion of present-day literary criticism, but less immediately so to one of linguistics. We won't be looking at it here, but some suggestions are made in the 'further reading' section for those interested in this area. Of particular relevance to the difference between analytical and continental philosophy is the written debate between John Searle and Jacques Derrida. Derrida's criticisms of 'speech act theory', Searle's response to this, and Derrida's reply, show up the differences between their approaches to language and their styles of philosophy. Derrida's rejection of the possibility of reasoned analysis and rational discussion is reflected in his intricate, playful style of argument.

It isn't hard to find points of similarity between analytic philosophy and present-day linguistics. Both disciplines could be said to place a high value on logical argument, on attention to detail, and on the careful analysis of complex wholes into their constituent parts. The growing acceptance of language as a legitimate focus of philosophical study, for which the analytic school was largely responsible, can be seen as one of the factors which made linguistics as an academic subject possible.

The linguistics

Unlike many philosophers over the centuries, linguists take it for granted that *natural language* is an interesting and important subject to study in its own right. This term is generally used to distinguish naturally occurring human languages such as, for instance, English, Polish and Urdu, from artificial languages, such as those used in logic, in computing and in various forms of coding. Languages from these two categories may well have a lot in common, but natural languages are, nevertheless, seen as belonging to a separate and definable class. It is the task of linguists to describe and analyse the features of this class.

Almost any generalisation about natural language will be controversial, because so many different ideas and opposing theories are current in linguistics. Insofar as we need to make assumptions about natural language, and about the nature of linguistics, we will be using those outlined very briefly in the next three paragraphs. However, this book isn't intended to relate philosophical ideas to any one particular type of linguistics, and we'll be considering some other current ways of describing language in the final section of each chapter.

On one view, then, the description of a natural language is divided into three different categories: the phonological, the semantic and the syntactic. The phonological description of a language concerns the way in which its sounds are patterned and related. Semantics concerns the meanings of the individual words contained in a language, and also the meanings which result when these words are combined in various ways. Syntax is the study of these ways of combining words: the regularities which can be observed in the construction of sentences. These three branches of linguistic description are seen as totally separate and independent from each other, but together they make up the *grammar* of the language. A grammar can be described as what it is that people know when they can be said to 'know' a language, and is what linguists are attempting to model in describing a language.

Grammar, in this version of linguistics, is said to be *generative*. That is, it consists of a series of rules which are sufficient to generate, or produce, all the possible sentences of a language. In this way, a language can be described as a set of sentences. It is the set of all the sentences generated by the rules of the grammar, of all the grammatical sentences. The set is infinite; you could never produce a definitive list of all the possible sentences of, say, English. However, it is produced, or generated, by a finite number of rules which it is, in principle at least, possible to list. There are two types of rules in the grammar of any natural language: *generative rules* and *transformational rules*. The generative rules produce a series of deep structures. It is at the level of deep structure that semantics, or logical form, is determined. The transformational rules act on the deep structures to produce surface structures; at this level the details of structure and word order are determined.

The description of linguistics outlined above owes a lot to the American linguist Noam Chomsky, whose work we will consider in Chapter 5. As we shall see, Chomsky developed his influential ideas on language from the late 1950s onwards. However, some of the basics of present-day linguistics, and some which would be accepted even by those who would argue against a 'Chomskyan' approach to the study of language, date back earlier in the century. For instance, in 1938 the philosopher Charles Morris suggested that the study of language could be divided into a number of distinct branches. Particularly significantly, he argued that the study of syntax must be completely separate from semantics, and that it must consist of 'formation rules' and 'transformation rules'. Indeed, the idea that we need to distinguish between the 'underlying', logical form of a sentence, which is chiefly responsible for determining meaning, and its 'surface', grammatical form, can be traced back even further. As we will see, related ideas can be found in the work of the philosophers Bertrand Russell and Ludwig Wittgenstein.

In this book, we shall be looking at some of the ways in which philosophical thinking has contributed to current ideas about the grammar of natural language. We will be concentrating on syntax and semantics; we won't be looking directly at the interface between philosophy and phonology. Of course, not all linguists are engaged in the detailed study of the syntax, the semantics or the phonology of natural language. These are the three 'core' areas of linguistic description; they tell us a lot about language, but nothing at all about how people actually use language, how the context of use affects what they say and mean, or what consequences their use of it can have. These issues are studied in branches of linguistics such as pragmatics, discourse analysis and sociolinguistics. We will be just as interested in the contribution made by philosophy to thinking in these areas as we will in its contribution to 'core' areas of linguistic study.

Overview

Even within the restrictions outlined above, the range of philosophical writings relevant to linguistics is vast. What we will be studying in this book is by necessity only a selection of these, in terms both of subject matter and of individual philosophers. Each of the five chapters is concerned with one, necessarily broad, topic from philosophy. The philosophers whose work is used are chosen because they have been particularly significant in the development of thinking in this area, or can be seen as representative of ideas which are of current relevance to linguistics. Inevitably, much is left out, but the detailed study of philosophical topics, and even of the work of individual philosophers, is beyond the scope of this book.

Each chapter follows the same general format. In the introductory section some problems or general issues relating to language are presented. These are problems which are relevant to linguists, in that they are concerned with natural language as a focus of interest in its own right. The bulk of each chapter will be concerned with the ideas of philosophers who have discussed these issues, and where necessary with a comparison between different, sometimes competing, ideas on the same topic. Each chapter concludes with an assessment of what these have contributed to our understanding of the issues identified at the outset, and their influence, direct or indirect, on various branches of present-day linguistics. There is also a 'further reading' section in each chapter, which suggests directions in which the main topics can be explored further. This includes both some of the more readable of the works covered, and also introductory or more advanced discussions of them.

If there is a general theme which brings together all the topics we will be considering, it is the nature of meaning. Meaning is of central importance to all branches of philosophy concerned with the study of language. In this we can include not just the work of those philosophers who can be labelled as interested in 'the philosophy of language', but of all those who have worked in the philosophy of subjects such as mathematics, logic, knowledge and thought, who have had cause to think about the language in which their ideas are expressed. The questions which have confronted, and continue to confront such philosophers, are not generally, or not most strikingly, of the 'what does this word mean?' type. Rather, they have considered what it is to say that one thing 'means' another and, particularly, to say that some part of a language system 'means' something which is outside of that language system. This relationship between the linguistic and the non-linguistic is central to any attempt to describe language.

We begin, in Chapter 1, by considering what has been said about the most basic aspect of this relationship: the relationship between words and things. We will look at what philosophers from classical times onwards have claimed about what it is for a word to 'mean' some thing or concept, and consider the influence their ideas have had on the present-day study of lexical semantics. In Chapter 2 we broaden our study to include the meaning not just of individual words but of sentences, considering the propositions which they express. We will also consider the significance of basic logic, including logical relationships such as entailment and presupposition, in linguistics. Chapter 3 is concerned not so much with the relationships which exist between expressions of a language, but the relationships between those expressions and reality, and in particular the relationship between meaning and truth. We will be considering a number of ways which have been proposed by philosophers, and subsequently by linguists, to account for what it means to attach the labels 'true' and 'false' to sentences, or the propositions they express.

Chapter 4 broadens the discussion still further to consider not just language, but the contexts in which it is used. We will see that making statements of fact which can be labelled either 'true' or 'false' is just one of the many tasks in which speakers use language, and that a full linguistic account therefore needs to do rather more than simply assign truth-values to propositions. We will also see that logical relationships such as entailment simply aren't adequate for the purpose of explaining the many complicated ways in which people use and understand language. There are other relationships, such as various types of 'implicature', which often seem to be at odds with logic, but which describe more accurately what goes on in conversation. It is in this chapter that we will look at the branch of analytic philosophy known as ordinary language philosophy, and consider how it has contributed to the development of pragmatics.

Finally, Chapter 5 is concerned with the relationship between language and mind. A great deal has been written on this by both philosophers and linguists. We will concentrate mainly on the debate between 'behaviourist' and 'nativist' accounts of language: very generally, the question of whether language is best described as a type of behaviour observable within a community, or a type of knowledge complete in an individual. We will consider how these two philosophies have contributed to the development of 'empiricist' and 'mentalist' traditions in linguistics. In each of these traditions, work has been produced which attempts to explain the processes of language acquisition, and more generally the nature of language itself.

The book ends with a glossary of some of the key terms introduced. This concentrates on philosophical terms, which are likely to be unfamiliar to those studying linguistics.

Further reading

The introduction to Glock (1997) *The Rise of Analytic Philosophy* offers an interesting discussion of the development and possible definitions of the tradition. Glock argues that an interest in language isn't a defining characteristic; much continental philosophy also uses the terminology of linguistics. The book, which consists of a collection of essays on the subject, is itself a good illustration of the disagreement which exists about the appropriate definition, and the significance, of analytic philosophy. Dummett (1993) *The Seas of Language* is a much more extensive, and difficult, collection of essays on analytic philosophy, concentrating particularly on the work of Wittgenstein. In these essays, Dummett is particularly interested in the relationship between language and thought.

Many introductions to continental philosophy have been written, often concentrating on its application to literary criticism. See for instance Eagleton (1983) *Literary Theory*, especially Chapter 4, and Seldon (1989) *Practising Theory and Reading Literature*, also Chapter 4. The debate between Derrida and Searle can be found in the journal *Glyph* from 1977. All of Derrida's contributions to the debate are collected in the more easily available (1988) *Limited Inc*.

Chomsky set out what can perhaps be seen as the basic manifesto for the type of linguistics discussed here, particularly for transformational grammar, in his first, short book *Syntactic Structures* (1957); see particularly Chapter 3. There are many introductions to modern linguistics available, for instance O'Grady *et al.* (1997) *Contemporary Linguistics*. Rather more detailed, but restricted in scope, is Smith and Wilson (1990) *Modern Linguistics*. For a detailed introduction to transformational theory, see Haegman (1994) *Introduction to Government and Binding Theory*, and Radford (1988) *Transformational Grammar*. The ideas of Charles Morris referred to in this chapter were published in his (1938) article 'Foundations of the theory of signs'. We will look at the work of Russell and Wittgenstein in Chapters 2 and 3.

1 Words and things

Introduction

Much of what goes on in linguistics can be described under the general heading of 'analysis'. Linguistic analysis involves, for instance, identifying and describing the structures and sounds of a language, and attempting to explain the relationships between them. But that isn't the whole story. Linguistics is a discipline which concerns itself with the study of language in all its aspects and, as linguists, we need to consider how the individual elements of a language relate not just to each other, but to the world outside. We need to study not only the relationships *within* a linguistic system, but also those *between* this system and the things it describes. After all, it is only through such relationships that language functions as it does in communication. To study only the internal structures and relationships of a language might tell us a lot about its complexities and regularities, but it would somehow 'miss the point'; we would be no nearer to being able to explain how language actually 'works' than we were when we started.

Part of the task of explaining how language works is to account for the obvious difference between examples such as 1) and 2); in general, 1) is accepted to be 'true', while 2) is labelled 'false'.

1) A kangaroo is an animal.
2) Zebras have wings.

Another part of the task is to describe how speakers use language for particular purposes: how 3) might count sometimes as a question and sometimes as a request, and how 4), although labelled 'false', might sometimes be used to communicate something which is true.

3) Can you reach the top shelf.
4) My flatmate is a machine.

These are issues which we will address in Chapters 3 and 4, but first we need to establish how the component parts of these sentences contribute to our interpretations. Our examples are made up of individual words such as *kangaroo*, *zebras* and *flatmate*. Before we can discuss what sentences 'mean', and what speakers might 'mean' by what they say, we need to establish what we are talking about when we discuss the meanings of these words.

There might not seem to be much of a problem here. 'Surely', a cynical non-linguist might say, 'if you want to know what *kangaroo* means you only have to look it up in a dictionary – the whole point of dictionaries is to give the meanings of words'. If we do as the cynic suggests and reach for our dictionary, we will read that a kangaroo is 'a large Australian herbivorous marsupial'. But this hasn't got us any further forward. We haven't got outside the linguistic system at all; we have simply complicated things by introducing other words such as *marsupial*. What we have obtained from the dictionary is not in fact the meaning of the word, but a definition of one word by means of a series of other words.

Our cynical friend is not going to give up that easily. He takes us on a trip to a zoo and positions us in front of a certain enclosure. 'There', he says, pointing at a particular animal, '*That* is a kangaroo. That's what the word means'. Again we have to explain patiently that it's not quite as simple as that. It might seem reasonable (although it's far from uncontroversial, as we will see) that the brownish creature over there, or the group of such creatures, is the meaning of the word *kangaroo* in 1) above. But our friend might find it harder to point at the meaning of, say, *bird*. He would need to decide on one particular creature to point at, making a choice between, say, the penguins, the ostriches and the parrots. Drawing a picture of a bird-like figure would hardly help; our friend would need to make a series of decisions about what counted as an essential feature of 'bird-hood'. Whatever his final drawing looked like it would be bound to bear little resemblance to some of the creatures in the zoo labelled 'bird'; if his drawing bore a reasonable resemblance to a canary it could hardly pass for a sketch of a flamingo. Finally, no matter how carefully he searches the zoo, our friend won't be able to point at anything and say 'There, that's what *unicorn* means'. But that is hardly grounds for saying that the word *unicorn* is meaningless; it's a perfectly acceptable word of the English language. At this point our friend is forced to admit that there is more to linguistics than he thought.

The problems which we have just been considering have been discussed in philosophy for well over two thousand years. Many of the philosophers who have contributed to the discussion have done so because they were interested in its implications for their study of knowledge, or of logic, or of the nature of reality. Their contributions have therefore had varying degrees of relevance to linguists and, as we will see, some have been taken on as basic premises of linguistics, while others have been more or less abandoned. Nevertheless, it's worthwhile for linguists to study a discussion which has concerned itself with so many of the questions raised by the relationship between words and things.

One of the earliest points of discussion, and one which has remained central, is the question of whether words can in fact be said to refer directly to things at all. This may at first appear an odd, even an unnecessary question to ask, but we saw earlier that it was one which caused problems for our cynical friend, especially when he tried to relate the word *bird* directly to an object. He knew very well what it meant for something to be called a bird, and could identify any number of individual birds; he could also talk about birds when there were none actually present. But there was no one specimen which met the definition completely. One way of answering the question might be to say that it's not objects themselves to which words refer, but our *idea* of objects; the word *bird* refers to an idea, or mental image, of what a bird is like. This answer has been suggested by those philosophers who subscribe to an **ideational** account of meaning. According to such accounts, we use words to refer to our internal impressions, which are derived from our experiences of the world. One of the biggest problems facing ideational accounts of meaning, however, is related to the problem our friend encountered when he tried to draw an explanatory picture of a bird. It's the problem posed by 'general ideas'; an idea of 'bird' would have to be general enough to be compatible with any individual example of a bird, but would therefore run into danger of being *too* general to count as a coherent meaning.

An alternative approach to meaning, one which avoids the problem of general ideas, is known as the *direct reference* account. This is more or less the account adopted by our friend when he tried pointing at animals to explain meaning. The meaning of a word such as *bird* is simply the set of individual objects to which it applies. The meaning of an individual name such as *Charles Darwin*, or description such as *the head keeper*, is simply the particular individual referred to. This is to describe meaning in terms of **denotation**. A word or phrase denotes a certain object or objects in the world. However, in many cases direct reference on its own is not enough to explain meaning. Remember the problem our friend had explaining why *unicorn* is a legitimate word in English. If meaning were simply reference then *unicorn* should be a nonsense word, because there is nothing which it denotes. But we could taunt our friend with 5) and not be accused of talking nonsense.

5) Search as hard as you like, you won't find any unicorns.

And furthermore, we can assure him of the truth of 6) without having any idea what the denotation *of the biggest animal in the zoo* is. To find out what this phrase refers to would require a lot of hard and potentially dangerous work with a tape measure, but we can use the phrase, and use it perfectly coherently, without knowing, or caring, what animal actually fits the description.

6) That gate has to be wide enough for the biggest animal in the zoo to get through.

Examples such as these are generally explained by saying that words don't just have denotations, they also have connotations. The word **connotation** is used informally to describe properties which are implied or suggested; you might, for instance, be advised to avoid using a word because it has 'bad connotations'. In linguistics and philosophy the word has a much more specific meaning. It is used to describe the particular properties which make a word or phrase applicable. The phrase *the head keeper* will denote one particular individual at any one time, and its denotation will vary from time to time depending on retirements, promotions and so on. But it connotes a property, the property of being head keeper, and the property itself remains constant. A similar distinction is made between the **extension** and **intension** of an expression. The extension of a singular term such as *the head keeper* is, again, just the person who happens to hold that post at any one time, while the extension of a general term such as *elephant* is the set of all individual elephants. The intension of a word or phrase, like the connotation, can be seen as a property, or set of properties, which remain constant. These properties describe the relevant individual or individuals, and can therefore be seen as a set of criteria for determining the extension at any given time.

We are now in a position to explain examples 5) and 6). The term *unicorn* doesn't denote anything; it has no extension. But 5) is nevertheless a meaningful sentence because *unicorn* has a connotation, or intension; we know what type of (non-existent) animal we are talking about, just as we know that no such animal exists. Similarly, *the biggest animal in the zoo* connotes a particular property, and we can discuss the animal which has that property without knowing what specific animal it is, without knowing the denotation of the phrase. In both these cases, then, it is intension rather than extension which is central to explaining the 'meaning' contributed to sentences by individual words and phrases. There are, of course, situations in which the opposite is true: in which extension is central. Imagine the question in 7) appearing in a history exam.

7) *Q* Who was the Monarch of England in 1600?
   Ai Elizabeth I.
   Aii The person with supreme power over the laws and government of the kingdom.

The first answer would get you full marks. It gives the extension of the term *the Monarch of England in 1600*, by indicating the actual individual it refers to. The second answer, however, would probably be considered to be facetious, or else to have seriously missed the point of the question. It gives the intension of the term by describing the properties which determine its application. Both answers might be argued to give 'the meaning' of *the Monarch of England in 1600*, but it is quite clear that the 'right' answer to the question is the extensional, rather than the intensional, meaning.

There is a particular type of sentence which highlights the distinction between intension and extension, and which would be problematic for an account of meaning which didn't distinguish between the two. Consider the following scenario. A stockbroker, let's call him Clarence, frequents his local Conservative club most Friday evenings, and knows several of the other members, at least to nod to. One in particular, whom he knows only as Archibald, he occasionally has a chat with while they wait at the bar, and Clarence is inclined on the whole to think that Archibald is a good sort. Now it so happens that Clarence falls on hard times. Due to an unprecedented slump in the stock market his regular income all but dries up, and before he knows it, he is overdrawn at the bank. Much to his chagrin he receives a particularly stern letter from his bank manager, whom he doesn't know, but whose signature he makes out to be 'A. Braeburn-Twinsett'. He concludes that Braeburn-Twinsett must be a very rude and unsympathetic fellow. However, on the occasions when he visits the Conservative club, now rather less frequently, he still occasionally chats to Archibald, and still gets on well with him. Now it just so happens that 'A. Braeburn-Twinsett' is Archibald, who has never told Clarence what his surname is, or what he does for a living. In this context, we would be justified in saying that 8) is an accurate statement of Clarence's views, but we would have to admit that 9) is most definitely not true.

8)   Clarence believes that Archibald is a jolly nice chap.
9)   Clarence believes that Braeburn-Twinsett is a jolly nice chap.

The problem is that the names *Archibald* and *Braeburn-Twinsett* denote the same individual, so if 8) is true it seems logical that 9) must be true as well, or else Clarence must hold two opposing views about the same person. The solution, of course, is that although the two names have the same extension, they don't have the same intension. As far as Clarence is concerned, *Archibald* is 'the chap in the Conservative club' and *Braeburn-Twinsett* is 'my bank manager'. It is the intension of the names which is relevant to the 'meaning' of 8) and 9).[1] These examples couldn't be explained if meaning consisted simply of the object denoted, as our cynical friend originally suggested when he tried to explain meaning by pointing to animals in the zoo. As we shall see, examples such as these have been described as involving 'intensional contexts', precisely because they present situations in which the intension of an expression, rather than its extension, are relevant to questions of meaning and related decisions about truth and falsity. Examples 8) and 9) are also known as *referentially opaque contexts*, or simply **opaque contexts**. To be opaque is the opposite of being transparent; in these contexts you can't 'see through' to the reference of the relevant names.

Before we look at some of the ways in which philosophers have approached such questions, we need to consider one other function which words sometimes serve. Again, it's easiest to do this by considering a pair of examples.

10) Writers are often troubled people.
11) Writers rhymes with lighters.

Example 10) is not a problem for the account of meaning we have outlined so far. The word *writers* is here being used to refer to a group of people who are the extension of the term, and of whom it is said that they are often troubled. But the same cannot be said about 11). Here *writers* can't be referring to a group of people at all; it makes no sense to say that people 'rhyme' with anything. It is only words which can be said to rhyme, and so 11) can only be understood as a statement about the word *writers* itself. It's the word itself, rather than its extension, which is being referred to. As further evidence of this, note that 11) only makes sense with the singular verb, *rhymes*. The sentence would make no sense if we changed it to *rhyme* to agree with the plural noun *writers*, as in 'Writers rhyme with lighters'.

The distinction between examples such as 10) and 11) is generally referred to as the difference between the *use* of a word and its *mention*. Example 10) includes a use of the word *writers*; it refers to its usual extension. In 11), however, the word is mentioned without being used; it refers only to the word itself. Note that the word *lighters* is also mentioned here rather than used; 11) is concerned with the word *lighters*, not with its extension. This distinction is conventionally signalled by putting a word which is being mentioned into quotation marks. We therefore get pairs such as:

12) Gladys has a nice name.
13) 'Gladys' is a nice name.

Example 12) is about a particular person, denoted by *Gladys*, of whom it is said that she has a nice name. Example 13), however, is about a particular name, denoted by *'Gladys'*, of which it is said that it *is* a nice name. Later, we will look at some of the consequences of this account, and at some of the objections which have been raised to it.

In this chapter we will be concerned mainly with the relationship between objects and the words which name them. In other words, we will be considering the meanings of concrete nouns and noun phrases. This in part reflects the emphasis of much of the philosophy we will be studying. From the earliest times, philosophers have been interested in the relationship between physical objects, together with the impressions they impart to the five senses, and the words which people use for them. As we will see, however, there is also a long tradition of discussing the terms which are used to describe properties, such as *just* and *good*. As linguists, we are used to labelling these *adjectives*, but in philosophical discussion they are more often described as *predicates*; they can be predicated of nouns in statements such as 'Caesar is just' and 'peace is good'. We will touch on the meaning of predicates where relevant in what follows, but we will reserve more detailed study of them for Chapter 2.

Classical philosophy

Interest in the relationship between words and things can be traced back to classical philosophy, often described as the foundations of the Western philosophical tradition. The terms 'classical philosophy' and, less common nowadays, 'the philosophy of the Ancients', are used to refer to the philosophical writings which have survived from ancient Greece and Rome. Perhaps the most influential of classical philosophers, as well as the best known, are Plato and his pupil Aristotle, who lived and worked in ancient Greece in the fifth and fourth centuries BC. The origins of the philosophical treatment of such topics as politics, ethics, science, aesthetics and indeed language have been traced to their work.

Most of Plato's philosophical writings are in the form of dialogues. In these, two or more characters discuss and debate philosophical issues, often in an informal and conversational style. In general in Plato's dialogues there is one character who acts as teacher, and guides one or more pupils towards a better understanding of the chosen topic by asking a series of leading questions. In Plato's early writings at least, the teacher is called 'Socrates', and is generally taken to represent the character and ideas of Plato's own teacher Socrates. It's only through these dialogues that we know of the teachings of Socrates, who didn't himself leave any written record of his ideas.

To understand Plato's account of the relationship between words and objects, we need to look at one of his most famous ideas, the 'theory of Forms'. Plato posits the existence of **Ideal Forms**, sometimes known as *Platonic Ideals*. These are the ideal, or perfect versions of qualities and objects which enable us to make sense of the world around us. Our knowledge of them is innate, meaning that we are born with it as part of our human nature rather than gaining it through experience. Platonic Ideals are not themselves tangible objects; it's perhaps easiest to think of them as being the templates, or patterns, of all individual objects. As such, they are absolute and unchanging. There exists an ideal version of, for instance, Justice, although we don't experience this Ideal when we experience some individual manifestation of justice. Similarly, there are Ideal versions of Table, Dog and Triangle, but all we ever experience are individual, imperfect tables, dogs and triangles. These Forms are sometimes also described as 'Ideas'. This term shouldn't be taken to suggest that Platonic Forms exist only in the human mind. Plato seems to understand Ideal Forms as being universal properties which have a real, but intangible existence.

Plato's account of Ideal Forms is developed over a number of his dialogues. One such dialogue is *Phaedo* which, like many of them, is named after one of the pupils whom Socrates instructs. Socrates conducts a dialogue with a group of his pupils, in which he leads them to understand that any judgement that two objects display 'equality' must be based on knowledge of a perfect version of Equality, which serves as an 'absolute standard'. He goes on to argue that the same must hold for other characteristics, such as beauty, goodness, uprightness and holiness. Our judgements of all these qualities depend on knowledge of Ideal Forms. Socrates distinguishes between individual, 'concrete' objects, observable by means of the senses, and the Forms, which are 'constant': 'And these [concrete objects] you can touch and see and perceive with the senses, but the unchanging things you can only grasp with the mind – they are invisible and are not seen' (79a).[2]

Plato's account of how words relate to, or name, objects and qualities depends on the relationship between imperfect concrete individuals and constant Ideal Forms. If we see something with the appropriate properties, we call it beautiful, not because it is the same as the Ideal of Beauty, but because it is similar enough to it to be given that name. In the discussion reported in *Phaedo*, Socrates establishes that 'the Forms exist individually, and that other things participate in them and derive their names from them' (102b). In our example, we might say that the individual derives its name from, or is called after the Ideal of Beauty, although it is not, and could not be, of the same form as the Ideal. So the meaning of the word *beauty* is precisely that Ideal Form which serves as a template against which any individual can be measured. This early account of meaning is, therefore, very different from the direct reference, or extensional accounts we have considered. The extension of the word *beauty* is the set of individual entities to which it can appropriately be applied. But the meaning of the word, according to Plato, is not this actual set, but the Ideal Form of Beauty, which the individuals all, imperfectly, resemble. Plato makes clear that we don't experience Ideal Forms except by thinking about them, but it's necessary to his account that we have some 'inborn' or 'innate' knowledge of them, to which our individual experiences can be compared. In other words, we must have an innate knowledge of the proper, or real meanings of words before we ever experience individuals which those words can name.

Plato's account is concerned with abstracts. In order to explain the way in which words are applied to objects and concepts, he talks not just of the actual objects but of other types of entity, entities which have no concrete existence and which we can therefore never experience by means of our senses. It is therefore a **metaphysical** account, and indeed is regarded as one of the first metaphysical theories in the Western tradition. Metaphysics can be very generally defined as the discussion of that which exists, but exists out of reach of our senses and therefore can't be directly observed and studied. So, for instance, religious theories are metaphysical in that, in general, they are concerned with the existence of things we can't see: things which are 'other than' physical reality.

Like Socrates before him, Plato was dedicated to the teaching of philosophy. He established the Academy of Athens, sometimes described as the earliest university in the Western world. By far his most famous pupil at the Academy was Aristotle. Most of the work of Aristotle which has survived is in the form of published lectures, originally delivered at the Academy and elsewhere. Aristotle's work was heavily influenced by his teacher Plato, but he by no means subscribed to all of Plato's ideas. Perhaps most significantly, he rejected the notion of Ideal Forms upon which Plato's philosophy of objects and names depended. This rejection was consistent with his attempts to explain the world from what is sometimes described as a 'common sense' point of view; there was no place in his description for entities of which we have no direct evidence.

For Aristotle, the ultimate reality is what we experience through our senses. In this, his approach can be described as essentially **empirical**. He sees our knowledge of the world as being derived from our experience of it, rather than from unobservable metaphysical concepts. We have a concept of a property such as 'justice' because we have learned about it from our experience of individual, actual acts of justice. This is very different from Plato's account, in which individual acts of justice are recognised as such because of the extent to which they partake in the universal and unchanging concept of Justice.

The different accounts of reality offered by Plato and Aristotle naturally have different consequences for the nature of words, and their relationship to objects. We have seen that Plato's metaphysical account suggests that words are the names of Ideal Forms. Concrete objects may be given names by being 'named after' the Ideal Form to which they approximate, but can never be identical. For Aristotle the picture is reversed. All we have access to is information from our senses, in other words our experiences of the appearance, smell, taste, sound and texture of actual objects. So words must stand not for abstract Ideals, nor even for concrete objects, but for the impression which we have received from our senses. When we describe something as, say, a dog, we are giving a name to the impression we receive from the sight of a four-legged animal of a particular type, as well perhaps as a characteristic 'doggy' smell and 'shaggy' texture of which we are also aware. And when in the absence of any such impressions we talk generally about 'dogs', we are referring to the collection of experiences we have gained from individual dogs. Similarly, in using an abstract noun such as 'justice', we refer to the impressions we have received from individual acts of justice.

The collection of impressions which Aristotle describes us as receiving from our encounters with the world are sometimes labelled 'Ideas'. The term is used rather differently here than when it is applied to Platonic Forms, because in this case we really are dealing with something which exists in the human mind: with what are sometimes called 'mental likenesses'. Aristotle discusses the role of these Ideas in, for instance, the work entitled *de Interpretatione*. He describes 'signs' as varying between individuals, but 'affectations of the soul', or mental experiences, as being the same for everyone:

> And just as written marks are not the same for all men, neither are spoken sounds. But what these are in the first place signs of – affectations of the soul – are the same for all; and what these affectations are likenesses of – actual things – are also the same.
>
> (Chapter 1)[3]

So for Aristotle, words are effective because they are signs, or symbols, of the collection of impressions which form a mental experience. These experiences in turn are the 'likenesses' of actual entities, which have a reality and an existence of their own, although we can have access only to the experiences.

In Aristotle's work, then, we can see the beginnings of the ideational account of meaning. The meaning of a word is a particular idea, or mental image, which we have formed as a result of our experience of the world. His views on experience, and also on the relationship between words and objects, have, as we will see next, influenced philosophical debate in more recent centuries. But Plato's account has also remained important, and we will be returning to it, and to some of the ideas it influenced, in later chapters.

The British Empiricists

For Aristotle, it was 'ideas', in the sense of mental images, or impressions of external objects, which were the meanings of words. This type of definition of meaning was fundamental to the work of a number of individual philosophers of the seventeenth and eighteenth centuries who are often described as setting the agenda for modern philosophy, much as Plato and Aristotle did for ancient philosophy. These philosophers are sometimes referred to collectively as the British Empiricists, but they didn't work as a group and their work in fact differs from each other's in a number of ways. What they do have in common, however, as the title suggests, is an empirical approach to philosophy. They were committed to explaining our knowledge and understanding of the world around us in terms of our experience of it.

The British Empiricists were philosophers of the *Enlightenment*. This is the name which is often given to the intellectual and political developments of the period between the 1680s and 1780s. This was a time of great change in Britain and in Europe generally, when many of the traditional beliefs and values of the medieval and early modern periods were being challenged by the developing natural sciences. In particular, people were gradually becoming less happy to accept the authority of the church over all aspects of life, and were therefore becoming reluctant to accept the 'divine right' of monarchs to rule with absolute power. Instead, ideas of the natural equality of all people were advanced, which in turn led to an interest in what we would now call 'human rights'. During this period, various programmes of social and educational reform were attempted. If the political movements of the Enlightenment saw a rejection of authority in favour of egalitarianism, then in philosophy too there was a tendency to reject traditional wisdom in favour of the individual's use of reason. There was a growing belief in the power of human progress, and the resultant obligation on people to make sense of the physical universe for themselves, rather than relying on mysticism and superstition.

One of the early philosophers to voice such views, and a leading British Empiricist, was John Locke. Born in 1632, Locke studied traditional philosophy at Oxford, but his influences also included the new ideas which were becoming established in Europe, and the developing experimental sciences. He wrote extensively on science, on politics and economics, and also on the philosophy of knowledge. Probably his best known work is the lengthy treatise on science and knowledge entitled *An Essay Concerning Human Understanding*. This was first published in 1690, but underwent several extensive revisions, the fourth edition appearing in 1700, just four years before Locke's death.

In this work, Locke considers the nature of human understanding, or knowledge, and attempts to explain how it is possible. He emphasises the central importance of observation and of reason. In so doing, he rejects the view current at the time that human beings, by virtue of their status as the culmination of Creation, have certain innate knowledge which enables them to make sense of the world. We can recognise in this a view similar to Plato's idea that we must be born with knowledge of universal Forms, before we can make judgements about actual, concrete objects. Locke allows that our basic cognitive capacities, our abilities to think, reason, and remember, must be innate, in the sense of being a necessary part of human nature. But he argues that all actual knowledge must be acquired. He declares that his intention is to show 'how men, barely by the use of their natural faculties, may attain to all the knowledge they have, without the help of any innate impressions, and may arrive at certainly without any such original notions or principles' (Book I, Chapter II, 1).[4]

Locke holds that all that we have direct access to are our ideas, which we can contemplate by use of our understanding, and it is to these ideas that we refer when we use words. So for Locke the meanings of words are the various simple and complex ideas which humans are capable of forming. Indeed, in a section of his *An Essay Concerning Human Understanding* dedicated to the discussion 'Of Words' Locke introduces the idea that a speaker is able to use words '*as signs of internal conceptions*, and to make them stand as marks for the *ideas* within his own mind, whereby they might be made known to others, and the thoughts of men's minds be conveyed from one to another' (Book III, Chapter I, 2, original italics). So when we use a word, say *tree*, we are describing the idea, or the impression, we receive from our sense experiences of a tree. Note that Locke sees the purpose of language as being to convey ideas from the mind of the speaker to that of the hearer. This picture of the function of language, which has been voiced in different ways by many philosophers over the centuries, is one we will return to later.

Words can also be used to convey 'general ideas'. When, in the comfort of our study, we talk about the properties of 'trees', we are referring to the idea we have formed from all our experiences of trees. Indeed, it's only by means of the word *tree* that we are able to classify all these individual experiences as being in some way 'the same'. As Locke explains it, the introduction of general terms meant that 'one word was made to mark a multitude of particular existences' (Book III, Chapter I, 3). The existence of a word *tree* groups together a collection of simple ideas derived from separate sensory experiences.

This account of general ideas runs into similar problems to those which faced our friend at the start of this chapter when he tried to present us with the meaning of *bird*. Remember that when he tried to draw a picture to explain the meaning he encountered all sorts of difficulties. Now imagine that the picture he draws is to represent the general idea which he has in his head. He will need to produce an image which is identifiably bird-like, but has no specific characteristics which would make it incompatible with particular birds. It couldn't be of any particular colour, since birds come in all sorts of colours. This would seem to demand the impossible: that when we use the word *bird* generally, we have access to an image of a bird which is of no particular colour, or for that matter size or shape. Yet even a colourless image will not do, if such a thing is possible, because all birds are of some colour, and therefore 'colour' must be one of the properties of the general idea.

This very problem was pointed out a few years after Locke's death by George Berkeley, another of the British Empiricists, but one who differed from Locke on several important points. In his *Principles of Human Knowledge*, published in 1710, Berkeley takes as an example his own inability to contemplate a suitably general idea of 'man':

> The idea of man that I frame to myself, must be either of a white, or
> a black, or a tawny, a straight, or a crooked, a tall, or a low, or a

middle-sized man. I cannot by any effort of thought conceive the abstract idea above described.

(Introduction, 10)[5]

Berkeley pays homage to Locke's work, describing him as 'a late deservedly esteemed philosopher' (Introduction, 11) but argues that he has been led into the error of proposing general ideas by the nature of language itself; the fact that there are general terms seems to suggest that there must be general ideas to which they refer. Berkeley argues that, on the contrary, general words must be capable of being given broad definitions, for instance that a triangle is a 'plain surface comprehended by three right lines', but that such definitions are compatible with a vast number of individual, separate, ideas. He sums up: 'It is one thing for to keep a name constantly to the same definition, and another to make it stand everywhere for the same idea: the one is necessary, the other useless and impracticable' (Introduction, 18).

George Berkeley is often referred to as Bishop Berkeley, the position he rose to in the Anglican Church. He was born in Ireland in 1685 and spent much of his life there, although he also spent time on the Continent, in America and in England, dying in Oxford in 1753. His lively personality and novel philosophical ideas made him popular in society, and he forged many friendships among the intellectual and literary figures of his day. Berkeley's religious beliefs were the foundation of much of his philosophy. Like Locke, he argued that the mind has direct access only to itself and its own ideas. He also claimed that knowledge of God is present in the mind itself. His account of the mind gave rise to his philosophy of 'immaterialism', for which he is probably best known, and which has led to various parodies of his work. These parodies tend to play on his insistence that we have no conclusive evidence that the material world exists in the absence of our perception of it. Berkeley was anxious to counter 'materialist' philosophies which claim that the only real existence is the existence of physical matter. Such accounts rule out the validity of discussing minds, spirits and, indeed, God.

In this Berkeley can be distinguished from Locke. Locke, as we have seen, described words as standing only for our ideas of the material world. But he allowed that we generally assume that those ideas are formed from information from our senses about real objects: 'It is therefore the actual receiving of ideas from without that gives us notice of the existence of other things and makes us know that something doth exist at that time without us which causes that idea in us' (Book IV, Chapter XI, 2). Locke's views here can perhaps be likened to those of Aristotle, who as we have seen, maintained that words stand for individual ideas, but allowed that the material objects which formed those ideas were actual and constant.

Berkeley drew the contrary conclusion, namely that, since the only things we have access to are our ideas, the only things which we can be sure have real existence are those ideas. We have no sufficient evidence that the material world exists independently of our idea of it. Just as we have no reason to believe that the objects of our imagination exist other than in our mind, so we have no reason to believe that our ideas, however formed, have any existence other than in our mind. So for instance, we can't say with certainty that a tree which we are observing will continue to exist once we cease observing it; to say so is only to imagine that we could observe it if we were present:

> For as to what is said of the absolute existence of unthinking things without any relation to their being perceived, that seems perfectly unintelligible. Their *esse* is *percipi*, nor is it possible they should have any existence, out of the minds of thinking things which perceive them.
>
> (*Principles of Human Knowledge*, 3)

The Latin in this passage is generally translated as 'to be is to be perceived'. Berkeley offers a number of arguments in favour of this conclusion, encouraging his reader to perform a series of mental exercises as proof that it is impossible for 'unthinking', or inanimate beings to have any reality independent of the minds of those who observe them. He suggests, for instance, that we consider what differences we would be able to observe, first if there were an external reality and then if there were none; his suggestion is that there would be no difference, hence that we have no reason to believe in an external reality. He goes on to argue that it is not in fact possible to imagine the existence of an unobserved object without thereby imagining it observed. He presents all these ideas as if he is simply reminding his readers of what must be common sense:

> But say you, surely there is nothing easier than to imagine trees, for instance, in a park, or books existing in a closet, and nobody by to perceive them. I answer, you may so, there is no difficulty in it. But what is all this, I beseech you, more than framing in your mind certain ideas which you call books and trees, and at the same time omitting to frame the idea of anyone that may perceive them? But do you not yourself perceive or think of them all the while? This therefore is nothing to the purpose.
>
> (23)

Despite Berkeley's insistence that we have no valid evidence for the existence of the material world, he was by no means a **sceptic**. That is to say, he didn't hold with the view that nothing can be known for certain and that all that is possible are judgements of probability based on observation. The sceptical approach to knowledge, which can be dated to ancient times, was current when Berkeley was writing, and indeed one of his chief motives was to counteract such trends. Its currency was related to the challenge posed to old orthodoxies, and particularly to the validity of religious knowledge, during the Enlightenment. Berkeley was keen to provide an alternative to scepticism, with its claims that no knowledge can be certain and therefore that we can have no certainty of the existence of God. Along with other theologians of his time, he equated this position with atheism. As we have seen, he claimed that the mind does indeed have certain knowledge, but only of itself and of God. Material objects exist only in being perceived, but this, he argued, doesn't mean that we need doubt their existence. All objects are constantly being perceived, so they all continue to exist. Even when no humans are around, the material world is perceived by God, and exists in the mind of God.

Before leaving Berkeley's response to Locke, it is worth taking note of one other point he raises. Remember that Locke described language as existing mainly for the purpose of transferring ideas from the mind of the speaker to that of the hearer. Berkeley observes, however, that:

> The communicating of ideas marked by words is not the chief and only end of language, as is commonly supposed. There are other ends, as the raising of some passion, the exciting to, or deferring from an action, the putting the mind in some particular disposition; to which the former is in many cases subservient, and sometimes entirely omitted, when these can be obtained without it, as I think does not infrequently happen in the familiar use of language.
>
> (Introduction, 20)

Berkeley is here chiefly concerned with occasions when words may have some effect on the hearer, particularly an emotional one, without that effect necessarily being associated with any idea. But his observation can perhaps be seen as a precursor to the discussion of meaning in use, a topic which we will consider further in later chapters. We will also refer back to the work of the British Empiricists in the final chapter, when we will consider its implications for the question of how children first learn language. First, however, we need to consider some of the responses to their views, and the ways in which they influenced later thought. In these we can see the beginnings of a recognisably 'modern' account of meaning.

Names

George Berkeley was one of a large number of philosophers and theologians to respond to Locke soon after the publication of *An Essay Concerning Human Understanding*. Another such response was that of the German philosopher Leibniz, who wrote *Nouveaux Essais sur l'Entendement Humain*, translated into English as *New Essays on Human Understanding*, between 1703 and 1705, although it was not published until 1765.[6]

Gottfried Wilhelm Leibniz lived and worked in Germany in the late seventeenth and early eighteenth centuries. Like Locke, he was deeply interested in the scientific developments of his time. Indeed, he was a true polymath, familiar with many disciplines besides philosophy, and writing on topics as diverse as medicine and theology. His professional life was spent in court rather than in university appointments; despite being offered a number of professorships, he preferred to remain in the service of the Duke of Brunswick, who later became George I of England. His official duties seem to have left him plenty of time for his studies. The only main philosophical work which was published during his lifetime was *Theodicy*, which first appeared in 1710, but he wrote extensively, and many other books were published after his death, including *New Essays on Human Understanding*.

Leibniz's response to Locke is presented in the form of a dialogue between two characters: *Philalethes* presenting Locke's arguments and *Theophilus* replying to them with Leibniz's responses. Leibniz offers a *rationalist* account of understanding; he sees knowledge as being derived from the application of reason, rather than adopting the 'common sense' view of the empiricists that knowledge is derived from experience. He also challenges Locke's claims about what words mean. Philalethes repeats Locke's claim that words refer only to our ideas of objects; Theophilus responds that: 'In each case words indicate the things as well as the ideas' (287).

Through Theophilus, Leibniz is claiming that words stand not just for our ideas, or impressions, of things, but for the things themselves. He doesn't go as far as to claim that words refer *just* to actual objects or sets of objects. This, as we have seen, is known as the 'direct reference' account of meaning, in which words are said to refer directly to mind-external objects or events without the mediation of our ideas. One name closely associated with the direct reference account of meaning is that of John Stuart Mill. Mill can perhaps be seen as beginning a discussion of 'names', which was developed over the period of a century by a number of different philosophers. Before we consider Mill's account and the debate it generated, however, it's worth looking at the passage which immediately follows the claim from Leibniz we have just quoted. It can perhaps be seen as an early reference to the distinction we have already encountered between 'use' and 'mention'.

Use and mention

In *New Essays on Human Understanding*, after making his claim about words, things and ideas, Theophilus goes on to make the following observation, which is not subjected to any further discussion:

> Sometimes words themselves are spoken of materially, and in such a context one cannot precisely replace the word by its signification, i.e.

by its relation to ideas or to things. This happens not only when one speaks as a grammarian but also when one speaks as a lexicographer, giving the explanation of a name.

(287)

Leibniz is noticing here that words are not always used to refer to objects or ideas; sometimes we need to refer to words themselves, most often when, as he suggests, we are concerned with the actual linguistic properties of words. The use of words to talk about words, or more generally of language to talk about language, is sometimes described as 'metalinguistic'; language is both the means of description and the object described. We have already looked at some examples of this type when we considered the difference between the use and the mention of a word, at the start of this chapter. We could say that when a word is being used it refers to something outside of the linguistic system, but when it is mentioned, which Leibniz describes as the word being used 'materially', it refers to the word itself, part of the linguistic system.

As we have seen, it has become customary to distinguish between the use and the mention of a word by presenting the latter in quotation marks. The implications of this are discussed by the philosopher Leonard Linsky in the introduction to a book which he edited in 1952 entitled *Semantics and the Philosophy of Language*. He comments that 'in order to say something about (or mention) anything it is necessary to use a name or other means of designation for that thing' (4). Metalinguistic statements therefore pose a possible problem, because there are no independent names by which words can be designated. Linsky argues that there is no possible confusion between a thing and its name in an example such as 14):

14) John is tall.

This sentence makes reference to, or mentions the person John, but it's not John himself but his name which appears in the sentence. John is mentioned in the sentence; John's name is used in it. This distinction is not so easily made, however, in the case of 15):

15) 'John' consists of four letters.

This sentence is clearly not about the person John, but about the word *John*; it is the word *John* which is being mentioned. Yet the word *John*, the name for the person John, does not itself have a separate name. As we have seen, the use of quotation marks is a conventional way of indicating that the word is being mentioned, not used. Another way of explaining this is to say that 'John' is in fact the name of the word *John*; we can create a name for any word by placing the word itself inside quotation marks. This gives us a way of mentioning the word when we want to say, for instance, that it has four letters, just as we have a way of mentioning the person when we want to say, for instance, that he is tall.

The distinction between use and mention, and the notation which accompanies it, have not always been accepted without criticism. One of the most common objections to be raised is the rather unsatisfactory logical consequence of this account. In 15) we saw an example of the use of the name for the word *John*; now imagine that we want to mention *this* name. Following the convention we have established, we would need to give the name a name of its own by placing it inside quotation marks. This would give us ' 'John' ', and the name for this, should we want to mention it, would have to be ' ' 'John' ' ', and so on. Several writers have expressed reservations about the infinite process of naming-of-names which the distinction between use and mention seems to imply. Some of these are listed in the 'further reading' section at the end of this chapter.

In his critique of Locke, then, Leibniz was perhaps the first to raise the possibility of this 'special' function of words. He also, as we have seen, differs from Locke in his account of words used 'normally', and the way they relate to objects. In the rest of this section, we will consider the discussion by John Stuart Mill and others of this relationship between names and objects. In the context of Mill's work the term *name* is used, as indeed it had been in the work of previous philosophers, to indicate any word, or indeed any noun phrase, which can be used to identify a particular person or object. This usage is not consistent throughout the debate that followed; the term is also sometimes used with the restricted meaning of 'proper name', such as *John, Mary*, or *Mr Jones*, and we will need to bear these different uses in mind in what follows.

Mill on direct reference

John Stuart Mill was born, just over a century after John Locke's death, in 1806. Like Locke, and indeed like Leibniz, he didn't base his career at a university; he worked as an administrator in the East India Company and later as a Member of Parliament, before his death in 1873. Nevertheless, he published many books and pamphlets during his lifetime. He is probably best known for his moral and political philosophy and his views on social and economic reform. He argued for a scientific approach to the understanding of these subjects, and this is one concern of his *A System of Logic*, first published in 1843. In this book, Mill also engages in the development of a precise method of logical analysis and reasoning, seeing a clear account of language as a necessary prerequisite for this. Indeed, he begins with a chapter called 'Of the necessity of commencing with an analysis of language', arguing that language is a necessary tool of scientific and logical analysis, and therefore needs to be as precise and accurate as any other scientific instrument.

Mill poses himself the question of whether words are best described as names of things or of our ideas of things. He describes the first as the description 'in common use' and the second as an invention by 'metaphysicians'. Mill suggests that 'there seems good reason for adhering to the common usage, and calling ... the word *sun* the name of the sun, and not the name of our idea of the sun' (23–4). His argument in favour of this decision is the 'common sense' view that, when we use words to say something, for instance in saying 'the sun is the cause of the day', we are talking about the physical entities involved, and not about our idea of them.

Mill distinguishes between 'general' and 'individual' names. The former are words which can be applied to an indefinitely large class of objects, while the latter can each be applied to only one individual, as is the case with proper names:

> Thus *man* is capable to being truly affirmed of John, George, Mary, and other persons without assignable limit; and it is affirmed of all of them in the same sense; for the word man expresses certain qualities, and when we predicate it of those persons, we assert that they all posess these qualities. But *John* is only capable of being truly affirmed of one single person, as least in the same sense.
>
> (27)[7]

Mill further distinguishes between 'connotative' and 'non-connotative' names, describing this as one of the distinctions 'which go deepest into the nature of language' (31). To understand this distinction we need to recall the examples used above to illustrate the difference between 'denotation' and 'connotation', the denotation of a word being simply the thing referred to, and the connotation being the property or group of properties which determine the denotation. For instance, we distinguished between 'Elizabeth I' as the denotation, and 'the person with supreme power over laws and government of the kingdom' as the connotation of the phrase *the monarch of England in 1600*. In distinguishing between connotative and non-connotative names, Mill is suggesting that not all names have connotations. Those which he identifies as being non-connotative are what we would call 'proper names'. Mill describes proper names as words which serve only to identify individuals. Apart from this purpose, it is inappropriate to ask what the word 'means', or to consider the 'reason' for an individual to have a certain name. A general term like *man*, however, denotes all individual human beings, and also connotes the attributes of being human; 'it is a connotative name' (32). Mill stresses that a connotative name such as this is still a name *of* what it denotes; the connotation can offer an explanation of why it can serve as a name for this. He considers the proper name *Sophroniscus* and the denotationally equivalent expression *The father of Socrates*:

Both these are names of the same individual, but their meaning is altogether different; they are applied to that individual for two different purposes: the one, merely to distinguish him from other persons who are spoken of; the other to indicate a fact relating to him, the fact that Socrates was his son.

(38)

So Mill classifies the proper name *Sophroniscus*, and the noun phrase *the father of Socrates* as two different types of individual name. Used successfully, both serve to pick out an individual. But the proper name does no more than this, while the noun phrase also gives some definition of that individual. It's possible to ask why some descriptive phrase is applicable to an individual, but not to ask why some proper name is. We can explain why the description *the father of Socrates* is appropriate by saying 'because he was the father of Socrates', but if asked the same question about *Sophroniscus*, we can only say 'because that's his name'.

It is, of course, possible to state explicitly the relationship between the name and the description which Mill discusses. We can say 'Sophroniscus is the father of Socrates'. But if, as Mill claims, the proper name *Sophroniscus* is non-connotative, this statement can be concerned only with the denotation of the two terms. In effect it says that two expressions which denote the same individual are equivalent. The statement should, therefore, be totally trivial and uninformative; it shouldn't even be worth saying. However, expressions such as this are in fact often used, and used to convey non-trivial information; they are often worth saying. This particular problem was addressed by the German philosopher Gottlob Frege, whose work we will consider next.

Frege on sense and reference

Born in 1848, Gottlob Frege was Professor of Mathematics at the University of Jena. The work for which he is now best known, on logic and on language, developed late in his career out of his interest in mathematics. In 1892 he published an article entitled 'Über Sinn und Bedeutung'. This has been translated into English variously as 'On sense and meaning' and 'On sense and reference'.[8] The term *meaning* has been used in such a number of different ways that it can become confusing to try to reserve it for the very precise idea of Frege's *Bedeutung*. In particular, Frege's term is applied to something quite different from *meaning* as used by Mill who, as we have seen, comments that two expressions can refer to the same individual but have different meanings. For this reason we will use the terms *sense* and *reference* when discussing Frege's work.

Frege's starting point is with what he describes as 'expressions of equality'. Using Mill's example to illustrate Frege's point, we could say that while 16) can offer some valuable information, 17) is a simple, necessary truth, which tells us nothing new.

16) Sophroniscus is the father of Socrates.
17) Sophroniscus is Sophroniscus.

Frege points out that, if this 'equality' is a relation between the individuals denoted, 16) should be no more informative than 17); both would merely state that a certain individual is identical with himself. Rather, he suggests, what we are saying in 16) is that *Sophroniscus* and *the father of Socrates* both denote the same individual; we are making a statement about the relationship between two different ways of naming an individual, not between the individual and himself. Hence, what we say is significant and far from a trivial tautology. The difference between the two expressions which makes 16) significant is not a difference in their denotation, but 'a difference in the mode of presentation of the thing designated' (57).[9]

This observation leads Frege to propose that every name has an element concerned with this mode of presentation, which he calls its *sense*, as well as a denotation, which he calls its *reference*. To illustrate this, Frege uses the pair of names *the evening star* and *the morning star*. These names were given to the bright lights seen at different points in the sky in the evening and the morning, respectively. Now eventually it was discovered that these two lights were actually the same body, seen in different places because of the rotation of the earth (they are both, in fact, the planet Venus). When this discovery was made, it would have been possible to report it using 18):

18) The evening star is the morning star.

Like our example 16) above, this is a perfectly informative statement. This is because, as Frege notes, although *the evening star* and *the morning star* are now known to have the same *reference*, they have different *senses*; the same object is identified in both cases, but two different ways of identifying it are being used. We could equally well identify this same object yet another way and say:

19) The evening star is Venus.

So far it may not appear that Frege is saying anything so very different from Mill. He is using different terminology, but his *reference* seems very close to Mill's *denotation*, and his *sense* to Mill's *connotation*; if confronted with an example like 18), Mill would presumably explain that *the evening star* and *the morning star* denote the same individual but have different connotations. And indeed, like Mill, Frege adopts a 'direct reference' account; he explicitly states that the meaning of a name is a physical object, not an idea:

The meaning and sense of a sign are to be distinguished from the associated idea. If what a sign means is an object perceivable by the senses,
my idea of it is an internal image. ... The idea is subjective: one man's
idea is not that of another.

(59)

So while ideas of an object may vary from individual to individual, the
object itself, the meaning of a name, is a constant, mind-external entity.

But Frege does differ from Mill; briefly, he allows that proper names
have sense as well as reference. Remember that Mill distinguished between
connotative and non-connotative names; *Sophroniscus* denotes an individual but has no connotation, whereas *the father of Socrates*, while
denoting the same individual, also connotes a certain property which
distinguishes that individual. Frege doesn't make this distinction. He in
fact uses the term *proper name* to refer to anything which serves to denote
a particular object. 'The designation of a single object can also consist of
several words or other things. For brevity, let every such designation be
called a proper name' (57). So for Frege, there is no need to distinguish
between *Sophroniscus* and *the father of Socrates*; they both have sense as
well as reference.

It's fairly easy to work out the sense of a descriptive noun phrase. In
19), for instance, the object denoted by *the evening star* is identified by
means of one particular property; we might paraphrase and say it is 'the
light which can be seen in the sky in a particular place in the evening'. But
the sense of a proper name is less apparent. We may know what, or who,
they denote, but we can't necessarily say *how* an individual is picked out
by *Venus* or *Sophroniscus* or, to use Frege's own example *Aristotle*. Frege's
answer is that such names work in exactly the same way as the descriptions; they denote an individual by means of some identifying property.
According to this account, if you know the meaning of a name then you
associate some particular property with that meaning; this, for you, is the
sense of the name.

This account works well enough for many names, particularly those of
historical figures. It is fairly likely that for most people nowadays the name
Lloyd George, for instance, will refer to a particular person and will have
a sense along the lines of 'the British Prime Minister during the First World
War'. But, as Frege acknowledges, there may not always be agreement
about the sense of names. To use his example, we may find that for one
person the name *Aristotle* has the sense 'the pupil of Plato and teacher
of Alexander the Great', while for another it has the sense 'the teacher of Alexander the Great who was born in Stagira'. Frege's response to this is that
'so long as the thing meant remains the same, such variations of sense may
be tolerated', although he stipulates that they 'ought not to occur in a
perfect language' (58n). Frege in fact sees sense as the essential property of

all names; it is possible for name to have sense but no reference, but not vice-versa. This is an issue to which we will return in the next chapter.

Frege then considers the implications for his account of what is known as *Leibniz's Law*, or the *Law of Substitution*. This can be paraphrased as follows:

20) If two expressions are denotationally equivalent, one can be substituted for another in a formula *salve veritate*.

Salve veritate is Latin for 'with truth unchanged', so the principle states that substituting an expression for another with the same reference should not alter the truth, or falsity, of the sentence in which it occurs. And this works in practice for many examples. If we can agree that *Charles Dickens* and *the author of Great Expectations* have the same reference, we should agree that 21) and 22), for instance, must both be the same in terms of truth (and that they are, in fact, both true), as must 23) and 24) (which are both false):

21) Charles Dickens lived in the nineteenth century.
22) The author of *Great Expectations* lived in the nineteenth century.
23) Charles Dickens was French.
24) The author of *Great Expectations* was French.

However, we seem to run into difficulties when we try to apply the Law of Substitution to examples like 25) and 26):

25) Joe said 'Charles Dickens was French'.
26) Joe said 'the author of *Great Expectations* was French'.

Here again we have formed 26) by replacing an expression in 25) with one with the same reference, but the meaning of the whole formula does not remain the same; its truth has changed. If Joe in fact said 'Charles Dickens was French', then 25) is an accurate way of reporting this but 26) is not. Frege explains this by means of a type of use–mention distinction. What we are talking about in an example like 25) is not the usual meaning of Joe's words, but the words themselves. We therefore have 'signs of signs', indicated as such by the presence of the quotation marks: 'Accordingly, a word standing between quotation marks must not be taken as having its ordinary meaning' (58–9). But the problems for the Law of Substitution do not end with direct quotations, with their helpful quotation marks. We can recall from the introduction to this chapter that there are certain types of sentence, known as intensional contexts, in which it isn't possible to substitute extensionally equivalent expressions. As a reminder, let's consider the following pair:

27) Pip believes that the author of *Great Expectations* is a genius.
28) Pip believes that Charles Dickens is a genius.

It's possible that if 27) is true then 28) is also true but this isn't necessarily the case. Pip may have read and admired the novel without noticing who wrote it; he may not remember who wrote it; he may even believe that Walter Scott wrote it. In all these cases we would want to say that 27) was true but 28) false. Similarly, Pip may have read only *Oliver Twist*, and on this basis 28) might be true. But if he doesn't know that Charles Dickens also wrote *Great Expectations*, then we certainly couldn't claim that 27) was true. These examples involve what are known as 'propositional attitudes'. They are concerned with an attitude of the subject to a particular proposition. In this case the attitude is one of belief, but the same effect is achieved, with a number of other attitudes, such as hoping, fearing, wishing and so on.

Frege's explanation of examples of this type relies on his distinction between sense and reference, and on his claim that everything which he describes as a 'proper name' has a sense. He claims that in cases such as 27) and 28), as well as in the direct quotation examples such as 25) and 26), the relevant names 'do not have their customary meaning but designate what is usually their sense' (59). So in 28), for instance, the name 'Charles Dickens' is being used to denote not its reference, the individual, but its sense. As we saw earlier, what counts as the sense of a name can vary from one person to another. *Charles Dickens* is here being used to denote the sense which Pip attaches to this name. As we have suggested, this sense may be 'the author of *Oliver Twist*', and may not be 'the author of *Great Expectations*', depending on the extent of Pip's individual knowledge. Frege labels these uses, where a word denotes its sense, as *indirect* uses, which he distinguishes from *customary* uses, in which a word is used to denote its reference. 'The indirect meaning of a word accordingly is its customary sense' (59).

We are now familiar with three sets of expressions to discuss the difference between the actual object identified by a name, and the properties which determine how the name is applied: *extension* and *intension*, Mill's distinction between *denotation* and *connotation*, and Frege's *reference* and *sense*.[10] These same distinctions, particularly the last one, have been employed to talk about the meaning of sentences, a topic which we will investigate in the next chapter.

Russell on descriptions

The next major contribution to the discussion of the nature of names and descriptions came from Bertrand Russell. Russell was one of the most influential figures in twentieth-century British philosophy, publishing many books and articles during his long career. He was also a noted political activist and social reformer, a high-profile pacifist and, in later life, a leading member of the Campaign for Nuclear Disarmament. Born in 1872 into an aristocratic family, Russell spent much of his professional life at Cambridge. However, his pacifism during the First World War, which led to his being briefly imprisoned, caused him to be dismissed from his post, and he didn't return to the University until 1944, when he became a Fellow of Trinity College.

Like Frege, Russell's first and primary philosophical interest was in mathematical logic. His approach was essentially an analytic one, concerned with the analysis of the language in which the ideas of logic are expressed and, ultimately, with a refinement of that language. This in turn led to an interest in meaning, and in particular in the logic of linguistic meaning as it relates to issues of human knowledge and understanding. Russell claims in his *Autobiography*, published in 1967, that it was while he was in prison during the First World War that his interest in meaning developed. Certainly it was there that he wrote the manuscript which was published after the war in 1919 as *Introduction to Mathematical Philosophy*.

Bertrand Russell was the first to use the now-familiar term *definite description* for phrases such as *the father of Socrates, the evening star*, and so on. Such phrases offer a defining description of an individual and, crucially, convey the idea that there is only one such individual.[11] They are introduced by what is known in linguistics as the *definite article*, and it is this which introduces the idea of 'uniqueness'. With the *indefinite article* the effect is different; *an evening star* doesn't pick out any particular star, in Russell's term it introduces only the 'concept' of evening stars, while *a father of Socrates* is bizarre precisely because it seems to suggest that Socrates didn't have just one particular father.

Remember that Frege differed from Mill in arguing that both definite descriptions and names (for Frege both classed as 'proper names') have a sense as well as a reference. In the chapter on 'Descriptions' in his 1919 book, however, Russell argues that definite descriptions and proper names should be classed as very different entities. That isn't to say that Russell advocates simply returning to Mill's version. Unlike Mill, Russell proposes to restrict the property of direct reference to actual proper names (and, as we will see, to one particular type of use of proper names) and to exclude definite descriptions from the class of referring expressions altogether. In support of this claim, Russell argues that it isn't possible simply to substitute names for definite descriptions which apparently have the same reference. Like Frege, he considers the evidence from 'identity statements'. Both 29) and 30) may in fact be true but, as Russell puts it, 'the first is a fact of literary history, the second a trivial truism' (174).

29) Scott is the author of *Waverley*.
30) Scott is Scott.

According to Russell's explanation, the difference between 29) and 30) is due to a difference between *Scott* on one hand and *the author of Waverley* on the other, which is more significant than just a difference in Fregean 'sense'. This difference is based on the apparently straightforward fact that *the author of Waverley* is a more complex expression than *Scott*. An ordinary proper name, such as *Scott*, is what Russell describes as a 'simple symbol ... directly designating an individual which is its meaning' (174); it can't be analysed into individual parts. A definite description such as *the author of Waverley*, however, is made up of a number of parts, each of which itself has meaning; the meaning of the whole expression is dependent on the fixed meanings of these individual parts.

So Russell subscribes to the 'direct reference' account of meaning for proper names; they denote some particular individual, such as the particular author. Definite descriptions, however, don't refer to, but rather describe, an individual. When they appear in a sentence their effect is to specify that an individual meeting a certain description exists, so that something can then be said about this individual. Since proper names serve simply to denote some individual, it's essential that there must exist some individual for them to denote. A name which doesn't denote is simply meaningless. The same is not the case for definite descriptions which don't describe. Russell's examples are *the golden mountain* and *the round square*. There aren't in fact individuals which correspond to these descriptions, but the descriptions themselves are still meaningful, 'the reason being that it is a *complex* symbol, of which the meaning is derived from that of its constituent symbols' (179). Russell also discusses what happens when descriptions such as these occur in sentences; we will look at this part of his theory in Chapter 2.

Such an account of proper names would seem to raise problems for the use of fictional or historical names. It might be quite easy to agree that a completely made-up name, which refers to nothing, is meaningless, but we can hardly claim to be puzzled as to the meaning of examples such as the following:

31) Hamlet saw his father's ghost.
32) Homer was blind.

Russell discusses both these proper names, although not these actual examples. We know what 31) means, even though we know that *Hamlet* is a character in fiction who never actually existed. We know what 32) means, even though we accept that there is no conclusive evidence that the person we call *Homer* ever lived. But Russell's explanation is not to say that *Hamlet* and *Homer* do exist, if not in real life then at least in imagination or in fiction; he vehemently rejects any such explanation, calling it 'a most pitiful and paltry evasion' (169). Rather, he suggests that in such cases what appear to be proper names are not in fact being used as proper names, to refer directly to individuals, but rather as 'abbreviated descriptions'; the names actually stand in for the descriptions we associate with them, and serve to describe an individual so that something can be said of it. What these descriptions are will of course vary from individual to individual, as Frege noted in his discussion of *Aristotle*, but for a lot of people *Hamlet* might be an abbreviation for 'the hero of Shakespeare's most famous tragedy', and *Homer* for 'the author of the *Iliad* and the *Odyssey*'. Using these names as they are used in examples 31) and 32) therefore involves the mental association of the names with these descriptions.

Russell in fact suggests that proper names function as abbreviated descriptions in *most* uses. The occasions when they function as proper names must be limited to those occasions when you actually have direct sensory experience of someone, for instance you can see them, and you associate a name with that person. In these cases proper names can be said to refer directly to individuals. But in many other cases, even when using a name for someone you know personally, you will probably actually associate a description with that name, such as 'my brother', 'the local postman', 'the woman I sit next to at evening class', and so on. In these cases, using the name (*John*, *Mr Jones*, *Evelyn*) will involve applying this description, rather than referring directly to the individual. Russell suggests that 'the same considerations apply to almost all uses of what look like proper names' (179).

Remember that Russell's interest in language was derived from his work on logic on the one hand and the theory of knowledge on the other. He was not particularly concerned with language as a means of communication; these claims about the uses of proper names have more to do with what goes on in the minds of individuals when they use – or even think about – a name, than with the ways in which names can be used to communicate information. It's relatively easy to see how a name may be associated directly with someone who is present, or indirectly with the description of someone who is absent, when these associations take place in your own mind. It's perhaps harder to see any of these processes going on when you use sentences such as those we have been considering to communicate with someone else. As we will see in the next chapter, Russell was explicit in his purely 'philosophical', or logical interest in language. Nevertheless, it's the issue of how names are in fact used, and their role in communication, which has led to some of the strongest criticism of his account.

Kripke on naming

Perhaps the best known account of names offered as an alternative to those put forward by Frege and Russell is that proposed by Saul Kripke, an American philosopher who became a professor at Princeton University in 1977. In an article published in 1972 called 'Naming and necessity',

Kripke identifies problems for any account of names which relates them to descriptions.[12] These are problems for Frege's claim that names, as well as descriptions, have both reference and sense, and for Russell's suggestion that most of what appear to be proper names are actually acting as 'abbreviated descriptions'. We have already seen that such descriptions must be allowed, in natural language, to vary from individual to individual. Frege allowed that for one person the name *Aristotle* may have the sense 'the pupil of Plato and teacher of Alexander the Great' and for another 'the teacher of Alexander the Great who was born at Stagira'. It's also the case that such descriptions aren't always 'reliable'. We can imagine certain ancient documents coming to light which indicate, for instance, that Alexander the Great was never taught by Aristotle. This might well make us revise certain of our views on classical history, but it would hardly force us to rethink the actual meaning of the word *Aristotle*. We might think to ourselves 'so it turns out that Aristotle wasn't the teacher of Alexander the Great', but not 'so it turns out that Aristotle wasn't Aristotle'. Kripke offers the following example of this: Columbus might be identified by many people as being the first European to land in America. It's quite likely that this wasn't in fact the case; it's quite likely that America was reached by the Vikings long before Columbus. However, people who associate that description with Columbus don't use the term *Columbus* to refer to 'some Norseman' (264).[13] They use it to refer to the particular historical figure called Columbus; they just happen to have a false belief about him. Such beliefs needn't in fact be true of any individual for a name to be meaningful:

> Biblical scholars ... think that Jonah really existed. It isn't because they think that someone ever was swallowed by a big fish or even went to Nineveh to preach. These conditions may be true of no one whatsoever and yet the name 'Jonah' really has a referent.
>
> (264)

Kripke's explanation is that names, unlike descriptions, are 'rigid designators'. Like Mill before him, he sees names as directly denoting individuals, without the mediation of any sense or description. The connection between name and individual is unaffected by any incidental changes in what descriptions can appropriately be applied to the individual, and indeed is the same for all speakers of a language, regardless of individual differences in knowledge or point of view. Kripke's emphasis is therefore on the way in which a name is used by a community of speakers, often the set of speakers of a particular language, to refer to a particular individual. Central to his account is the use of a name in communication, and in particular the way in which an individual speaker comes to use a name on a certain occasion so that it is understood. This account is sometimes described as the 'causation' theory of names, and can be summarised as follows.

Every individual which has a name is given this name on a particular occasion. Kripke refers to this as an 'initial baptism', but it needn't take the form of an official ceremony. It may be, for instance, when parents first tell their family what they have decided to call their child, or when a town council passes a motion to give a particular name to a new road. After such an occasion, the name is passed on within a community of speakers simply by being used to refer to that individual. So when any speaker uses a name to refer to an individual, it is in theory possible to trace a continuous 'chain of communication', in which the name has been used with the same reference right from the time at which it was originally given. In Kripke's words, 'it's in virtue of our connection with other speakers in the community, going back to the referent himself, that we refer to a certain man' (265).

The meaning of a name is therefore assigned not by individuals, as it is in Russell's account of names as abbreviated descriptions, but by an entire community of speakers. This explains why speakers can use names, and use them successfully, even when they wouldn't be able to offer a definite description with the same reference. For instance, Kripke suggests that 'the man in the street' might use the name *Feynman*, and when asked, may say 'well he's a physicist or something'. Kripke's claim is that even though he can't produce a unique referring description, he is using the name appropriately, that is 'he uses the name "Feynman" as a name for Feynman' (262). This is precisely because of the way in which he has heard the name used by other speakers in the community.

Kripke's work on naming was produced more than half a century after Russell started taking an interest in meaning, and longer still after Frege applied his interest in mathematics to the problem of identity statements. We certainly shouldn't dismiss Frege and Russell's accounts; indeed we will return to them in the next chapter, and assess their impact on another area of linguistic enquiry. But it is Kripke's work which has been the focus of interest for linguists. Although he too is primarily a logician, Kripke demonstrates an implicit understanding of the relevance of 'speakers' and 'communities' when it comes to discussing meaning. He shows an awareness, which is taken for granted in many branches of modern linguistics, that meaning isn't just something which is attached to a certain word, or combination of words, but something which involves the individual speakers, and the community of speakers, of a language. As we have seen, Frege's interest in meaning relates closely to his interest in mathematics, and Russell's to his interest in logic and knowledge. In neither of these interests is communication of primary relevance.

Words and things in linguistics

The philosophical works we have studied in this chapter, and particularly the accounts of names in the last section, have been influential in a number of areas of linguistics. As we will see in later chapters, they have informed work on the ways in which words contribute to making sentences 'true' or 'false', and on the relationship between language and mind. But, as we saw at the outset of this chapter, linguists as well as philosophers have cause to be interested in the relationship between words and things in its own right. The area of linguistics concerned with the meanings of individual words of a language, and the relationships between them, is the branch of semantics known as *lexical semantics*. These relationships include, for instance, those of synonymy (two words with the same meaning), antonymy (two words with opposite meanings), polysemy (one word with many meanings) and homophony (two separate words which sound the same).

The classification of such relationships might appear to be relatively straightforward, but in making decisions about them the issues which we have explored in this chapter are highly relevant. If two words are synonymous, for instance, they should in theory be interchangeable in all contexts. We might want to claim that the words *lad* and *boy* are synonyms because they have the same meaning; after all, they can both be paraphrased as 'young human male'. But once we become aware of the issues we have been studying here, the case becomes a lot less clear-cut. To begin with, the two words certainly don't seem to be exactly intensionally equivalent. To see this we only need to try them out in a set of intensional contexts, such as the statements of propositional attitude in 33) and 34):[14]

33) Gus likes to think that he is a bit of a lad.
34) Gus likes to think that he is a bit of a boy.

Now it certainly seems to be the case that 33) could be true while 34), in which an apparently synonymous expression has been substituted, could be false. *Lad* and *boy* are not intensionally equivalent because one has associations which the other lacks. And indeed, once we consider the extensions of the words, the exact set of individuals they could be used to refer to, we would probably be reluctant to agree that they have exactly the same extensional meaning either. The word *lad*, for instance, might generally be agreed to allow for a higher upper age limit than *boy*. This suggests that its extension is a larger set of individuals, which in turn suggests that the two are not extensionally equivalent.

The same seems to hold, to a greater or lesser degree, for many pairs of words which are conventionally classed as synonyms. Think of pairs such as *snake/serpent*, *car/automobile*, *hall/vestibule*, or any of the words grouped together in a thesaurus, and you will probably be able to detect intensional and/or extensional differences between them. It has been suggested that no natural language in fact includes any exact synonyms, pairs of words which are both extensionally and intensionally equivalent. Indeed, it would seem to introduce an unnecessary redundancy into a language; if two words had exactly the same meaning, one of them would be unnecessary. For similar reasons, it has been suggested that exact translation between two languages is never in fact possible. No word in the first language could ever have a precise counterpart, in terms of both extension and intension, in the target language.

Definite descriptions, of the type identified by Bertrand Russell, have continued to be a source of interest to philosophers and linguists alike. We will look at some of their work, particularly as it relates to the ways in which speakers use definite descriptions in different contexts, in later chapters. As suggested, much of the criticism of Russell's account has been focused on its inability to deal with 'real life' uses of definite descriptions. As just one example of the type of problem which has been raised, consider the following question:

35) Who is the man drinking a Martini?

We can imagine this question being asked at two parties by two different people, giving two very different interpretations. In one case, at a fashionable reception, a woman notices a man with a commanding air drinking a clear liquid from a Martini glass. She utters 35) to a fellow guest in order to find out whether he is anyone famous. She uses the definite description *the man drinking a Martini* successfully to refer to that particular distinguished-looking person if her fellow guest recognises who she means; it doesn't matter that it in fact turns out that all he has in the glass is water. The second scene is set at the annual gathering of a local temperance society. Someone has just informed the president that a man has been spotted slyly drinking a Martini. The outraged president utters 35); his intention is to discover the identity of the miscreant, and he uses the definite description to refer to this character, whoever he may be. This example is discussed by the philosopher Keith Donnellan in his 1966 essay 'Reference and definite description'. He labels the first case an example of the *referential* use of a definite description. The second, which he argues is a common type of use of definite descriptions, but one not considered by Russell, he labels an example of the *attributive* use.

Before we move on to study the relationship between language and truth, it's worth sparing a thought for the ideational accounts of meaning. Recall that these are accounts which claim that, since all we have certain knowledge of is our own ideas and impressions, it must be these which are the meanings of words. The last we heard of ideational accounts of meaning was in the eighteenth century, when they seemed rather to be foundering on the problems posed by general ideas, and on the extremes of immaterialism. But they weren't entirely sunk. Indeed, the notion of 'mental image' as meaning became central to the work of the *Structuralist* linguists of the twentieth century, of whom Ferdinand de Saussure is perhaps the most famous. We will be studying some of this work in the final chapter.

Further reading

The British Empiricists

Locke's *An Essay Concerning Human Understanding* is available in a number of modern editions. The Everyman version used here is slightly abridged, but contains all the parts relevant to Locke's account of language. This is set out chiefly in Book III of the work, 'Of words', part of which is reprinted in Martinich (1996): 500–5.

George Berkeley actually wrote two parts to *The Principles of Human Knowledge* but lost the manuscript of Part II before publication and never rewrote it. The published version, which is available in a number of modern editions including Penguin, therefore consists only of the Introduction and Part I. It is short and lively.

Ideational accounts of meaning are considered in Hacking (1975) *Why Does Language Matter to Philosophy?* in his section on 'The heyday of ideas', including reference to some philosophers not discussed here.

Use and mention

Searle (1969) *Speech Acts* includes a discussion of 'Reference as a speech act' which begins with a staunch criticism (73–6) of the notion that to mention a word by producing it in inverted commas is to give a name for that word. Searle argues that the word itself is produced, but not in the normal way; it is *presented* for discussion. Another attack on the distinction between use and mention, this time one which deals specifically with Linsky's account, can be found in Roy Harris' (1996) *Signs, Language and Communication* (100–4).

Names

Mill's account of names is set out in Book I of *A System of Logic*, mainly in Chapter 2. References here to Frege's 'On sense and reference' are to Geach and Black (1980) *The Philosophical Writings of Gottlob Frege*. Russell's essay 'Description' forms a chapter of his (1919) *Introduction to Mathematical Philosophy*. Kripke's 'Naming and necessity' was originally published in a book of the same name in 1972. Russell considers reference in a number of his other philosophical works. For instance, names and descriptions are discussed in Part II of *Human Knowledge* (1948) and proper names are the subject of Chapter 6 of *An Inquiry into Meaning and Truth* (1940).

A lot of work has been produced in this area. Carnap (1956) *Meaning and Necessity* gives a detailed analysis of the terms *intension* and *extension*, and compares them with the work of Russell and, in particular, of Frege. Evans (1982) *The Varieties of Reference* offers a detailed but difficult account, with separate chapters of Part I devoted to Frege, to Russell and to recent work such as that of Kripke. He links Russell's account to his interest in the philosophy of the mind in detail. Evans himself argues that there are 'non-Russellian referring expressions', in other words that names and expressions which Russell would class as descriptions can in fact be explained in terms of reference.

One philosopher who has written about the particular problems posed by opaque contexts is the American W. V. O. Quine, whose work we will look at in the final chapter. He deals with these topics in his (1961) book *From a Logical Point of View*. Much of his argument there, including the suggestion that it is necessary to consult intension when considering statements of belief, can be found in his (1956) article 'Quantifiers and propositional attitudes'.

Many expository accounts of the discussion of names are available. R. Martin (1987) *The Meaning of Language* discusses Russell's and Kripke's accounts of proper names in Chapters 16 and 17. Stainton (1996) *Philosophical Perspectives on Language*, Chapter 3, is concerned with direct reference accounts in general and Russell's account of descriptions. The debate is treated in some detail in Part II of Devitt and Sterelny (1987) *Language and Reality*.

2 Propositions and logic

Introduction

So far we have been concerned almost entirely with the way in which language names, or picks out, individual objects. We have looked at some possible explanations of the relationship between the material world and the words used to describe it. But of course language doesn't just provide names for objects. Being able to use a language involves much more than simply knowing a long list of words and meanings. Imagine that a group of aspiring linguists succeed in listing all the words of a language, and giving their intensional and extensional meanings. They would still have a lot of work left to do before they could claim to have described what it is that people 'know' when they are able successfully to use and understand the language.

If we were trying to explain to the struggling linguists what was missing from their description of a language, we would probably find ourselves saying something like, 'All you've done is produce a list of the words in the language. You haven't said anything about the ways in which the words can combine together, or the effects on meaning when they are combined'. In effect, we would be complaining that the linguists had said everything they could about the words of the language, but nothing at all about its phrases and sentences. These are, of course, the subjects of a great deal of analysis and description in linguistics. The ways in which words can legitimately combine together to form phrases, clauses and sentences are studied in syntax. The meanings which result from these combinations are the subject of semantic analyses. And here, as in the study of the relationship between words and things, linguists have taken up topics first discussed in philosophy.

At the beginning of the last chapter we considered linguistics as a discipline which necessarily concerns itself with both the relationships *between* language and the outside world and the relationships *within* a linguistic system. In the study of sentence meaning, both these types of relationship are relevant, and both have been considered by philosophers over the centuries. We are concerned with the relationship *between* language and the world when we ask what it is that makes a sentence an appropriate description of a particular state of affairs: essentially, when we consider what it is for a sentence to be 'true'. This will be our main concern in the next chapter. When we consider the relationships which exist between the sentences of a language, we are also primarily concerned with relationships which are based on the properties of truth and falsity. However, in this case we are concerned not so much with what makes individual sentences true or false, but with the ways in which *truth-values* can be predicted for groups of related sentences.

For the time being, let's assume that every sentence in a language can be labelled either 'true' or 'false'. The truth-value of any sentence, then, is whichever of these labels applies. There are only two possible truth-values for any sentence: true and false. Speakers of a language in fact know a lot about relations between truth-values. As a speaker of English, you know that if 1) below is true, then 2) must also be true, while 3) must be false.

1)   Braeburn-Twinsett owns a Volvo Estate.
2)   Braeburn-Twinsett owns a car.
3)   Braeburn-Twinsett doesn't own a car.

If you asked any speaker of English to explain the connection between 1) and 2), they would probably say that 2) 'follows logically' from 1), or that '2) has to be true if 1) is true'. This particular relationship between sentences is known as **entailment**. It is what is known as a **truth-functional** relationship; the function, or effect, of entailment is to predict the truth-value of one sentence from what is known of the truth-value of another. Example 3) contains **negation**, which is also truth-functional, because we can predict the truth-value of 3) if we know the truth-value of 1); if 1) is true then 3) must be false. On the other hand, knowing that 1) is true will leave us none the wiser about the truth-value of an example such as 4).

4)   Braeburn-Twinsett lives in a detached house.

We could explain this by saying that there is no truth-functional relationship between 1) and 4). We might be able to make informed guesses about whether 4) is likely to be true, but we would have no firm evidence.

Truth-functional relationships between sentences are studied in the branch of philosophy known as logic. Logic is primarily concerned not with language but with formal relations involving constants and variables. But because these relations can tell us something about what is going on when we interpret sentences such as 1)–3) above, logic is an important area of philosophy for linguists.

There are other types of relationship between sentences which speakers of a language can, in general, agree on, and which linguists therefore need to be able to explain. You may have noticed, for instance, that if you are assured that 1) is a true sentence you learn more from it than simply the contents of Braeburn-Twinsett's garage. You are also led to understand that Braeburn-Twinsett must actually exist. After all, if he didn't exist, we couldn't truthfully say anything about him. In other words, from our example 1) we also understand the following piece of information:

5)   Braeburn-Twinsett exists.

Now the way in which 1) leads us to understand 5) is rather different from the relationship of entailment which holds between 1) and 2). Braeburn-Twinsett's existence, and his ownership of a car, are both necessary conditions for 1) to be true. But while using sentence 1) when you knew Braeburn-Twinsett didn't own a car would just involve saying something false, using it when you knew that no such person actually existed would involve doing something very odd indeed. This relationship between 1) and 5) is known as **presupposition**. As further evidence that presupposition is, at least, different from logical entailment, consider the following:

6)   Braeburn-Twinsett doesn't own a Volvo Estate.

Example 6) is the negation of 1), and as a result it doesn't share its entailments. Specifically, 2) is not a logical entailment of 6). But, in contrast, 6) does still seem to suggest the truth of 5). So while negation has a strong effect on the relationship between a sentence and its entailments, it has no such effect on presupposition. Presupposition has been the subject of much discussion in linguistics, and is talked of variously as a relation between words, between sentences and between speakers. But the roots of this discussion are planted very firmly in philosophy and in fact, as we shall see, in the work of some philosophers with whom we are already familiar, including Gottlob Frege and Bertrand Russell.

This chapter, then, will be largely concerned with the different types of relationship which can exist between sentences, and with the ways in which what we know about the truth-value of one can tell us about the truth-value of other, related sentences. In order to understand what has been said about these relationships, we will need to explore some basic ideas from philosophical logic. First, though, we need to be a bit more familiar with what can be said in general about sentence meaning. In particular, we need to think about **propositions**, and their significance in distinguishing between individual sentences.

Propositions

We saw in the previous chapter that the meanings of words are often described as being made up of both an extension, an actual object or property named, and an intension, the characteristics by which that object or property is distinguished. In fact a very similar claim has been made for sentences. In the case of a sentence, the extension is not an object or property, or even a state of affairs; it is a truth-value. We have seen that there are generally said to be just two truth-values: true and false. So it follows that every sentence in a language has one of two extensions; it is either true or false. Now, we can't explain sentence meaning just in terms of these two extensions. In effect, this would leave us no way of distinguishing between all true sentences on the one hand, and all false ones on the other. If we explained sentence meaning only in terms of extension, and even if we could accept that 7)–9) are all true, we wouldn't be able to say anything about the differences in meaning between them.

7)   Pandas are black and white.
8)   The Earth is larger than Mars.
9)   Columbus discovered America.

This certainly seems to be an unacceptable state of affairs. Despite all having the same extension, it's clear that 7), 8) and 9) have individual meanings which are distinct from each other. Furthermore, it's clear that 8) means the same as 10), while 9) means the same as 11), but that neither 10) nor 11) mean the same as 7).

10) Mars is smaller than the Earth.
11) America was discovered by Columbus.

When we are concerned with meaning which differs from one true sentence to the next, we are concerned with a different aspect of sentence meaning: with intensional meaning. The proposal that the overall significance of a sentence needs to be divided into two separate elements can be found in the work of Gottlob Frege. In his 1892 article 'On sense and reference' which we studied in the last chapter, he proposes that the sense of a sentence is a particular 'thought'. He also describes the 'truth-value of a sentence as constituting what it means' (204). Remember that for Frege what something means is its 'reference', or extension. He goes on to explain:

> If now the truth-value of a sentence is its meaning, then on the one hand all true sentences have the same meaning and so, on the other hand, do all false sentences. From this we can see that in the meaning of a sentence all that is specific is obliterated. We can never be concerned only with the meaning of a sentence; but again the mere thought alone yields no knowledge, but only the thought together with its meaning, i.e. its truth-value.
>
> (204)

Frege specifies that what forms the sense, or intension, of a sentence is to be understood as the 'content' of a thought. This is what is often described as a proposition. In philosophy and linguistics, as in some of its 'everyday' uses, the term is often associated with thoughts, statements, claims and beliefs. Propositions are sometimes described as able to be introduced by 'that ... ' clauses. If, for instance, you believe that Mrs Solomon, your next-door neighbour, is wise, then the proposition that Mrs Solomon is wise is the content of your belief, and you can express this belief in any of the following ways, among others.

12) Mrs Solomon is wise.
13) My next-door neighbour is wise.
14) Madame Solomon est sage.

The sentences 12)–14) are certainly not identical, but they all contain, or express, the same proposition. To put it another way, 13) and 14) are intensionally equivalent to 12): 13) by means of paraphrase within the same language, and 14) by means of translation into another language.[1] If we were asked whether 12)–14) were true, we would need to find out about the truth or falsity of this one proposition. If it in fact turns out that Mrs Solomon is not wise, then the belief, and therefore all the sentences used to express it, will be false. So propositions are entities which can be true or false, and therefore have consequences for the truth or falsity of the sentences which express them. Remember that the intension of a word can be said to determine what counts as its extension. In just the same way the intension of a sentence, a proposition, can determine whether its extensional meaning is 'true' or 'false'. It may help to think of a true proposition as being equivalent to a 'fact'. If you believe or state a fact then your belief or statement will be true. If what you believe or state is not a fact, your belief or statement will be false.

Notice also that our examples 12)–14) involve a subject, by means of which an individual is named, and a predicate in which some property is ascribed to that individual. The association of an individual with a property is often taken to be the basic form of a proposition. In fact, it is part of some definitions of propositionality. Such an association is generally expressed in simple declarative sentences, as in examples 12)–14) above. It's important to bear in mind that declarative sentences are not themselves propositions, but that they generally express propositions. This important point is made particularly clearly by the German philosopher Rudolf Carnap. In his (1956) book *Meaning and Necessity*, originally published in 1947, Carnap defines the term *proposition* as being used not 'for sentences or for sentences together with their meaning but for those entities which themselves are extra-linguistic but which, if they find expression in a language, are expressed by (declarative) sentences' (26–7).

Carnap is here stressing that the intensional meanings of sentences, like those of individual words, can't themselves be explained within the linguistic system; for words and sentences to be meaningful they must relate to the world outside this system. Of course there is the added complication that when we want to produce a proposition, for purposes of discussion, we generally need to do so by producing a declarative sentence which expresses the proposition. All the examples we have considered in this section have taken the form of declarative sentences. This is one instance of the general problem which linguists and philosophers face of having to use language for the purpose of discussing language.

We will be returning to propositionality throughout the following chapters, where we will consider its implications in more detail. For the time being, however, we are equipped with enough information to enable us to examine the ways in which propositions have been used in formal logic.

Formal logic

The term *logic* is often used in normal, non-philosophical conversation to mean something similar to 'reasoning' or 'argument'. People say 'I don't follow your logic' or 'I don't see the logic in that' when they mean that they can't understand how a particular conclusion was reached, or agree with a particular line of argument. In philosophy, the term is used with a related, but more precise meaning, to talk about how we can get from a particular starting point, say the truth-value of one sentence, to a separate conclusion, such as the truth-value of another, related, sentence. We are interested in logic because of its significance in linguistics, but many of the philosophers who have worked in this area, some of whose work we will consider in this chapter, have been concerned primarily with mathematics, and only secondarily with language.

With this in mind, it's perhaps not surprising that the expressions used in logic can look rather like mathematical equations. This can make them look distinctly off-putting at first glance to students of language, but with a bit of decoding we should find that the parts of logic we need to understand for our purposes are not too daunting. The 'mathematical' look is partly due to the fact that logic employs *variables* to stand in for specific entities, so as to be able to make general statements, or *formulae*, which will hold good whatever specific values are given to the variables. You are probably familiar with mathematical terms such as $\sqrt{x}$ which means 'the square root of any number' and $x+1$ which means 'any number plus one'. In just the same way in logic we find formulae such as $\ulcorner p \wedge q \urcorner$ where the variables p and q stand for propositions, and the symbol $\wedge$ is a logical version of $+$.

Notice that as well as the use of variables to stand for propositions we are using the symbols $\ulcorner \ \urcorner$ in place of the quotation marks ' '. These are known as *corner quotes*, and are used to indicate that what is being quoted is a general formula rather than a specific sentence. The use of corner quotes generally implies that we could be talking about any expression which has this particular form: any expression which can be obtained by replacing the variables with appropriate words or phrases. With appropriate substitution, the formula ⌜p∧q⌝ could be instantiated, or exemplified, by any of the following, and of course by any other similar expression:

15) Rover has four legs and Tommy has two legs. (where p = *Rover has four legs* and q = *Tommy has two legs*)
16) Alice is ten and Ben is five.
17) My neighbour's car runs on petrol and my car runs on diesel.

The branch of logic we are considering here, the one most centrally concerned with relationships between propositions, is known as *propositional*, or *sentential* logic.

Propositional logic

Propositions such as 'Rover has four legs' and 'Ben is five' are known as *simple propositions*; they each represent what Frege would describe as the 'content' of a single thought. Propositional logic is largely concerned with the ways in which simple propositions can combine together to form *compound propositions*, propositions which can be analysed as involving the contents of more than one thought. Examples 15)–17) above are all compound propositions. Propositional logic is also known as *propositional calculus*; it involves working out, or calculating, the truth-value of a complex proposition from the truth-values of its parts. So doing propositional calculus sometimes seems a bit like 'doing sums' with propositions. If it looks at times as if we might be getting too far away from language, then remember that for the output of propositional calculus to make sense it must always be possible to replace the variables such as p, q, r with simple propositions. In fact this is often a good way of checking what a propositional formula means.

So in studying propositional logic we are considering the possible operations, or procedures, which can be performed on propositions. Propositional logic includes a number of symbols for these, which are known as *operators*, or sometimes as *truth-functional operators*, because they tell us the truth-value of the compound proposition from what we know to be the truth-values of the simple propositions. Unlike the symbols such as p, q, r, these symbols always stand for the same operations; they each have a unique value. These operators are therefore known as *logical constants*. The operators which we will consider here are **conjunction**, negation, **disjunction** and condition. They can be related to the linguistic expressions *and*, *not*, *or* and *if ... then*, although the exact nature of these relationships is something we will need to look into in more detail later.

Conjunction

Logical conjunction acts, as its name suggests, to join two or more propositions together. The symbol for logical conjunction is ∧, so the conjunction of two simple propositions, p and q, is represented by the formula ⌜p∧q⌝. Other symbols which are sometimes used for this are ⌜p·q⌝, ⌜Kpq⌝, ⌜p&q⌝ or simply ⌜pq⌝. They all mean the same; we will stick with ⌜p∧q⌝ for simplicity. We have seen that operators such as conjunction are sometimes described as 'truth-functional' because they determine the truth of a compound proposition from the truth of simple propositions. Now consider the simple propositions 18) and 19), and the compound proposition 20):

18) Mary is happy.
19) Fred is sad.
20) Mary is happy and Fred is sad.

The compound proposition combines the information contained in both the simple propositions. If these pieces of information are both true then the compound proposition will be true. But if either piece of information is false, that is if either Mary is not happy or Fred is not sad, then the compound proposition in 20) will be false, because it will contain a piece of false information. If Mary is not happy, for instance, then it simply can't be the case that Mary is happy and Fred is sad. And of course if both simple propositions are false then the compound proposition will be false. In other words, the only situation in which ⌜p∧q⌝ can be true is if both p and q are true. In any other situation, ⌜p∧q⌝ will be false.

There is a more concise way of expressing the sort of information contained in the last paragraph. Describing the truth-functional effects of an operator in all possible situations can be a long-winded process. This information can instead be contained in a *truth table*, a chart which gives the truth-value of the compound proposition in every possible situation. The meaning of an operator consists in its effects on truth-values, so such a table constitutes a definition of the operator. A truth table employs columns to list the possible truth-values and rows to show how the operator relates them to each other. Here is the truth table for conjunction:

p	*q*	*p∧q*
t	t	t
t	f	f
f	t	f
f	f	f

Each column is headed with a simple or complex proposition. Each row represents a possible situation, and states the truth-values of each proposition in that situation. So the first row under the headings can be read as, 'if p is true and q is true then ⌜p∧q⌝ is true', and the second as 'if p is true and q is false then ⌜p∧q⌝ is false', and so on.

Negation

Negation is different from conjunction in that it operates on only one proposition at a time. Informally we might say that if we add *not* to a positive statement we get the denial, or the opposite, of that statement. So 22) and 23) both act to deny, or to negate, what is said in 21):

21) The moon is made of green cheese.
22) The moon is not made of green cheese.
23) It is not the case that the moon is made of green cheese.

In propositional calculus, the symbol for logical negation is ~. So if we replace the simple proposition in 21) with the variable p, we can represent 22) or 23) as ⌜~p⌝. Now we have said informally that a negative proposition will be the 'opposite' of the corresponding positive. In terms of truth-values, the operation of negation inverts the truth-value of a proposition. So if we take a true proposition and negate it we must get a false one, but if we take a false proposition (such as what we in fact have in 21]) and negate it we get a true proposition (such as 22] or 23]). In other words, it's not possible for a proposition and its negation to be both true or both false.

Here is the truth table for negation:

p	*~p*
t	f
f	t

As the headings indicate, each row gives a possible value for p and the corresponding value for ⌜~p⌝. So the table states that whenever p is true, ⌜~p⌝ is false, and whenever p is false, ⌜~p⌝ is true. That is the meaning of logical negation. Certain other facts follow from this, of course. The table rules out the possibility that p and ⌜~p⌝ could ever both be true. Remember we saw that a conjunction will be false whenever at least one of the simple propositions conjoined is false. It follows that a compound proposition of the form ⌜p∧~p⌝ must always be false. Example 24), and indeed any proposition with this form, is a **contradiction**.[2]

24) Alice is a child and Alice is not a child.

Notice also that if we take a proposition of the form ⌜~p⌝ and feed it back through the table, negation will again reverse the truth-value; if ⌜~p⌝ is true then ⌜~~p⌝ will be false. By having the opposite value from ⌜~p⌝,

⌜~~p⌝ will always have the same truth-value as p. So in logic, if not always in natural language, two negatives cancel each other out, or 'make a positive'. This can be expressed logically by the formula in 25). Although it sounds distinctly odd, it is quite easy to interpret 26) as false, like 21):

25) ~~p = p
26) It is not the case that the moon is not made of green cheese.

Disjunction

Disjunction is like conjunction, rather than negation, in that it combines two or more propositions. These propositions are described as *disjuncts*. The disjunction of two simple propositions, p and q, is symbolised as ⌜p∨q⌝. Disjunction can be related in meaning to *or* although, as is often the case with logical operators and natural language expressions, their meanings are not always equivalent. However, as the similarity to *or* suggests, disjunction differs from conjunction in that only one, not both, of the disjuncts need be true for the disjunction as a whole to be true. To illustrate this, we can use the simple propositions 27) and 28), and the disjunction 29).

27) William has gone to play tennis.
28) Martha has gone to her violin lesson.
29) William has gone to play tennis or Martha has gone to her violin lesson.

Imagine that you pass by William and Martha's house, spot that their car is not on the drive, and produce 29) by way of explanation. If it turns out that one of the simple propositions 27) and 28) is true, you would be justified in concluding that what you said in 29) was true. If, however, it turns out that neither 27) nor 28) is true, then you were mistaken and what you said in 29) was false. This is the only situation in which a logical disjunction can be false. The truth table for disjunction is as follows:

p	*q*	*p∨q*
t	t	t
t	f	t
f	t	t
f	f	f

This shows up the difference between logical disjunction and natural language *or*. This difference occurs in the first line of the truth table. If, in our example, it turns out that in fact William was at tennis *and* Martha was at her violin lesson, you might well be accused of having been wrong in stating 29); you didn't allow for the possibility that both disjuncts might be true. But the truth table for logical disjunction allows for the disjunct to be true when *both* disjuncts are true.

Condition

Finally, we need to consider logical **conditionals** which, as noted earlier, can be related to natural language *if … then*. A statement of the form 'if p, then q' is represented in logic as ⌜p⊃q⌝. As with conjunction, there are some alternative ways of symbolising this operator, and you may sometimes come across the forms ⌜p→q⌝ or ⌜Cpq⌝, which are exactly equivalent. The two propositions involved in a conditional are known as the *antecedent* (p) and the *consequent* (q). Imagine that a friend says to you:

30) If you wash the car I will take you out for lunch.

It would, of course, be perfectly reasonable to expect that, sometime after you have washed the car, you will be taken out for lunch. So reasonable, in fact, that if you washed the car but were then disappointed in this expectation, you would be justified in claiming that your friend had lied: that 30) was false. From this we learn that the conditional as a whole is false where the antecedent is true but the consequent false.

Now imagine that you decide that your friend is not offering a very good bargain, that you decline to wash the car, and that you are then taken out for lunch anyway. You will probably be pleasantly surprised, but this turn of events doesn't make 30) false. In fact we can go further and say that if the antecedent is false (if you don't wash the car), then the conditional as a whole will be true whatever happens. This may at first seem to be a rather strange claim to make. We might be inclined to wonder how 30) can be a true statement if you refuse to wash the car. Well, it will be true just because it is concerned only with the consequences of your washing the car; it has nothing to say about what will happen if you don't wash it, so no possible consequence can make it false. So the truth table for logical conditional is as follows:

p	q	p⊃q
t	t	t
t	f	f
f	t	t
f	f	t

There is one particular consequence of this which seems bizarre when translated into natural language sentences, but is perfectly consistent logically. As we have seen, a conditional will always be true when its antecedent is false. It follows from this that any conditional with a false

antecedent will be true, regardless of the nature of its consequent. So 31) and 32) must both be described as true statements:

31) If the world is flat then London is the capital of England.
32) If ice sinks in water then whales are fish.

This is because a purely logical conditional is concerned only with truth-functional relationships, and not at all with the nature of, or possible connections between, the propositions p and q. It is sometimes referred to as a *material* conditional, a name suggested by Bertrand Russell. With natural language *if*, on the other hand, we generally expect the antecedent and the consequent to be related in some way, for instance in terms of cause and effect.

Before we finish our brief survey of logical operators we should consider the curious-looking expression ***iff***, which also occurs in complex propositions, and which needs to be clearly distinguished from the examples we have considered so far. Put briefly, *iff* is an abbreviation for *if and only if*. Now the expression *if and only if* does occur in natural language, although it's less common than the simple *if*, and describes a different relationship. Imagine that, instead of 30) above, your friend had said to you:

33) I will take you out for lunch if, and only if, you wash the car.

You would still be justified in expecting to be taken out for lunch after washing the car, but this time you have no reason to hope that your friend might take you out for lunch even if you decline. In fact, 33) would prove false if you decided not to wash the car but were taken out for lunch anyway. An expression of the form 'q if, and only if, p' is represented in logic as ⌜q iff p⌝, or alternatively ⌜p≡q⌝, ⌜p↔q⌝, or ⌜Epq⌝. Its truth table is as follows:

p	*q*	*q iff p*
t	t	t
t	f	f
f	t	f
f	f	t

Propositional logic can, of course, get a lot more complicated than the examples we have considered here, but we have now defined its general notation and basic operators. As well as the ways in which simple propositions can be combined to form complex ones, however, logic is also concerned with the form of the simple propositions themselves. This is the concern of the branch of logic known as *predicate logic*, which we will consider next.

Predicate logic

Predicate logic offers a more detailed form of analysis than propositional logic, in that it describes not just relationships between propositions, but also the internal structure of propositions themselves. It enables us to describe how a proposition can, for instance, make statements about the existence of entities, associate an entity with a particular property, and generalise over classes of entities. It also, in a sense, includes propositional logic, in that it uses the logical constants we have considered so far to explain relationships between propositions. In predicate logic, variables are used to stand in for entities and the predicates which can be applied to them. So in a formula such as ⌜Fx⌝, F stands for a predicate and x for an entity. So F can be replaced by any predicate and x by any entity giving us, among numerous others, examples such as:

34) This house has three bedrooms.
   (where x = *this house* and F = *three bedrooms*)
35) The floor is rotten.
   (where x = *the floor* and F = *rotten*)[3]

As well as assigning a predicate to one entity, predicate logic allows us to describe a relationship between two entities. To give the formula for this, we place a variable standing for the relationship first, followed by variables standing for the two entities, for instance: ⌜Fxy⌝. Just as with the simple formula, we can suggest a huge number of instantiations of this formula, such as:

36) George was the father of Elizabeth.
   (where F = *father of*, x = *George* and y = *Elizabeth*)

37) Clarence admires Archibald.
   (where F = *admires*, x = *Clarence* and y = *Archibald*)

38) Martha plays the violin.
   (where F = *plays*, x = *Martha* and y = *violin*)

Predicate logic also includes a number of **quantifiers**. In linguistics, this term is used to refer to words which express quantity, words such as *all, every, each, any, most, many, some, no*, etc. There are operators in predicate logic which correspond to words of this type, the most commonly discussed of which are the *existential* and the *universal* quantifiers.

Existential statements

The existential quantifier, as its name suggests, is used to make logical statements about the existence of entities. It is represented by the symbol ∃; a statement to the effect that an entity, x, exists, would take the form ⌜∃x⌝. This can be added to any formula in which a particular predicate is assigned to a variable, giving something which can be given a definite truth-value. So for instance ⌜red x⌝ specifies of any individual which can be substituted for x that it is red. As it stands, without knowing *what* individual is under discussion, we can't say anything about its truth-value. But now let's add the existential quantifier, giving us 39):

39) (∃x) (red x)

We now have a formula which states that there exists some particular entity, and further that this entity is red. We could paraphrase it informally as 'there is something which is red'. This statement *can* be assigned a truth-value. In fact, we could point at any one red thing to indicate that it is true that there exists an entity which is red. Note that this formula doesn't say anything about whether there is one or more than one relevant entity which fits the description. So alongside 39) above we could suggest:

40) (∃x) (Pope x)

Again, we could point to an individual who exists and who is the Pope, to demonstrate that this is true. In fact, there is only one individual we could point to in order to prove 40) true, but a choice of many for 39); there is only one Pope but there are many red things. The existential quantifier doesn't allow for this distinction; it can best be read as stipulating that there is *at least one* entity of a certain type.

Universal statements

The other quantifier commonly used in predicate logic is the universal quantifier. It is used to make statements about the whole of any set of entities, or to generalise over a class. Its natural language counterparts include *all*, *every*, *each* and *any*. The symbol for the universal quantifier is ∀. This can be combined with the other operators we have considered to make universal statements. Suppose we want to generalise over a particular class of entities, say all politicians, and to state that they all have a particular property, say that they are all corrupt. Using P to stand for the predicate *is a politician* and C to stand for the predicate *is corrupt*, we can express our generalisation as follows:

41) (∀x) (Px→Cx)

This can be read as 'for every entity x, if x is a politician then x is corrupt' or, more informally, 'all politicians are corrupt'.

The universal quantifier can also be used to generalise over relationships between entities or, more precisely, over relationships between classes of entities. Remember that we saw above that 'George was the father of Elizabeth' is one possible instantiation of the formula ⌜Fxy⌝, where F = *father of*. Now of course the pair *Elizabeth, George* is only one of a huge number of pairs which would fit that formula. If we wanted to suggest a universal statement from this we could say that everybody has a father, or that for every person, there is someone who is his or her father. Now we already have a quantifier for describing existence, the existential quantifier. So our generalisation could be stated in logical form as follows:

42) $(\forall y)\ (\exists x)\ (Fxy)$

This can be read as: 'for every entity y there exists an entity x such that x is the father of y', or simply 'everyone has a father'.[4]

These are of course only a few of the many types of proposition which can be expressed using predicate logic. But the operators with which we are now familiar are enough to enable us to understand some of the main ideas which have been put forward concerning logical relations. For the rest of this chapter we will concentrate on the two particular relationships we considered in the introduction to this chapter: entailment and presupposition.

Entailment and presupposition

In our study of propositional logic, we looked at some of the ways in which the truth or falsity of one proposition can have consequences for the truth or falsity of another. In particular, we considered a number of situations in which the truth-value of a simple proposition affects the truth-value of the compound proposition of which it is a part. So, for instance, from what we know about the logical properties of conjunction, we can say that if 44) is false then 43) must also be false; or, to put it another way, for 43) to be true it is necessary for 44) to be true.

43) It's a sunny day and Tommy has four tickets for the test match.
44) Tommy has four tickets for the test match.

The truth-functional properties of conjunction tell us that if a proposition q is false then a proposition ⌜p∧q⌝ is also false, so if Tommy doesn't have four tickets for the test match then not only 44) but also 43) must be false. Notice that if 44) is true, however, we can't say anything definite about the truth-value of 43); it might be true, but to decide whether it is or not we need to know something else, that is whether it's a sunny day or not.

What we have just established about the relationship between 43) and 44) is, in fact, that 43) entails 44), or that 44) is an entailment of 43). If a proposition p entails a proposition q, we can represent this relationship as ⌜p→q⌝. Remember that this is one of the symbols which is sometimes used for the relationship of material condition. In fact the two logical relationships are very similar; if p entails q then the truth of q follows logically from that of p, just as the truth of a consequent follows from the truth of an antecedent.

We can summarise the relationship of entailment by saying that, if p entails q, then the truth of q is a necessary precondition for the truth of p. There are two predictions we can make about the truth-values:

45) If p is true then q is true.
46) If q is false then p is false.

As we have seen, we can't predict anything about the truth-value of q if p is false, or the truth-value of p if q is true. A proposition may have any number of entailments. For instance, 43) above entails both 44) and also the proposition that it's a sunny day. Each one of these entailments must be true in order for p to be true. The truth of each one of its entailments is a *necessary* condition for the truth of p, but only taken altogether does the truth of the entailments count as a *sufficient* condition for the truth of p.

There are propositions other than logical entailments which follow from the truth of sentences such as our two statements about Tommy. We would probably, for instance, understand that there was someone called Tommy, even if we were not previously aware of his existence; we would understand 47):

47) Tommy exists.

As we saw in the introduction to this chapter, we can describe this as a presupposition. Unlike a logical entailment, it is shared by a positive statement and its denial; 43) and 48) share 47) as a presupposition:

48) It's a sunny day, but Tommy doesn't have four tickets for the test match.

This, in fact, sums up the most common definition of semantic presupposition. We will look at this definition and its implications in more detail soon. But first we need to consider some of the philosophical work which was influential in shaping our understanding of presupposition and its relationship to logic. To do so, we need to return to the debate about the nature of names which we studied in the last chapter, and specifically to the opposing views of Gottlob Frege and Bertrand Russell.

Frege on logical presupposition

Frege was perhaps the first to use the term *presupposition* for this type of logical relationship, although he does so only in passing. In 'On sense and reference', he notices the shared element between a statement and its negation. Here is his explanation:

> If anything is asserted there is an obvious presupposition that the simple or proper names used have meaning. If therefore one asserts 'Kepler died in misery', there is a presupposition that the name 'Kepler' designates something; but it does not follow that the sense of the sentence 'Kepler died in misery' contains the thought that the name 'Kepler' designates something. If this were the case the negation would have to run not
>
> Kepler did not die in misery
>
> but
>
> Kepler did not die in misery, or the name 'Kepler' has no reference.
>
> That the name 'Kepler' designates something is just as much a presupposition for the assertion
>
> Kepler died in misery
>
> as for the contrary assertion.

(69)

Remember that in Frege's terms, to say that a name 'has meaning' is to say that it refers to some actual entity. So Frege can be paraphrased as saying that an assertion which contains a name introduces a presupposition that this name does in fact refer. This is not, however, part of the proposition expressed (part of the 'sense of a sentence'). 'Kepler did not die in misery' doesn't entail that Kepler died in misery, but it does presuppose that Kepler exists.[5]

Frege further argues that the denotation of a complex expression is dependent on the denotations of its parts. So if *Kepler* doesn't denote, if there is no such person as Kepler, the sentence 'Kepler died in misery' can't denote either. Now, according to Frege, the denotation of a sentence is its truth-value, so a sentence which has no denotation has no truth-value. This is not, of course, to say that 'Kepler died in misery' makes no sense, or expresses no proposition. For Frege all 'proper names' have sense, or connotation. So we can still attribute sense to the name, and hence to the sentence which contains it, even if Kepler doesn't exist. An assertion of the sentence when Kepler doesn't exist would be an example of what is sometimes known as 'presupposition failure'. Such uses are in fact quite common in natural language. But Frege was interested in developing a logically perfect language. He saw the existence of referring expressions which fail to denote, and hence of sentences without truth-value, as an 'imperfection of language' (70).

Frege's account of this type of example was challenged twenty-three years after 'On sense and meaning' was first published, in an article by Bertrand Russell written in 1905 and entitled 'On denoting'. In the last chapter we looked at Russell's later article, 'Descriptions', and saw that, unlike Frege, he drew a distinction between proper names, such as *Kepler*, and definite descriptions, such as *the Prime Minister of Britain*. He claimed that these latter don't in fact refer to individuals; they describe but do not denote. As evidence of this, Russell drew attention to definite descriptions such as *the round square* and *the golden mountain*. We postponed discussion of the question of what happens when such phrases occur in sentences, a question which Russell addresses in his 1905 article.

Russell on denoting

In 'On denoting', Russell observes that 'a phrase may be denoting, and yet not denote anything; e.g., "The present king of France" ' (471). By virtue of its form, just because it is a definite description, this phrase would appear to denote a unique individual. Yet in 1905, and indeed today, there is no individual named by this phrase; there is nothing to which the expression refers. The question then is how to interpret a sentence with an expression such as *the king of France* as its subject. Here is Russell's own, now famous, example:

49) The king of France is bald.

It's clear how a Fregean account of this example would go. Frege doesn't in fact discuss definite descriptions in this context, but his explanation would necessarily be the same as for his 'Kepler died in misery' example, because he classes descriptions and names together as 'proper names', having both sense and reference. For Frege, an assertion of 49) would introduce a presupposition that the definite description does refer, that the individual exists. In situations when this is not in fact the case, 49) would fail to have a truth-value, an unfortunate example of an imperfection in language. Russell looks at the problem in a rather different way. His claim is that 49) does have a truth-value: 'it is plainly false' (484).

In explaining how 49) can be described as false, Russell concentrates on the meaning of the sentence as a whole, rather than just that of the subject. Indeed, his claim is that the meaning of a definite description can only be described in terms of the meaning of expressions in which it occurs; 'a denoting phrase is essentially *part* of a sentence, and does not, like most single words, have any significance of its own' (488). He distinguishes between the grammatical form of a sentence, a purely linguistic matter, and its logical form, something which can be expressed in predicate logic of the type we have been studying. The expression *the king of France* may be the grammatical subject of 49), but it isn't the logical subject. Indeed, this sentence has no logical subject. Unlike a sentence with a proper name in the subject position, 49) is not, despite appearances, logically in subject-predicate form. Instead, the meaning of the sentence involves quantifiers, variables and identity. The sentence states that there exists one, and only one, king of France, and also that all entities which are king of France are bald. It is false because one of its entailments, the proposition that there exists a king of France, is false.

The logical form which Russell assigns to his example can be summarised in the following formula of predicate logic.

50) $(\exists x) (kFx \wedge (\forall y) (kFy \rightarrow y = x) \wedge Bx)$

This may at first appear rather daunting, but this is only because it's a bit longer than the logical forms we have considered so far. It's entirely made up of variables and logical operators with which we are familiar. So it's helpful to consider it as a series of small 'chunks' of logic:

$\exists x$	kFx	$\wedge$	$\forall y$	KFy	$\rightarrow$	$y = x$	$\wedge$	Bx
There exists an entity x	such that the entity x is the king of France	and	for any entity y	if that entity y is the king of France	then	the entity y is identical to the entity x	and	the entity x is bald

Informally, this can be paraphrased as 'there is one, and only one, king of France and he is bald'. As Russell explains, this offers a way of reducing any proposition with a denoting phrase as a constituent to one which doesn't involve a denoting phrase. The sentence needn't be dismissed as meaningless because it isn't a sentence 'about' about the king of France. It's a series of statements about existence and identity. Such statements can indeed be meaningful, even in the absence of a king of France.

Remember that Frege used the relationship between a statement and the denial of that statement to argue that certain propositions must be presupposed rather than entailed. Russell also considers the effect of negation, but he uses it to support his analysis of examples such as 49) as not being logically of subject-predicate form. He argues that 51), the negation of 49), is in fact logically ambiguous.

51) The king of France is not bald.

His claim is that this could be interpreted in two ways, as a denial of either of two of the logical entailments of 49): that is, of the baldness or of the existence of the king. The acceptability of both of the following illustrates this apparent ambiguity:

52) The king of France is not bald; he has a full head of hair.
53) The king of France is not bald; there is no king of France.

This is often described as an ambiguity in the 'scope' of the negation. Using the logical form in 50) above, we can express this ambiguity in the scope of negation as an ambiguity between 52b) and 53b):

52b) $\sim(\exists x)\ (kFx\ \&\ (\forall y)\ (kFy{\rightarrow}x = y)\ \&\ Bx)$
53b) $(\exists x)\ (kFx\ \&\ (\forall y)\ (kFy{\rightarrow}x = y)\ \&\ \sim Bx)$

Again, these formulas look complicated at first glance, but on closer inspection consist only of a series of symbols with which we are familiar. In 52b) the negation is attached to the statement of existence; this formula states that there is no unique entity which is the king of France and is bald. In 53b) however, the negation is attached only to the statement of baldness; there is a unique king of France, but he is not bald. Now of course in 1905, and also today, the interpretation offered in 52b) makes 51) true, while with the interpretation in 53b) it is false. Russell doesn't recognise presupposition as a separate logical relationship. He analyses both the existence of the king of France and his baldness as logical entailments of 49). In effect, for Russell, 51) can be read as 'Either the king of France is not bald or there is no unique king of France'.

Russell's account of definite descriptions, and of 'denoting phrases' which fail to denote, was widely accepted and remained practically unchallenged for forty-five years. Then in 1950 Peter Strawson published an article entitled 'On referring', in which he offered an alternative approach to the questions Russell had been concerned with. Strawson was one of the leading members of what came to be known as the **ordinary language** school of philosophy, the school which argued that natural language and language use are as valid subjects for philosophical investigations as are the formalised languages of logic and mathematics.

Strawson on referring

Strawson's interest in natural language use is apparent in his approach to the problem of denoting expressions which fail to refer: the 'the king of France' problem. He begins his article with the comment that 'We very commonly *use* expressions of certain kinds to mention or refer to some individual person' (320, emphasis added). It is the speaker, not the expressions themselves, which Strawson regards as doing the referring. Strawson argues that ' "Mentioning", or "referring", is not something an expression does; it is something that some one can use an expression to do' (326). It is this very point which, he suggests, has been missed by 'logicians' when they have discussed meaning.

Strawson's explanation of the relevant examples is remarkably similar to Frege's account. Both depend on the idea that proper names and descriptions introduce a presupposition of the existence of the individual denoted. In fact, philosophers and linguists now sometimes talk about the 'Frege–Strawson' definition of logical presupposition, almost as if they had worked on it together. This similarity may at first seem rather surprising. After all, the two philosophers, working more than fifty years apart in separate countries, took very different approaches to the study of language. Frege was principally interested in developing a logically perfect language which would be adequate for the purposes of mathematical analysis. He would seem to be an obvious candidate for the criticism levelled by Strawson at 'logicians' interested in meaning. Strawson, on the other hand, was dedicated to the idea that natural language was a legitimate topic of study in its own right. To criticise it for being 'imperfect' would, according to Strawson, be to miss the point; language doesn't need to be 'purified' or 'perfected' in order for it to be worthy of serious study.

Nevertheless, both philosophers reached the conclusion that the relationship between a denoting expression and the proposition that its referent exists is one of presupposition rather than entailment. This conclusion, however, followed for each of them from very different premises. For Frege, it was a logical consequence of his distinction between sense and reference, itself an attempt to explain logically certain types of sentence, most importantly statements of identity. For Strawson, the conclusion was part of his rejection of Russell's account of sentences containing definite descriptions: an account in terms of a logical form very different from grammatical form. In particular, Strawson criticises Russell for his 'preoccupation with mathematics and formal logic' (337). Russell, he suggests, insists on a classical system of logic, one in which every proposition must be either 'true' or 'false'; he insists on applying this to what are, in fact, specific types of natural language use. Russell therefore fails to take account of how most people would react on hearing his *the king of France* example (in which, for some reason, Strawson changes *bald* to *wise*). Strawson explicitly rejects the claim that an expression such as 'the king of France is wise' must be either true or false. He allows for cases in which a speaker uses this sentence but 'the question of whether his statement was true or false simply *didn't arise*' (330, original emphasis). These are instances in which the statement fails to say anything true or false simply because it fails to mention any individual.

In Strawson's analysis, then, the proposition that there exists a unique king of France is not an entailment of the sentence. It is, rather, implied in what he describes as a 'special' way. In *Introduction to Logical Theory*, published in 1952, he uses the term presupposition for this special type of implication. It is here that he offers a definition of presupposition as truth-functionally distinct from entailment. He reminds us that if a proposition, say *q*, is a logical entailment of another proposition, say *p*, then *q* is a necessary condition only for the truth of *p*. He compares this with the relationship between two statements, which he labels S and S', in which 'S' is a necessary condition of the *truth or falsity* of S ... let us say, as above, that S *presupposes* S'' (175, original emphasis). Another way of expressing this is to say that S' is presupposed by S if it is logically necessary for both S (the truth of S) and ~S (the falsity of S). This is what is generally accepted to be the standard logical, or the *Frege–Strawson* definition of presupposition.

In effect, Strawson abandons the idea that what is known as *bivalent* logic must be sufficient to explain ordinary language. Bivalent logic, also known as classical logic because of its origins in ancient philosophy, is the logic we have been working with in this chapter. It allows a choice between precisely two truth-values for any proposition: 'true' and 'false'. Strawson argues that in some contexts a statement may have neither of these values, because the question of its truth or falsity may just not arise. Some logicians have proposed a three-valued, or *trivalent* logic which is sometimes described as containing the values 'true', 'false' and 'neither-true-nor-false'. An example such as Russell's *the king of France* sentence, when the presupposition necessary for it to be either true or false fails, must be classified as having this third truth-value. Other logicians have suggested that it is possible to retain a bivalent system, as long as a 'truth-value gap' is included to account for such examples.

It is a testimony to Bertrand Russell's longevity and enduring interest in philosophy that in 1957, fifty-two years after originally publishing 'On denoting', he produced a response to Strawson's challenge, in an article entitled 'Mr Strawson on referring'. This response is short and polemical, and serves to highlight the differences between the approaches to the study of meaning adopted by Russell, with his interest in mathematical logic, and by Strawson. Russell sums up this difference, from his own point of view, by describing how many philosophers of the time, including Strawson,

> Are persuaded that common speech is good enough not only for daily life, but also for philosophy. I, on the contrary, am persuaded that common speech is full of vagueness and inaccuracy, and that any attempt to be precise and accurate requires modification of common speech both as regards vocabulary and as regards syntax.
>
> (387)

Russell saw the task of the philosopher as being, in part, to modify imprecise natural language to reflect 'correct' logical structure. In his response, he reiterates his commitment to the idea that every meaningful sentence must, in accordance with classical logic, be either true or false. His aim had always been to find an adequate way of explaining this logic; 'My theory of descriptions was never intended as an analysis of the state of mind of those who utter sentences containing descriptions' (388).

Russell's response to Strawson indicates that the debate between their different accounts of non-denoting definite descriptions was not resolved, and that it in fact remains unresolvable. The two philosophers, and the schools of thought which they can be seen as representing, approach the problems from two very different perspectives. Strawson's account is the one which has been of most enduring interest to linguists. This is perhaps not surprising, given Strawson's interest in speakers and their use of language. After all, Russell accused him of being concerned with 'common speech' and with 'the state of mind' of the speaker, two topics which have become of central importance in modern linguistics.

There is, however, another reason for the popularity of Strawson's account of logical presupposition, clearly distinguished as it is from logical entailment. It seems to capture the intuitive response that many people have to examples such as 'the king of France is bald'. That is, that there are important differences between the proposition that the king of France is bald and the proposition that he exists. The first, a logical entailment, is what is explicitly stated; it is set out for discussion. The second, however, seems to be not so much stated as assumed, or taken for granted. The distinction is sometimes discussed in terms of *foregrounded* (entailed) propositions and *backgrounded* (presupposed) ones. Russell's account, dependent as it is on a series of logical entailments, doesn't allow for any explanation of this apparent difference. For Russell, this isn't really a problem since, as we have seen, his interest isn't in speakers' (or hearers') states of mind. However, it's important for an explanation of this difference to be available when presupposition is discussed, as it has been, as a relationship between speakers. Such accounts involve what is known as *context-bound* or *pragmatic* presupposition.

Pragmatic presupposition

The story of work on presupposition in linguistics can very broadly be summarised as a debate between two opposing points of view. Some linguists have seen presupposition as a semantic feature of the language, determined by the structure and vocabulary of sentences, while others have characterised it as a pragmatic feature of speakers' behaviour, determined by the utterances they produce in particular contexts. When presupposition was first discussed in linguistics, it was the 'logical' aspects of presupposition which received most attention, generally discussed in terms of the Frege–Strawson account of the difference between entailment and presupposition. Linguists in this tradition have concentrated on analysing the presuppositional properties and behaviour of different words, structures and complex sentences. We will consider a few of these in the final section of this chapter.

Around the beginning of the 1970s, linguists began to work on the idea that presupposition is best described as a relationship between utterances, or even the speakers who produce them. Such descriptions drew on the claim that what is presupposed is often dependent not just on logical properties, but on context of use. They were based on the idea that the reasons why some information may be presupposed rather than asserted, and therefore be presented as 'background', are dependent on contextual factors such as the speaker's beliefs, the purpose of the discourse and so on. Despite the clear difference of emphasis between semantic and pragmatic accounts, both can be seen as drawing on ideas put forward by Strawson.

Strawson's influence on the development of a pragmatic account of presupposition shouldn't in fact be too much of a surprise. He was, as we have seen, keen to emphasise the importance of distinguishing between sentences and the uses they are put to, or the statements they can be used to make. In *Introduction to Logical Theory*, he states explicitly that his 'presuppositional' logic applies to statements, not to sentences: 'It is about statements only that the question of truth or falsity can arise; and about these it can sometimes fail to arise' (175). In assigning truth-values to statements rather than to sentences, he makes it clear that he sees them, and related properties such as presupposition, as dependent on context. And in 'On denoting' he comments on the presupposition of unique existence attached to the use of the definite article (in a phrase such as *the king of France*) in a way which again highlights the importance of context. The occurrence of the definite article acts as a signal either that previous reference has been made to the entity in question, or that 'the context (including the hearer's assumed knowledge) is expected to enable the hearer to tell *what* reference is being made' (342, original emphasis).

It is facts which can be treated as background, such as the existence of certain individuals, which are most likely to be presupposed. One clear reason why a fact, in a particular context, might be treated in this way is if it is 'old information', in that it is already known. In Strawson's terms, this is information which has already been mentioned, or is obvious from the context. Indeed, linguists have often equated 'background' information, which is generally presupposed, with 'old', or 'given' information, while what is 'foregrounded' is generally information which is 'new'. Strawson himself illustrates this point by encouraging his readers to consider the different contexts in which 54) and 55), which express the same proposition, would be appropriate.

54) That is the man who swam the channel twice in one day.
55) That man swam the channel twice in one day.

Example 54), unlike 55), contains the definite description *the man who swam the channel twice in one day*, together with its associated presupposition of existence. Strawson's explanation of the difference between the two is phrased in terms of knowledge and belief on the part of the speaker and hearer. He suggests that: 'You would say [54] instead of [55] if you knew or believed that your hearer knew or believed that *some one* had swum the channel twice in one day' (343, original emphasis). Note that Strawson is, in effect, discussing the difference between these two examples in terms of the situations it which each would be *appropriate*, a notion which has become central to pragmatic descriptions of use.

According to Strawson's account, then, what is presupposed can be seen as a reflection of the speaker's beliefs about the situation in which she is speaking. In particular, what is presupposed is what the speaker believes to be already known by the hearer. There would, after all, be little point in 'foregrounding', and drawing attention to, what is already known. However, as Strawson himself observes, it simply doesn't seem to be the case that a speaker will only ever presuppose what she has reason to believe the hearer already knows. Information which is in fact 'new' may sometimes be presupposed. Strawson's own account of this is in 'On denoting'. He notes that if he were to use a sentence such as 'all my children are asleep', he would introduce the presupposition that he has children. He goes on to observe that he may use this sentence:

> with the intention of letting someone know that I have children, or of deceiving him into thinking that I have. Nor is it any weakening of my thesis to concede that singular phrases of the form 'the so-and-so' may sometimes be used with a similar purpose. Neither Aristotelian nor Russellian rules give the exact logic of any expression of ordinary language; for ordinary language has no exact logic.
>
> (344)

Strawson here observes that presupposing expressions may sometimes introduce information which is new to the speaker, but doesn't offer any explanation of the contexts in which they can be used in this way. Various subsequent attempts have been made to define presupposition in a way which makes it consistent with uses of the type Strawson noticed. Many of these date from the 1970s, when interest was renewed, in philosophy and linguistics, in pragmatic aspects of presupposition.

One philosopher to take up the issue of presupposing expressions which are used in the absence of the necessary background knowledge was Paul Grice. Grice was another of the Oxford philosophers of the ordinary language school. Initially Peter Strawson was his student, and the two philosophers later collaborated on joint work. Grice is now best known for his theory of 'conversational implicature', which we will consider in Chapter 4. But his contribution to the discussion of presupposition can be found in 'Presupposition and conversational implicature', an article which he worked on during the 1970s, although it was first published in 1981.

In this article Grice considers the hypothesis, which he makes quite clear he doesn't want to commit himself to, that Russell's theory of description gives an accurate account of '*the* phrases', and that certain pragmatic principles can be found as alternatives to the 'theory of presupposition'. We needn't concern ourselves here too much with the details of this account, which is not as fully developed, and has not been nearly as influential, as Russell's or Strawson's. However, Grice's general approach, and his commentary on some of his examples, are interesting developments of the topic. Significantly, his account is dependent on conversational use of language. He suggests that in conversation speakers tend to express their message in such a way as to 'facilitate' an appropriate response. One type of appropriate response to a statement of fact would be a denial. One of the propositions to which the use of a sentence commits a speaker 'is, in some way, singled out as the one that is specially likely to be denied' (273).[6] Other information has 'common-ground status and, therefore, is not something that is likely to be challenged'. This common ground could be shared knowledge, but need not be. Grice argues that we might well hear someone uttering an example such as 56) in a context in which a particular concert is being discussed, but the speaker has no reason to believe that her audience knows that her aunt has a cousin, or even that she has an aunt.

56) My aunt's cousin went to that concert.

The use of the referring expression *my aunt's cousin* presupposes the existence of that relative, just as the use of the expression *the king of France* presupposes the existence of the monarch. Grice's explanation is that a proposition need only be 'non-controversial', or 'something we would expect the hearer to take from us (if he does not already know)' (274). We might expand on this and say that, even if we don't know that the speaker has an aunt who has a cousin, this fact is perfectly consistent with our background knowledge and assumptions; people tend to have families, which are quite likely to include relatives such as aunts and cousins.

Grice's account suggests that, in terms of language use, the difference between presupposition and assertion is perhaps best characterised as a difference in levels of commitment. One reason why a speaker might be so deeply committed to a proposition that she presupposes rather than asserts may, of course, be that it is known by both speaker and hearer. It would be simply pointless, or redundant, to say, for instance 57) instead of 58) if you are sure that your hearer has some basic knowledge about French politics.

57) There is a president of France, and he lives in Paris.
58) The president of France lives in Paris.

Similarly, to borrow Grice's own example, it would be unnecessarily complicated to use 59) instead of 60).

59) I have an aunt who has a cousin who went to that concert.
60) My aunt's cousin went to that concert.

Even if your hearer doesn't know much about your family connections, 60) will tell him all he needs to know without being unnecessarily wordy. It will also steer him in the right direction as far as a response is concerned. What you are talking about is the concert in question. Your family tree is not really 'the point'; your hearer would be rather changing the subject if he responded with 'Gosh, I never knew that you had an aunt'.

The balance between presupposed and asserted information seems to offer one way of examining how speakers use language to present their ideas succinctly, to direct their hearers towards relevant information, and also to exercise control over conversations. Some work in this area is mentioned under 'further reading', below. The final section of this chapter is concerned with some more general ways in which linguists have picked up on this, and on other areas originally discussed in logic, and have considered their significance for the study of natural language.

Logic and linguistics

The work of Frege, Russell and Strawson which we have considered in this chapter has been very influential in linguistics. As suggested, it is Frege and Strawson's work on logical presupposition which has been the focus of most interest, but Russell's work shouldn't be ignored. In particular, Russell's distinction between 'apparent' grammatical form and 'hidden' logical form has been seen as a basis for developments in linguistics such as Chomsky's distinction between 'surface' structure and 'deep', logical structure. Meanwhile, by the end of the 1970s, logical presupposition had received so much attention that Grice was able to comment, in 'Presupposition and conversational implicature', that

> In recent years, linguists have made it increasingly difficult for philosophers to keep their eyes glued on a handful of stock examples of (alleged) presuppositions, such the king of France's baldness and the inquiry about whether you have left off beating your wife.
>
> (279)

Much of the work which was conducted in linguistics was aimed at identifying expressions and constructions which might be said to introduce presuppositions. As Grice suggests, philosophers had on the whole been content to discuss presupposition in terms of a very few examples. Indeed, we have been able to follow the discussion so far by considering only what are known as existential presuppositions, presuppositions of existence associated with using expressions such as proper names and definite descriptions. If presupposition is to be a valuable tool for explaining language, we really need a few more examples than that. Let's start with Grice's veiled reference to wife-beating. What he has in mind here is the presupposition which had been noticed in connection with the use of the verb *stop*. If you say that you have stopped doing something you generally presuppose, but don't actually assert, that it is something which you used to do. So if you're presented with 61), it's impossible to answer either way without committing yourself to having been a viewer of daytime TV at some point (we'll take the liberty of changing wife-beating to daytime TV-watching).

61) Have you stopped watching daytime TV yet?

This example contains what is known as a *presupposition trigger*; the presence of the verb *stop* introduces the presupposition that the habit has existed. Many other presupposition triggers have been identified.[7] A few examples of these are illustrated in examples 62)–65); in each case the triggering word is highlighted.

62) John *regrets* sending a defamatory e-mail to the whole list.
63) The workers *knew*/believed that the management were lying.
64) The students *managed* to finish their essays during Reading Week.
65) John read 'On denoting' *before* he went down the pub.

Regret and *know* are both examples of *factive verbs*; they introduce the presupposition that the action described in the sub-clause did actually occur, in this case that John did actually send the e-mail and that the management were actually lying. Note that this presupposition doesn't arise with the verb *believe*; if we read 63) with *believe* instead of *know* we don't actually learn whether the management were lying or not. The verb *manage*, as in 64), entails that the task was completed, but it also presupposes that the task was a difficult one. Finally, the presence of *before* in 65) introduces the presupposition that the action did actually take place; John did go down the pub. One way in which these have all been identified as presuppositional, one which is easily tested, is that they are all 'preserved under negation'; if you try negating any of these examples you'll find that the entailments are lost but the presuppositions we have identified remain.

The same test can be applied to presuppositions which have been identified as being attached to particular grammatical structures, rather than to individual words. Examples 66) and 67) both include negation but share the same presuppositions as their positive counterparts.

66) It wasn't Columbus who discovered America.
67) *New Essays Concerning Human Understanding*, which is a very good
   read, wasn't published during its author's lifetime.

In 66) the presence of the *cleft* construction introduces the presupposition that *someone* performed the action described, in this case that someone discovered America. In 67) it's the presence of the *restrictive relative clause* which introduces a presupposition: in this case that the book in question is a good read.

It has also been noticed that the presence of a particular word or construction isn't always enough to ensure that a presupposition is introduced. Semantic presuppositions of this type can be *defeated* in appropriate contexts. As just one very simple example of this, consider the difference between the following:

68) Hamlet washed himself before he killed the king.
69) Hamlet stopped himself before he killed the king.

In 68), the presence of *before*, as expected, introduces the presupposition that the action (the killing of the king) did in fact take place. But in 69) this isn't the case; in the interpretation of 69) as a whole we simply don't get the impression that Hamlet killed the king. To find the reason for this, we need to look beyond the presence of the *before* clause, and consult what we know about the meaning of the verb *stopped*. Because this verb is incompatible with the action having been performed, the presupposition which we would expect to be associated with *before* isn't associated with the sentence as a whole. Examples of this type have been used to argue that pragmatic presupposition must at least take precedence over, and perhaps completely supercede, semantic presupposition. It is the wider context in which the *before* clause occurs which determines what is presupposed. Pragmatic accounts have been suggested involving much larger contexts, in this way using presupposition as a means of analysing discourse.

The use of language in discourse, and the effect of context on the logical properties of sentences, is something that we will return to in Chapter 4. First, however, we will look at some of the ways in which philosophers and linguists have accounted for the fact that we are able, often without thinking, to accept some statements as 'true' and to dismiss others as 'false'. In other words, we will consider the relationship between sentences, or the propositions they express, and the reality which they describe.

Further reading

Propositions

Some discussion of propositionality occurs in many general books on philosophy and the philosophy of language. Ayer (1971) *Language, Truth and Logic* is a good example (see especially Chapter 5); and Searle (1969) *Speech Acts* is particularly readable (see particularly Chapter 2). The basics of propositionality, correspondence, truth conditions, etc. are introduced in many textbooks on semantics. A good example is the introductory chapter to Cann (1993) *Formal Semantics*.

Logic

We have only scratched the surface in our study of formal logic. A good introduction to the subject is Guttenplan (1986) *The Languages of Logic*. Two books particularly aimed at explaining logical theory for students of linguistics are McCawley (1981) *Everything that Linguists Have Always Wanted to Know about Logic*, and J. Martin (1987) *Elements of Formal Semantics*. Both deal with far more complex material than is dealt with here, including the role of set theory in logic, but both are designed to be accessible to those without a mathematical background. McCawley's book is comprehensive; the first three chapters in particular deal with propositional logic and the logical operators, while Chapter 9 is concerned with presupposition, both logical and pragmatic. Martin introduces propositional logic in Chapter 1 and relates it to proof construction, a topic not considered here. He takes the discussion further in Chapter 5. Chapter 7 is concerned with presupposition; Martin concentrates in particular on presupposition failure, the notion of three-valued logic and the projection problem.

Presupposition

Since the three main articles by Frege, Russell and Strawson on the subject, much of the work on the topic of presupposition has been undertaken by linguists, and the literature in this area is vast. For this reason, most introductions to and commentaries on presupposition are found in books on linguistics rather than on philosophy. However, some introductions to the philosophy of language do include discussion of the primary philosophical texts, and in particular of Russell's account of definite descriptions. See, for instance, R. Martin (1987) *The Meaning of Language*, Chapter 13; Devitt and Sterelny (1988) *Language and Reality*, Chapter 3; and Stainton (1996) *Philosophical Perspectives on Language*, Chapter 3.

As we have seen, work in linguistics on presupposition has developed in a number of different directions, and each direction has its own body of literature. Chomsky's (1972) book *Studies on Semantics in Generative Grammar*, and particularly the chapter 'Deep structure, surface structure and semantic interpretation', introduces the idea that intonational highlighting, which Chomsky calls 'stress', can affect what is presupposed. Chomsky sees 'stress' as being grammatically determined, and therefore argues that these presuppositional phenomena must be explained semantically. Stalnaker's (1974) article 'Pragmatic presuppositions' is an early attempt to explain the role of speakers and of context in what is presupposed. A longer study of this is offered by van der Sandt (1988) *Context and Presupposition*. Burton-Roberts (1989) *The Limits to Debate*, on the other hand, proposes a purely semantic account of presupposition, but one which must be supplemented by a pragmatic account. He offers a revised version of the 'standard' (Frege–Strawson) logical definition of presupposition, and argues that a third truth-value need not, and should not, be identified with a 'truth-value gap', or lack of truth-value.

Surveys of work on presupposition can be found in Gazdar (1979) *Pragmatics*, who is of course concerned mainly with the development of work in pragmatic presupposition, and Wilson (1975) *Presuppositions and Non-Truth-Conditional Semantics*, who offers a purely semantic approach, in particular concentrating on a number of individual lexical items. Many introductions to semantics or pragmatics contain a chapter on presupposition, although of course the perspective and emphasis of these vary. Levinson (1983) *Pragmatics* considers the relevance to pragmatics of work on presupposition from the Russell/Strawson debate onwards. McCawley (1981) *Everything that Linguists Have Always Wanted to Know about Logic*, Chapter 9 is a short but detailed analysis of semantic presupposition, and particularly of the status and consequences of a three-valued logic.

3 Truth and reality

Introduction

As part of our investigation in the last chapter into how words can combine together to make meaningful statements, we studied the basics of propositional and predicate logic. These provided us with a system for describing the truth-functional properties of sentences, or of the propositions they express. They also gave us an insight into some of the relationships which can exist between propositions. They didn't, however, offer us any help in explaining how language relates to reality. As we have seen, language isn't just an autonomous system in which words are strung together to make sentences. In order to give a full account of language in general, or indeed of any particular language, the linguist needs to explain not just the relationships within a language, but those between a language and the world outside.

In Chapter 1 we addressed one part of this issue by considering how it is that words, by virtue of what we might call their 'lexical meaning', can identify actual objects in the world. To put this another way, we considered how it is that the intensional properties of a word are able to determine what object or objects form its extension. We are now in a position to ask the same question about sentences. We have defined the intension of a sentence as the proposition, or thought, that it expresses. The question we now need to ask is how this proposition determines the extension of the sentence, in other words whether it is 'true' or 'false'.

There's no question that we frequently need to look at the world outside of the language system when making decisions about truth-values. Taking any well formed sentence, we are unlikely to be able to say whether the proposition which it expresses is true or false without looking at what we might loosely describe as 'reality', or perhaps 'the world'.[1] That's not to say that there aren't some sentences to which we feel confident assigning the value 'true' or 'false' straight away, without first having to find out how things are in the world. We may, for instance, feel that while we're not prepared to make a judgement about the truth of 1) without first going to have a look in the garden, we are quite confident in saying that 2) is evidence before making a decision.

1) The cherry tree is in blossom.
2) An unhappy bank manager is not a bank manager.
3) All green frogs are green.

In saying that we don't know whether 1) is true or false we are, in effect, admitting that we don't know what its extension or, in Frege's terms, its reference is. But this isn't, of course, to say that the sentence makes no sense to us. On the contrary, we know exactly what proposition it expresses and we can probably picture to ourselves the situation it describes. We might say that we know what would be the case if it were true. In saying this we are saying that we know what conditions would have to hold for 1) to be classified as 'true'. In other words, although we don't know its truth-value, we do know its **truth conditions**. There is a certain state of affairs, which would have to be in place in order for 1) to be a true sentence, and the description of this state of affairs forms the truth conditions of 1). We might say informally that the relevant state of affairs is that the cherry tree under discussion must be in blossom at the time of speaking.

It's easier to make decisions about the truth-values of the second two examples. We might say that 2) is a **contradiction**. It has to be false, whatever the state of affairs; it is necessarily false because of the words it contains.[2] But 3), on the other hand, is a **tautology**; it has to be true because, in a sense, it says the same thing twice. In philosophical terminology, 3) is an example of an **analytic** sentence. The adjective *analytic* is, of course, related to the noun *analysis*. An analysis of syntactic structure, for instance, involves breaking down a complex whole, such as a sentence, into its component parts in order to understand how it is constructed. The same could be said of semantic analysis; it involves identifying the individual elements which make up the whole. Example 3) is necessarily true; we know it is true just because we know the meaning of the individual words it contains. Specifically, if we analyse the subject we find that *green* is a component part, and further analysis reveals that *green* also forms the predicate.

We will be looking at what has been said about analytic sentences later in this chapter. The central idea we will be concerned with, however, is that the sense, or 'propositional meaning' of a sentence can be defined in terms of its truth conditions, or the specific circumstances which have to hold for it to be true. As we will see throughout the chapter, various problems present themselves for a 'truth-conditional' account of meaning. To start with, notice the difference between examples like 1) above and 4) below. Intuitively, we know what they both mean, but when we set about describing how we would know if they were true or false, we are forced to admit that they are in fact very different.

4) There are fairies at the bottom of my garden, but they are invisible and make no sound.

We know what the truth conditions of 4) are; we know what facts, however, improbable, would make it true. What makes 4) different from an example like 1) is not so much the improbability of what is described, as the fact that we have simply no idea how to find out what its truth-value is. We know well enough how to use our knowledge of the sense of 1) to determine its truth-value; we can go into the garden and have a look at the tree. But while we are there we won't be able to check on the truth-value of 4), because we can't imagine what might count as evidence for accepting it as true or rejecting it as false. Examples such as this show up an important consequence of accounts of sentence-meaning entirely in terms of truth. If you can never decide whether 4) is true or false, and meaning is ultimately dependent on truth, it might be legitimate to question whether 4) can be said to be meaningful at all. This is the argument which has been put forward in **verificationist** theories of meaning, which we will consider in this chapter. These are interesting, at least in part, because it was the reaction against them which led to a growing interest in the way language is actually used, and in the significance sentences may have beyond the stark fact of being true or false.

Even if we concentrate on sentences for which we can make definite decisions about truth-value, we come across some important distinctions which a straightforward truth-based theory of meaning would miss. Let's consider the difference between the following pair of sentences:

5) Oil floats on water.
6) Thirty-four is a larger number than twenty.

We shouldn't have much difficulty in agreeing that these are both true, but we may well spot that there is a different 'type' of truth involved in each case. While we know that oil floats on water, and could prove it if neces-sary, we can imagine a situation in which it isn't true. We can imagine a context, say in a world created in science fiction, in which oil has very different properties from those we know it to have in fact, and in which it sinks in water. In contrast, it's impossible to imagine a world in which 6) is not true.[3] We can sum up this difference by saying that 6) is a *necessary* truth, while 5) is a **contingent** one; it so happens that 5) is true but it needn't be. This difference, and the idea, which we have suggested infor-mally, that we can imagine different 'worlds' in which things are other than we know them to be, has been taken up by another truth-based account of meaning, known as *possible world semantics*. As we will see, such accounts have suggested that meaning can be defined in terms of truth, but only with reference to the totality, or set, of **possible worlds** in which a sentence is true.

First, however, we need to go back to the beginning, and to start by looking at what has been said about the ways in which language relates to the world. In doing so, we need to be aware of the difference which has been described between a proposition having the property 'true' or 'false', and its having conditions which can determine truth or falsity.

Truth conditions

In Chapter 2, when we examined the nature of 'propositionality', we saw that a proposition can be the content of a thought, the object of a belief, or most significantly from our current point of view, the intension of a sentence. We have just established that one way of describing the content of a proposition is as a set of truth conditions. Now, if the intensional meaning of a sentence can be characterised as a series of conditions which must be fulfilled for it to be true, we have a clear way of explaining how the intension of a sentence determines its extension, or truth-value. Discussion of meaning in terms of truth conditions is, of course, one focus of semantics. Studies of meaning concerned with phrases and sentences, but not with contexts, is sometimes described as 'truth-conditional semantics'; it explains semantic meaning as the set of conditions, or restrictions, which the linguistic form of the expression places on what it can truthfully be used to say. But before linguistic semantics became a separate topic of study, such accounts had already been proposed in philosophy.

In search of a truth-conditional account of meaning, we can go right back to Aristotle. In *de Interpretione* he distinguishes between sentences which make statements (or express propositions) and those which don't; sentences which make statements are 'those in which there is truth or falsity' (4, 17a, 3). He makes it clear in *Categoriae* that, while a proposition is something which has the potential to be true or false, any statement or belief of that proposition may well depend for its actual truth-value on context. 'Statements and beliefs themselves remain completely unchangeable in every way; it is because the actual thing changes that the contrary [being false rather than true] comes to belong to them' (5, 4a, 35). Propositions, then, are independent of context, and specify conditions for truth. The individual quality of being true is dependent on these conditions being fulfilled.

Aristotle's definition is an early version of what became known as the **correspondence** account of truth; a proposition, or sentence, is true if it corresponds to reality.[4] Such an account became current again in the twentieth century, when it was generally summed up as follows:

7) 'p' is true iff p.

Note that there is some room for confusion here as to whether 7) is a rule about sentences or about propositions. The occurrence of *p* in quotation marks could be seen as referring either to any particular proposition, or to the form in which a proposition is expressed, such as a belief or a sentence. Correspondence accounts of truth have been criticised for being unclear on this point, and it's certainly possible to find different philosophers working with each of these interpretations. For instance, the philosopher Ludwig Wittgenstein explains in his *Tractatus Logico-Philosophicus*, first published in England in 1922, that: 'To understand a *proposition* means to know what is the case if it is true' (4.024, emphasis added). Bertrand Russell, in *Human Knowledge* (1992), adopts the other interpretation. He describes truth and falsehood as 'external relations', in that you can't tell whether a sentence or belief, for instance, is true simply by looking at its content. But Russell then points out that: 'although understanding the *sentence* does not enable you to know whether it is true or false, it does enable you to know what sort of fact would make it true and what sort would make it false' (128, emphasis added).

For our present purposes, however, we needn't worry about these different interpretations, but can concentrate on some of the consequences of correspondence accounts of meaning. As we have seen, there are some sentences, described as *analytic*, for which it doesn't seem to be necessary to state any particular conditions for truth. In other words, they don't need to be shown to correspond to any particular situation in order to be described as 'true'. In accounts of meaning dependent on truth and correspondence, a special case is often made for the class of analytic sentences, on the grounds that our judgements about them don't depend on experience.

Analytic and synthetic sentences

We saw in the introduction to this chapter that certain sentences are known as *analytic* because a process of analysis is all we need to decide that they are true; the individual words they contain make them necessarily true. In contrast, for many sentences, such as our 'cherry tree' example, we need to look beyond the individual meanings of the words to determine truth-value. Sentences such as these are known as **synthetic**. If analysis is concerned with breaking a complex whole down into its constituent parts, synthesis is the opposite process of building something from separate elements. A synthetic statement, then, is made up of separate, independent parts. There is no necessary connection between the meanings of these parts, so it isn't possible to establish the truth of a synthetic sentence just by considering the relationship between subject and predicate.

Knowledge of the truth of analytic sentences is said to be *a priori*. To say this is to say that no other knowledge needs to precede it; it is logically 'prior' to other knowledge. In other words, as we have seen, we don't need to refer to any experience of the world before we can judge such a sentence to be true. It used also to be common to claim that synthetic sentences couldn't be *a priori*, precisely because we need to know something about 'how things are' before we can decide on their truth-value. This apparently clear-cut distinction was challenged in the late eighteenth century by the German philosopher Kant.

Immanuel Kant's life was apparently uneventful, but his effect on modern philosophy profound. He lived in Knigsberg in East Prussia for all of his eighty years, gaining a reputation as a teacher at the university there. Kant was a philosopher of the Enlightenment. He was born in 1724, just twenty years after the death of John Locke, who, as we saw in Chapter 1, argued that the only phenomena of which we can have direct knowledge were those we can experience: in effect, our ideas of objects rather than actual objects themselves. Kant comments several times in his writings on the contribution made by 'the celebrated Locke'. However, he draws attention to the limitations of Locke's account in explaining the origins of knowledge. For Locke, all knowledge and understanding must be derived from experience; knowledge of general principles must be derived from an accumulation of experiences of particular instances. Kant, however, argues that many of the means by which we derive knowledge can't be empirical in origin.

In 1781, Kant published a collection of his writings, including his response to what he saw as the scepticism of the empiricists, in his *Critique of Pure Reason*, a work which he revised and republished in 1787. The title reflects his interest in determining those aspects of human knowledge which must be accounted for as dependent on 'pure', or natural understanding, as opposed to experience. Following the convention of the time, Kant distinguishes between classes of knowledge which are *a priori* and those which are *a posteriori*, or dependent on and following from experience. However, he departs from convention by arguing that it's not only analytic statements of which we have *a priori* knowledge. Rather, certain synthetic statements can be known to be true, and necessarily true, without reference to experience, as would be demanded by empiricism, and without demonstration by laws of reason, as would be required by rationalism.

Kant himself uses the examples 8) and 9), to which we could add the rather less technical pair 10) and 11), to distinguish between analytic and synthetic judgements. Kant explained that in 8) the predicate is contained in the concept of the subject, while in 9) the predicate is outside of the ideas contained in the subject. Any analysis of the meaning of 'body' (or anything which has substance) would necessarily include the idea of 'extended' (or taking up some amount of space), but not the idea of 'heavy'. Similarly all puppies are necessarily, by definition, young dogs, but they are not by definition adorable.

8) All bodies are extended.

9)   All bodies are heavy.
10) All puppies are young dogs.
11) All puppies are adorable.

Another way of looking at this is to say that an analytic statement such as
10) is logically necessary; the negation of it, as in 12), is self-contradictory.
A synthetic statement such as 11), however, is logically contingent; the
negation of it in 13) is not a logical contradiction because the concept
'adorable' is not present in the concept 'puppy'.

12) Not all puppies are young dogs.
13) Not all puppies are adorable.

Kant explains that 'judgements of experience, as such, are one and all
synthetic' (B11).[5] The 'pure reason' with which he is concerned, however,
is that class of knowledge which is synthetic but is not based on experience: knowledge which is synthetic and *a priori*. We might describe our *a
priori* knowledge as our 'intuitions' about how the world is, but it is in
fact, and can only ever be, knowledge of the world as we perceive it. This
is because we experience only our own perceptions of the world, themselves based on certain preconceived ideas, such as those about quantity,
space and relation. The world of which Kant writes, therefore, consists in
human experience of reality rather than reality itself. Indeed, for Kant the
world is simply not available to us without the mediation of our perception of it. He claims that 'what objects may be in themselves, and apart
from all this receptivity of our sensibility, remains completely unknown to
us' (A42).
   These 'things in themselves', of which we as human beings can never
obtain any certain knowledge, are described by Kant, and by many
philosophers who have followed him, as *transcendent*. This adjective is
related to the verb *transcend*, which means to go, or to be, beyond certain
limits. In this particular case, it is used to refer to that which goes, or is,
beyond the limits of experience and resultant knowledge. In this, Kant is
interested in what we understand, or infer, to be the case by exercise of our
reason but without any firm base in experience. In a related usage, he
refers to our intuitions about the world, or *a priori* conditions for knowledge, as *transcendental*; such aspects of human understanding are
necessary preconditions for our interpretation of any experience, but are
independent of it, so that they too exist beyond the limits of experience.
The more general term *transcendentalism* is nowadays used to refer to any
philosophy or belief which emphasises the importance of understanding,
or of emotion, above that of actual experience of the world.
   We have yet to specify what sorts of knowledge can be at once *a priori*,
or transcendental, and synthetic. Kant suggests that knowledge of this type
can be found in mathematics. He describes our knowledge of mathematical

propositions as being *a priori*, but the propositions themselves as not being analytic. We know that 14) is true because it is consistent with our view of how mathematics works. Our knowledge of this is dependent on, and derived from, our way of understanding the world. No degree of analysis of the individual elements of 14) can 'prove' its truth. So, unlike with analytic sentences such as 8) and 10), the meaning of the predicate *four* is not actually contained in the meaning of the subject *two plus two*.

14) Two plus two equals four.

If we refer to the 'real world', for instance by counting two beans together with two other beans and finding that we have four beans, we won't actually have proved that 14) is true. We find that we have four beans just because our system of mathematics, of organising entities and quantities, tells us that we have four. Whether the world aside from our perception of it actually makes '2 + 2 = 4' true or false is not something to which we have access. Kant's own presentation of this argument is summed up as follows: 'The assertion that 7 + 5 is equal to 12 is not an analytic proposition. For neither in the representation of 7, nor in that of 5, do I think the number 12' (A164).

For Kant, such mathematical, *a priori* knowledge presents a further problem for empiricism. We might be said to have *general* knowledge of the truth of such propositions, but we can only ever have *particular* experiences of the world. Of course, it's not just mathematical propositions of which we have general knowledge, but they need to be distinguished from genuine empirical generalisations, such as 15).

15) All birds have feathers.

The generalisation in 15) might be described as 'probable' – we believe it to be true because for every instance of *bird* that we have experienced, the predicate *feathers* has been applicable. We can imagine the type of experience which would cause us to doubt the validity of 15), however unlikely we think this might be. But we simply cannot imagine any experience which would cause us to doubt the truth of 14). We can imagine observing a featherless bird, but we can't imagine observing two objects plus two objects making five objects. The difference between these two types of knowledge is, Kant argues, something which a purely empirical account of knowledge just can't explain. 'Experience teaches us that a thing is so and so, but not that it cannot be otherwise' (B3); experience alone can't explain the certainty of our knowledge of 14).

Kant's chief interest was not in language but in the nature of knowledge and understanding, and it is in this area of philosophy that his influence has been most strongly felt. However, his work also provides a good starting point for a consideration of different types of truth. In what follows we will be concerned mainly with the meaning of sentences which are synthetic, but of which we can't claim *a priori* knowledge. In other words, we will be thinking about sentences which are neither necessarily true nor necessarily false: sentences which can be used to make informative statements about the world. It follows from Kant's account of these that to describe them as 'true' can never mean for certain that they correspond with reality, but at best that they correspond with our particular, human perception of it. Next, we need to consider the ways in which these problems, and the general theme of the relationship between meaning and truth, were approached by some of the main schools of philosophy in the twentieth century. We will start with the concept of *verification*, which received much attention in the middle part of that century.

Verification

In order to study explanations of meaning in terms of verification, we need to move forward some 150 years from the time in which Kant was writing, and consider the work of twentieth-century philosophers known as **logical positivists**. We will, however, still be concerned with the topics of understanding, knowledge and experience. Logical positivists are sometimes referred to as *logical empiricists*; their account of meaning is, crucially, dependent on experience of the world.

It isn't hard to trace the philosophical predecessors of the logical positivists. The branch of philosophical thought known generally as *positivism* had been current since the nineteenth century. This timing was no coincidence; the growth of positivism was closely linked to the expansion in scientific discovery and knowledge. Positivists were interested in knowledge which could be gained through scientific investigation, not in knowledge which didn't rely on observation and couldn't be tested by experiment. They therefore rejected all claims to metaphysical knowledge, such as those relating to religion or superstition. We can spot a similarity here with the ideas we considered in Chapter 1 in connection with the British Empiricists, and particularly with John Locke. Locke claimed that we have access only to our ideas of objects, dependent on information from the senses, not to objects themselves. The positivists, some decades later, claimed that the only type of knowledge which is possible is knowledge based on the experiences of the senses, and therefore that the only statements which we can make with any confidence are those about sense data. Positivism, then, was a radically empirical school of thought. Its name is related to the everyday meaning of the word *positive* as 'absolute' or 'definite'. The knowledge in which the positivists were interested was the absolute knowledge derived from observation of the world.

The terms *logical positivism* and *logical empiricism* are applied to the development of positivism in the twentieth century concerned particularly with meaning and truth. This development is most closely associated with a group of philosophers known as the Vienna Circle, who held weekly meetings in Vienna in the 1920s and 1930s to read papers together and discuss ideas. These were not exclusively philosophical ideas; the group was also concerned with politics, and published work on social reform and democracy. This brought them into conflict with the rising power of National Socialism, and many of them were forced to leave Europe for America in the years leading up to the start of the Second World War. As a result, the Vienna Circle ceased to meet in the 1940s. But by this time it had become extremely influential on Continental and, by influence, on British philosophy.

The individual members of the Vienna Circle were concerned with a variety of different areas of science and mathematics. Their aim as a group was to develop a form of language for expressing scientific observation. They were concerned with identifying the 'meaningful' statements of science, as opposed to the 'meaningless' statements such as those of metaphysics, religion, ethics and aesthetics. The statements which they classified as meaningful were of three types. First, there were analytical statements, of the type we have just considered, in which truth is apparent from an analysis of the statement itself, without any need to refer to external reality. Second, there were the statements of mathematics and of logic which, as we have seen from the work of Kant, can't be proved by observation of the world.[6] The third category of statements which they classified as meaningful were synthetic statements which could be subject to an explicit process of verification. This third category is the largest and most diverse, and contains all other statements which are permissible in scientific discussion.

A statement which can be subject to verification, or is *verifiable*, is one which is capable of being tested, and hence either accepted as true or rejected as false, by observation. So for a logical positivist, 16) and 17) would count as meaningful statements, while 18), 19) and 20) are meaningless, and therefore have no place in scientific discussion.

16) Water freezes at zero degrees Celsius.
17) The sun moves round the earth.
18) God is good.
19) Murder is wrong.
20) Dreams are an expression of subconscious fears and desires.

We know what the appropriate method of verification for 16) would be; with the help of a thermometer we could produce experimental evidence to show that it is true. Similarly, we know where to look to find evidence relevant to 17); modern astronomy in fact tells us that it is false. That is not to say that statements such as this are meaningless. Example 17) can be subject to a process of verification just as 16) can; it is just that this process will show that 17) is false. For examples 18), 19) and 20), on the other hand, there is no method of verification available. No one has been able to suggest experiments either to prove the truth or to establish the falsehood of statements such as these. Attitudes to them are based on speculation, argument and, of course, belief. For logical positivists these statements are simply meaningless, precisely because we can't produce observable evidence to demonstrate that they are either true or false. A theory of truth based on verification is therefore a type of correspondence theory; to be true, a statement must correspond with the facts. However, verification specifies a further necessary condition for truth. The facts to which the statement corresponds must be available to (some form of) observation.

In this way, verification offers a means of distinguishing between statements which are meaningful, and therefore scientifically valid, and those which are meaningless. But the logical positivists saw verification as more than this. They saw it as a method of describing the meaning of individual statements. For them, the meaning of a statement is defined by the method of verification appropriate for it. In performing the experiment necessary to verify 16), for instance, you will in fact be demonstrating its meaning.

One member of the Vienna Circle who produced particularly influential work on meaning was Rudolph Carnap, whose definition of propositionality we considered in Chapter 2. Carnap argues that many of the apparent problems of philosophy can in fact be reduced to problems of expression. In particular, he argues that problems of metaphysics are 'pseudo-problems', and that they can be revealed as such by a suitably rigorous analysis of the language in which they are expressed. In effect, metaphysical statements turn out to be meaningless. Carnap is anxious to make clear that in dismissing the statements of metaphysics, members of the Vienna Circle are arguing not against their content, about which they in fact have nothing to say, but against their form, against the language in which they are expressed. In *The Logical Syntax of Language*, published in England in 1937, Carnap complains that:

> When we of the Vienna Circle criticize, in accordance with our anti-metaphysical view, certain sentences of metaphysics (such as: 'There is a God') or of metaphysical epistemology (such as: 'The external world is real') we are interpreted by the majority of our opponents as denying those object-sentences and consequently affirming others (such as: 'There is no God' or: 'The external world is not real', etc.). These misunderstandings are always occurring in spite of the fact that we have already explained them many times ... and are constantly pointing out that we are not talking about the (supposititious) facts, but about the (supposititious) sentences.
>
> (309–10)

Like other members of the Vienna Circle, Carnap was interested in the analysis of the language of science. His aim in *The Logical Syntax of Language* is to establish a formal language, or at least the properties of a formal language, in which the results of analysis in mathematics and physics can be exactly expressed. A formal language is one in which categories of symbols, and rules by which expressions can be constructed from these symbols, are specified, but in which no reference need be made to the meaning of symbols or expressions. Carnap argues that such artificial languages are more appropriate to scientific discourse than any natural language. He sees natural language as imprecise and imperfect; 'the unsystematic and logically imperfect structure of the natural word-languages' (2) makes it impractical to try to formulate their rules and structures precisely. Significantly, though, Carnap doesn't see his discussion of formal, artificial languages as being necessarily irrelevant to the study of natural language; the 'general character' of the syntactic rules he is studying might be applicable to it. He compares the analysis of formal languages to the approach of the physicist, who is interested in the laws of nature but doesn't attempt to account directly for natural phenomena. Carnap continues:

> In the first place the physicist relates his laws to the simplest of constructed forms; to a thin straight lever, to a simple pendulum, to punctiform masses, etc. Then, with the help of the laws relating to these constructed forms, he is later in a position to analyze into suitable elements the complicated behaviour of real bodies, and thus to control them.
>
> (8)

The material which physicists work with may seem fragmentary and the context of the laboratory artificial, but their findings can nevertheless be relevant to those interested in explaining naturally occurring physical phenomena. In the same way an artificially constructed, and therefore fully described, language may appear to have little in common with a natural language in all its complexity, but can offer a way of explaining its regularities. More recent syntactic theories, developed in linguistics, have, of course, been more optimistic about the possibility of describing natural language. Even these, however, generally allow some degree of simplification, or idealisation of the language. Carnap's comparison with the isolated experiments of physicists suggests one way in which both philosophers and linguists might be considered justified in these simplifications.

As the logical positivists published and circulated their work, it became influential beyond the confines of Vienna and indeed of continental Europe. Bertrand Russell, for instance, acknowledged the influence which the logical positivists had on his work. Another British philosopher particularly interested in these ideas was Alfred Ayer, who had become familiar with them while spending some time in Vienna in the 1930s. After the

Second World War Ayer, who is most commonly referred to as 'A. J. Ayer', became a professor at the University of London and later at Oxford, where he had been an undergraduate. But it was in 1936, at the age of twenty-six, that he wrote one of his most successful books, *Language, Truth and Logic*.

In this short book, Ayer introduced an English-speaking readership to the ideas of logical positivism, a radically new approach in the context of Oxford philosophy at that time. He acknowledges his greatest intellectual debt as being to the Vienna Circle, and particularly to Rudolph Carnap. Ayer offers a particular version of the *criterion of verifiability* to define meaningfulness. This criterion, sometimes known as the *verification principle*, forms the central idea of logical positivism, and had been stated in various forms by members of the Vienna Circle. Ayer differs from these in that he sees the method of verification as being only the criterion of meaningfulness, rather than itself being the meaning of an expression. He therefore describes his principle as 'weaker' than that of the Vienna Circle, and expresses it as follows:

> We say that a sentence is factually significant to any given person if, and only if, he knows how to verify the proposition which it purports to express – that is, if he knows what observations would lead him, under certain conditions, to accept the proposition as being true, or reject it as being false.
>
> (48)

Many objections have been raised to the implications of the verification principle, in all its various forms. For instance, it has been suggested that it's impossible to find any sure method of verification for statements of events in the past, yet it doesn't seem reasonable to reject all such statements as meaningless. Another objection concerns the nature of the principle itself, for which no method of verification can be suggested. Hence, the argument goes, if we accept the principle as valid we must immediately dismiss it as meaningless. Ayer himself revised his opinion of the value of verification later in his career, for instance in *The Central Questions of Philosophy*, first published in 1973. However, he retained an essentially empiricist approach to knowledge and meaning. He maintained that it must at least be possible to identify the state of affairs which would make a proposition true or false, even if the relevant factors are not available to inspection. Of this more modest claim he commented in the later book: 'The only objection to this view which I can see is that it is not very illuminating' (30).

In attempting to develop a workable verification principle, the logical positivists were trying to produce a 'correspondence' account of truth sufficiently rigorous for the purposes of scientific discussion. They argued that it isn't enough to say that a true statement is one which corresponds with the facts; for the purposes of science it must be possible to specify what observable phenomena, or what sense data, would justify the scientist in accepting a statement as true, or rejecting it as false. The problems with such an approach, which A. J. Ayer acknowledged in his later work, were perhaps largely to do with the fact that it was just too rigorous to be workable outside of a laboratory; there are many statements which we would want to accept as perfectly meaningful, for which proof by observation is simply not possible. Verificationist accounts are also limited, along with other correspondence theories, to specifying conditions for the truth of declarative statements and the propositions they express. They can say nothing about the many other ways in which language is used. We will return to this limitation later in this chapter. First, we will look at another twentieth-century attempt to produce a rigorous account of truth, this time one which focuses on truth conditions themselves, rather than on the ability to determine empirically whether these conditions hold. These accounts are generally known as 'truth theories' or, in their later versions 'truth theories of meaning'.

Truth theories

The names most closely associated with accounts of this type are those of Alfred Tarski and Donald Davidson. Tarski was a logician, and worked at the University of Warsaw at much the same time as the logical positivists were developing their ideas in Vienna. He too was forced to move by events in Europe, leaving Poland in 1939. A few years later he took up a position at the University of Berkeley in California, where he continued work on his account of truth. Davidson later became a professor at the same university, building on and developing Tarski's ideas.

In 1944 Alfred Tarski published an article entitled 'The semantic conception of truth and the foundations of semantics'. His aim in this article is to develop a fully truth-conditional theory of language. However, Tarski isn't attempting to produce such a theory for any natural language, such as English. He is interested only in languages which could be thoroughly defined in terms of truth; he argues that these are all artificial, or technical languages. Like Carnap, Tarski rejects natural language as being too vague and too imprecise to be capable of full theoretical explanation. Tarski labels the language under scrutiny the 'object language'. In most of his writings the object language is in fact a fragment of English, but it's important to bear in mind that it's not English itself, or any other natural language, which he is describing. Tarski attempts to provide an account of any object language consistent with the 'classical' model of truth. Such a model defines all statements as either 'true' or 'false', such that: 'The truth of a sentence consists in its agreement with (or correspondence to) reality' (62).[7] However, he sees this notion of 'correspondence' as too imprecise to give a satisfactory account of any object language; he wants to refine it by making explicit the conditions for truth of every sentence.

The account of truth which Tarski proposes is one which entails a series of statements, each of which gives the truth conditions for a sentence in the object language. These statements are presented as a series of **T-sentences**, one for each sentence of the object language. Each T-sentence takes a sentence in the object language and states those conditions under which it would be true. In effect, then, Tarski's account pairs each sentence in the object language with a further sentence. He explains that no individual example of a T-sentence is itself adequate as a definition of truth. Each T-sentence is, rather, a partial definition of truth, accounting for one particular sentence in the object language. A complete definition of truth, on the other hand, 'has to be, in a certain sense, a logical conjunction of all these partial definitions' (63).

Tarski introduces a version of the formulation of the correspondence account which we considered earlier in this chapter. Every T-sentence takes the form:

21) X is true iff p.

In this formula, 'X' stands for any sentence in the object language, and 'p' for a proposition stating the conditions in which it is true. The example which Tarski uses to illustrate this is given in 22). Note that in this case 'X' is in fact a sentence of English, but it needn't be.

22) The sentence 'snow is white' is true iff snow is white.

This may at first sight appear rather disappointing as a partial definition of truth. It looks distinctly uninformative. But this T-sentence doesn't in fact do what it might appear to; it doesn't repeat itself, or say the same thing twice. To understand this, we need to note that 'snow is white' in the antecedent is contained in inverted commas, and then to remember what we learnt in Chapter 2 about the distinction between use and mention. In fact, the expression 'snow is white' is *used* only in the consequent of 22). We could say that it is used *as* the consequent of 22). In the antecedent it is only *mentioned*, or named; a particular sentence in the object language is identified, so that something can be said about it. This distinction will perhaps be clearer if we consider a T-sentence expressed in English but concerned with an object language other than (a fragment of) English. We could provide a T-sentence for the French sentence 'La neige est blanche' as follows:

23) The sentence 'La neige est blanche' is true iff snow is white.

Remember also that Tarski's account of truth doesn't consist just in specifying that a T-sentence must have the form in 21). It crucially includes his claim that a set of T-sentences, one corresponding to each sentence in the object language, is a sufficient definition of truth for that language. Now as linguists we know that all natural languages are infinite. It would be impossible to list all the sentences of a natural language, so it follows that it must be impossible to come up with a complete set of T-sentences. It might seem to be quite a problem for Tarski that, according to his definition, any account of truth for a natural language must always be incomplete, or partial. But remember that Tarski doesn't claim to be writing about natural language. He was a mathematician and a logician, not a linguist, and his interest lay in what he describes as 'theoretical' rather than 'descriptive' semantics: in providing an account of truth for an artificial language rather than explaining natural language. He saw himself, as did some of the members of the Vienna Circle, as contributing to the development of a restricted, fully specified language which would serve more precisely than natural language as a medium for scientific discourse. Also like the logical positivists, he saw natural languages as necessarily vague and inexact, and therefore not amenable to scientific study, at least without first being neatened and tidied up.

In many ways, then, Tarski's aims and methods were very different from those of modern linguists, and it wouldn't be fair to criticise his work for not fitting the requirements of a different discipline at a different time. It is, however, interesting to compare Tarski's work with that of Donald Davidson, particularly Davidson's 1967 article 'Truth and meaning'. Unlike Tarski, Davidson *is* interested in natural language. In the twenty-three years between the publication of Tarski's 'The semantic conception of truth' and Davidson's 'Truth and meaning', linguistics had started to take off as a separate academic discipline, and natural language had become a legitimate field of study in its own right. And some philosophers, too, had begun to take more of an interest in natural language and even in actual usage.

In 'Truth and meaning', Davidson is quite outspoken in his disagreement with Tarski as to the purpose of an account based on truth, claiming for instance that: 'The task of a theory of meaning as I conceive it is not to change, improve or reform a language, but to describe and understand it' (98).[8] Also unlike Tarski, Davidson sees the list of T-sentences as itself providing a description not just of truth, but of meaning. In other words, for Davidson a theory of truth is not just a necessary preliminary for, but is in fact adequate in itself as, a theory of meaning. His main claim, then, is that a full account of meaning for a natural language can be provided by a theory of truth conditions for its sentences.

Davidson identifies two particular problems with Tarski's account which call for it to be modified. The first wasn't a problem for Tarski because of his different goals; it's the problem which we have already noted in connection with the nature of natural language. The number of sentences in any language is infinite, so they would need to be matched with an infinite number of T-sentences, making a complete account of truth for any language unobtainable. The second problem which Davidson identifies is to do with the logical nature of the operator *iff*, which forms part of every T-sentence. As we saw in Chapter 2, the logical operators are concerned just with mapping truth-values on to further truth-values. Unlike the expressions which are sometimes described as their 'natural language counterparts', they don't suggest any further relationship between the variables which they connect. We saw in particular that 'material condition', including *iff*, requires no connection, in terms of subject matter or relevance, between antecedent and consequent. This has the unfortunate result that any T-sentence in which the consequent and the antecedent 'match up' in terms of truth-value must be acceptable, regardless of what sentences of the object language it is being used to describe. So as well as Tarski's 22) above, 24) below must be counted as an acceptable T-sentence.

24) 'Snow is white' is true iff grass is green.

The proposition that grass is green has the same truth-value as the proposition that snow is white; they are both true. In the purely logical formula of a T-sentence, therefore, it ought to be possible to substitute one for the other; 24) should be as valid as 22), as should any T-sentence which combines 'snow is white' with a true proposition. And it should be possible to provide T-sentences for all the true sentences of a language by combining each with any true proposition, or indeed all with the same true proposition. This, clearly, is not an acceptable state of affairs when trying to describe the meaning of a natural language by means of a set of T-sentences. The T-sentence in 24) may be logically valid, but it tells us very little about English. As Davidson himself expresses it, 'any two sentences have the same reference if they have the same truth-value. And if the meaning of a sentence is what it refers to, all sentences alike in truth-value must be synonymous – an intolerable result' (93).

The solution which Davidson proposes to both of these problems is to supplement the list of T-sentences with an *axiomatic theory*. Axioms can be defined as principles or rules, much like the rules of a grammar, which, when taken together, are sufficient to produce a series of formulae, or theorems. In the case of a grammar, of course, these formulae are the sentences of a language. In the case of Davidson's axioms, however, the theorems are the T-sentences for the language. His axiomatic system, in producing all the T-sentences of a language, provides an account of the meaning of the language. The types of axiom which his system requires are axioms of reference, of satisfaction, and of connection. We can illustrate these, very briefly, by considering what we would need to construct a T-sentence for example 25):

25) Fire is hot.

In order to specify a unique meaning for this sentence, one which distinguishes it from all other true sentences of the language, we need ways of specifying the meaning of each of its parts. Firstly, we need to explain the meaning of the subject, something we can do by using a maxim of reference. These take the general form ' "x" refers to x'. Again, we have here the *mention* of an expression in the subject and the *use* of that expression in the predicate. So the axiom of reference we need here is:

26) 'Fire' refers to fire.

Next we need a way of identifying and explaining the predicate in 25), and of distinguishing it from all other possible predicates. We need an 'axiom of satisfaction'. This explains the meaning of a predicate in terms of those entities of which it is true, or to which it can correctly be applied. An entity 'satisfies' a predicate if the combination of the entity and the predicate gives a true statement. Again distinguishing between mention and use, we get:

27) 'Hot' is satisfied by hot things.

Finally, we need to identify the way in which 'fire' and 'hot' are connected. The 'connection axiom' for *is* specifies that:

28) ⌜a is b⌝ is true iff what ⌜a⌝ refers to satisfies ⌜b⌝.

These three axioms, taken together and applied to the English sentence *Fire is hot*, give us as output the theorem, or T-sentence:

29) 'Fire is hot' is true iff fire is hot.

In this way, Davidson avoids both of the problems identified in Tarski's account. To describe any natural language the set of T-sentences must be infinite, but they can now be derived from a finite number of axioms, just as the infinite sentences of a natural language can be derived from the application of a finite number of grammatical rules. These axioms, together with a system of logical constants such as those we studied in Chapter 2, and a grammar of well-formedness, are sufficient to produce an infinite set of T-sentences. The axioms also ensure that not just any true proposition can be paired with a true sentence to give an accurate T-sentence. Expression 29) above is the only T-sentence which can be derived for the English sentence 'fire is hot' using Davidson's axioms.

Davidson has applied his axiomatic account in practice to only a tiny fragment of English, but maintains that a full account of this type would in principle be possible for any natural language. However, he acknowledges certain other complications for a truth-theoretic account of natural language. For instance, any such account is necessarily focused on language as a means of 'stating facts' rather than as a way of, for instance, asking questions or issuing orders. In grammatical terms, we could say that truth theoretic accounts of meaning are focused on declaratives, at the expense of interrogatives and imperatives.[9] For example, given a suitably elaborate axiomatic theory, we might be able to provide the truth conditions for 30), but we couldn't state conditions for the truth of 31) or 32), both equally acceptable sentences of English.

30) You will resign your position.
31) Will you resign your position?
32) Resign your position!

Davidson addresses this problem in a later article, published in 1979, called 'Moods and performatives'. He explains that any adequate account of meaning must be able to account for the differences between examples such as 30)–32), which he defines as differences in 'mood', while still capturing the fact that they all 'have a common element' (15) of meaning. He is aware of the implications of this for a truth theory of meaning, stating that if it can't explain mood 'then truth theory is inadequate as a general theory of language' (15). The problem is that truth-functional operators, the only type of elements of meaning allowed by such as theory, can't be used to give an explanation of mood. The solution which Davidson suggests is that non-declaratives can be seen as composed of two separate parts. One of these parts is concerned with the 'common element' of meaning, and the other with mood. In other words, the meaning of all uses of non-declaratives must be capable of being described in terms of a declarative sentence and a 'mood-setter'. These two parts must be seen as being produced simultaneously when a sentence is used, but, Davidson stresses, as totally independent of each other. For instance, our interrogative and imperative example in 31) and 32) above could be expressed in terms of the declarative 30) and an independent mood-setter, as in 33) and 34) respectively.

33) My next utterance is a question.   You will resign your post.
34) My next utterance is imperative.   You will resign your post.

Davidson explains that both these 'parts' are truth-conditional, thereby fulfilling the requirements of a truth theory. But, being totally independent, they aren't combined using any truth-functional operator, explaining why examples such as 31) and 32) can't be assigned truth-values. In Davidson's own terms, 'Each of the two utterances has a truth value, but the combined utterance is not the utterance of a conjunction, and so does not have a truth value' (20). In this way, Davidson claims, it's possible to retain a truth-theoretic account of meaning while taking into account uses of language other than those concerned with statements of fact.

Another major complication which natural language raises for any truth-based theory of meaning is that what counts as 'true' will often depend on individual contexts of utterance. Only a small proportion of uses of natural language involve statements of the 'snow is white', 'fire is hot' nature. Davidson comments in 'Truth and meaning' that 'the same sentence may at one time or in one mouth be true, and at another time or in another mouth be false' (100). This ability of sentences to be true in certain circumstances but false in others was the motivating factor behind the development of another type of account of meaning, that offered by 'possible world semantics', to which we turn next.

Possible worlds

We are by now familiar with the idea that one popular way of explaining 'truth' is to say that a proposition can be described as true, or as a fact, if it corresponds with reality. We haven't been too much concerned with the nature of this 'reality', but have seen that it can be equated with the way the world, or the universe, actually is.[10] Now of course reality might have been other than it actually is. Consider, for instance, the way in which we all, from time to time, indulge in imagining how things might have worked out if a particular decision had been made differently, or a particular turn of events had not occurred. In other words, we are all capable of imagining different possible versions of reality, which are often closely related to how things actually are, but differ in some particular respect. One way to describe our imagined state of 'what might have been' is to say that it is in fact reality, but reality in another possible world. Possible world semantics is based on this simple fact that things might be other than they are, and on what follows from this: namely that, in different versions of reality, different propositions must be true and false. These ideas have, as we shall see, been developed and worked on by a number of philosophers of the twentieth century. But the origin of possible world semantics can be found in the work of Leibniz.

As we saw in Chapter 1, Leibniz was familiar with many disciplines, including theology, and it is his theology which informs his account of possible worlds. For Leibniz, different possible worlds exist in the mind of God; in his words, different versions of reality all originate 'from the Supreme Reason' (*New Essays on Human Understanding*, 227). A version of reality, or possible world, consists of everything which exists and has existed.[11] The number of possible worlds is infinite, but only one of them is realised, or created, and again this is dependent on God:

> And even though one should fill all times and all places, it still remains true that one might have filled them in innumerable ways, and that there is an infinitude of possible worlds among which God must need have chosen the best, since he does nothing without acting in accordance with supreme reason.
>
> (*Theodicy*, 8, 128)

According to Leibniz, because God is good, the world which he actually creates is, necessarily, the best possible world. 'Best' in this context can be thought of as something similar to the simplest. The best possible world is that which contains the maximum number of states of affairs but the minimum of individual laws, or the maximum of effects for the minimum of causes.

In more recent philosophy, Leibniz's account of possible worlds has been given a semantic, rather than a theological application. If the truth of a sentence depends on correspondence to the world, it is argued, then a multitude of different worlds must mean that a sentence can be true in some while it is false in others. So one way of describing the proposition expressed by a sentence would be to specify all the worlds in which it was true. Let's take Tarski's example *snow is white*. We could offer an account of the circumstances in which this is true by listing all the possible worlds in which it corresponds with reality, while ruling out all those worlds in which snow is, for instance, red or blue or black. The proposition expressed by a sentence is, on this account, described not as a series of truth conditions but as a set of those worlds, and only those worlds, in which it is true.

The notion of 'possible worlds' has been used by a number of philosophers in different ways. Some see them as a convenient figurative or metaphorical way of thinking about complex issues. The American philosopher David Lewis, however, gives them a more concrete definition. According to his account, every possible world, our world included, is defined by the entities which exist in that world and the facts which are true of those entities. Our world is generally described in this context as 'the actual world', but is to be thought of as no different in status from all the other possible worlds. Other worlds differ from it 'not in kind but in what goes on in them' (85). Worlds other than the actual are not 'imaginary' worlds; they are worlds just like ours, but in which things are different, to a greater or lesser extent. So, for instance, another possible world might be exactly the same as ours except that in it snow is blue.[12] Yet another world might have blue snow and cold fire but be like ours in all other respects. The same goes for entities. There are possible worlds which are just like ours, but populated by a slightly different selection of people, or of dogs, or indeed of ants, than exist in the actual world.

This way of looking at things can require quite a leap of imagination. We normally think of it as a plain fact, as simply true, that, for instance, snow is white. Looking at the matter in terms of possible worlds, however, we need to consider that it is merely possible that snow is white, and that this just happens to be so in the actual world. To put this another way, the world we inhabit is just one of those worlds in which snow is white, and so on for many other facts we take for granted. Possible world semantics, then, is concerned not just with what *is*, but with what is possible, and, as we will see, with what is impossible. Possibility and impossibility are what

are known as **modal** concepts, and belong to a type of propositional lo,
which we haven't considered yet. We will need to find out somethin,
about modality, therefore, before we can understand some of the implications of possible world semantics.

Modality

The study of modality dates back to the classical logic of ancient Greece.
The following passage, from Aristotle's *de Interpretione*, gives a definition
of what it is for a proposition to be possible:

> It is necessary for there to be or not to be a sea-battle tomorrow; but it
> is not necessary for a sea-battle to take place tomorrow, nor for one
> not to take place – though it is necessary for one to take place or not
> to take place. So, since statements are true according to how the actual
> things are, it is clear that wherever these are such as to allow of
> contraries as chance has it, the same necessarily holds for the contra-
> dictories also.
>
> (19a, 30–5)

If a proposition, such as the proposition that the sea-fight will take place
tomorrow, is possible, it is neither necessarily true nor necessarily false.
Aristotle is also asserting that if it can be said that something is possibly
the case, for instance that the fight will possibly take place tomorrow, it
can equally well be said that it is possibly not the case, that the fight will
possibly not take place tomorrow. From this we have deduced the
following statements about modality:

35) If something is possibly the case it is not necessarily not the case.
36) If something is possibly not the case, it is not necessarily the case.

We can think of several other situations. So, for instance if it is necessary
that the fight will not take place, we are in effect saying that it is not
possible that it will take place. Similarly, if it is necessary that it will take
place tomorrow, it is not possible that it will not take place. We can add
the following observations to our list:

37) If something is necessarily not the case, it is impossible that it is the
case.
38) If something is necessarily the case, it is impossible that it is not the
case.

So far we have stuck with the rather cumbersome expressions 'it is
possible that … ' and 'it is necessary that … '. In natural language we in
fact have a number of different ways of expressing these modalities. To

express possibility, for instance, we have all the options below, as well as many others.

39) It is possible that the fight will take place tomorrow.
40) The fight may take place tomorrow.
41) Maybe the fight will take place tomorrow.
42) The fight will possibly take place tomorrow.

In formal logic, there is only one logical operator to cover all these natural language expressions. The symbol for possibility is ◊, or sometimes M. If we specify that p is the proposition that the fight will take place tomorrow, then we can represent all of 39)–42) above as ◊p. Similarly, the symbol for necessity is □, or L; □p means that it is necessary that the fight will take place tomorrow. Using logical notation, we can rephrase our four findings above as expressions of logic as follows:

43) ◊p→~□~p
44) ◊~p→~□p
45) □~p→~◊p
46) □p→~◊~p

Possible world semantics offers another way of looking at relationships such as these. In fact, it allows us to make the same generalisation without using the concepts of *necessary* and *possible*, concentrating instead on statements involving *some* and *all*. These terms, as we saw in Chapter 2, are dealt with in conventional predicate logic, and can therefore be defined in terms of truth-values. Now, as we have seen, a possible proposition can be seen as one which is true in some, but not all, possible worlds. It is possible that snow is white and, in fact, snow actually is white in our world; the actual world is a member of the set of worlds in which it is true. Now, we know from 46) above that a necessary proposition is one which is not possibly not true, so we can define a necessary proposition as one which is true in all possible worlds. Remember that the most clear-cut of necessary truths are analytic sentences such as 47) and 48). We can say that there are no logically possible worlds in which 47) and 48) are not true. The set of worlds in which they are true is the set of all possible worlds.

47) White lilies are lilies.
48) All thoroughbred racehorses are horses.

Similarly, a proposition which is impossible, such as one which is logically contradictory, will not be true in any world. The set of worlds in which, for instance, 49) is literally true, is empty.

49) This is a white lily and it is not a lily.

The potential of possible world semantics for explaining modal logic is a major interest of Saul Kripke, the American philosopher whose work on names we studied in Chapter 1. He suggests the foundations for such an account in an article published in 1959, when he was only nineteen years old: 'A completeness theorem for modal logic'. This is a difficult and very technical article, but contains at the outset a clear statement of Kripke's view of the relevance of possible worlds, which he also refers to as 'conceivable worlds'. He explains that 'in modal logic, we wish to know not only about the real world but about other conceivable worlds; P [a proposition] may be true in the real world but false in some imaginable one' (2–3).

Kripke explains that the evaluation of a proposition as either true or false relates to one particular world; in general if we say that something is true we mean that it holds in the actual world. To speak of necessary truths, however, we must refer to the entire set of possible worlds: 'a proposition □B is evaluated as true when and only when B holds in all conceivable worlds' (3). Kripke suggests that such an approach assures that 'at least a certain non-trivial portion of the semantics of modality is available to an extensionalist logician' (3). Once it is translated into possible world semantics, modality can be addressed by a logician concerned only with the extensions of sentences – their truth or falsity – and with truth-functional operators. This is because treating modality in terms of possible world semantics means explaining it as a relationship between the values of truth and falsity and the set of worlds.

We have established that possible world semantics offers us a way of discussing modality within the limits of truth-functional logic. But some modal sentences pose further problems for extensional logic, and to these also, possible world semantics offers a solution. These problems are similar to those we considered in Chapter 1 when we looked at *opaque contexts*. Remember that opaque, or intensional contexts are sentences in which substitution of one expression by another with which it is extensionally equivalent doesn't necessarily result in the truth-value of the whole remaining unchanged. It is generally accepted that *the author of Great Expectations* and *Charles Dickens* are extensionally equivalent, or refer to the same individual. But, as we saw, substituting one expression for the other in a pair such as 50) and 51) doesn't necessarily give us two extensionally equivalent sentences. It's quite possible, for instance, that 50) might be true while 51) is false.

50) Pip believes that the author of *Great Expectations* is a genius.
51) Pip believes that Charles Dickens is a genius.

These particular examples illustrate the problematic opaque contexts associated with propositional attitudes, but the same type of problem is raised by modal expressions. Consider the pair of examples 52) and 53) in which, again, one expression is substituted for another with which it is extensionally equivalent.

52) It's possible that Charles Dickens is not the author of *Great Expectations*.
53) It's possible that Charles Dickens is not Charles Dickens.

Far from this substitution resulting in extensionally equivalent sentences, it seems to be the case that 52) and 53) must have different truth-values. We can probably agree that 52) is true. It's possible that Charles Dickens didn't write the novel after all; we can imagine the sort of documentary evidence which might convince us that someone else wrote it. But we certainly wouldn't want to say that 53) is also true; indeed it's a logical impossibility. It isn't possible that the person referred to as *Charles Dickens* is not the person referred to as *Charles Dickens*.

An account of these opaque contexts in terms of possible worlds would go as follows. In discussing an opaque context, as we saw in Chapter 1, we need to consider not the extensions, or denotations of its parts, but their intensions. So we must consider not the reference of the subordinate clause, but its sense. Taking the example of the clause *Charles Dickens is not the author of Great Expectations*, we need to take account not of its truth-value in the actual world, but of the proposition it expresses. Now, a proposition can be described as a set of possible worlds, as the set of all the possible worlds in which it is true. So we need to take into account the set of possible worlds in which the subordinate clause is true.

To take the modal contexts in 52) and 53) to begin with, we can say that the proposition that Charles Dickens is the author of *Great Expectations* is true in a certain set of possible worlds, a set which happens to include the actual world. There is another set of possible worlds in which Charles Dickens is not the author of *Great Expectations*. Now to say that a proposition is true in one set of worlds and false in another set is simply to say that it is possibly true. We have established that there is a set of possible worlds in which 'Charles Dickens is not the author of *Great Expectations*' is true, hence 52) is true. However, the proposition that 'Charles Dickens is not Charles Dickens' is not true in any possible world. The set of possible worlds in which it is true is empty. Example 53), which states that this set of possible worlds is not empty, is therefore false.

A similar account can in fact be applied to the examples involving propositional attitudes. They can be thought of not as a relationship between the subject and the reference of the proposition, a truth-value in the actual world, but as a relationship between the subject and the sense of the proposition, a set of possible worlds. The belief described in 50) is Pip's belief in a world in which the author of *Great Expectations* is a genius. This is not to say that Pip necessarily believes in a world in which Charles Dickens is a genius, because as we have seen, Charles Dickens is not the author of the novel in every possible world but only in a certain set of possible worlds, a set which happens to include the actual world.

Counterfactuals

We could summarise the applications we have considered so far by saying that possible world semantics offers a way of describing 'unreal' situations, or states of affairs other than those of the actual world we inhabit. We wouldn't need to talk about possible worlds if we only ever wanted to make statements of fact about reality. But once we start talking about what could possibly be the case, or about what people believe or imagine to be the case, we are talking about things being other than they actually are.

There is a further type of expression used to describe 'unreal' situations. Remember that when we first encountered the notion of possible worlds, we considered the way in which we sometimes imagine 'how things might have been', or 'what could have happened'. Such thoughts are often expressed in the following type of construction:

54) If only I hadn't missed the train I would have been in time to meet him.
55) If John were here now he would be making us laugh.
56) If we were meant to fly we would have been born with wings.

Such examples might at first appear to be straightforward conditionals of the familiar *if ... then* type. But a problem arises when we try to make decisions about their truth-values. In each case we find that we can't calculate the truth-value of the whole by determining the truth-values of the antecedent and the consequent, as we have done before. This is because neither part refers to an actual situation, and so neither can be tested in terms of its correspondence to reality. Examples such as this, concerned as they are with 'unreal' situations, generally occur in the *subjunctive* case (*if John were here* rather than *if John was here*) which serves to indicate their distance from reality.

The use of the subjunctive generally indicates that the antecedent is, or is believed to be, false. We wouldn't expect to hear someone say 55), for instance, in a situation in which John is actually present. Now remember that in the case of material implication, the logical equivalent of *if ... then* which we considered in Chapter 2, if the antecedent is false then the conditional as a whole must be true; everything follows from a false antecedent. But we need to make an exception for cases like these. We might be happy to accept 54)–56) as true, but if we allowed all such examples to be true just because their antecedents are false, we would also have to accept an example as preposterous as 57) as true.

57) If there were no clocks we would all live for ever.

The way in which this conclusion has been avoided is by making a separate category for these 'unreal' conditionals. They are known as *counterfactuals*, or as *counterfactual conditionals*. They have played an important role in the development of possible world semantics, and are the subject of a short book by the philosopher David Lewis, a professor at Princeton University, whose definitions of possible worlds we considered earlier.

In *Counterfactuals*, published in 1973, Lewis argues that, 'although vague', counterfactual conditionals can be assigned truth conditions, and that it is therefore not necessary to dismiss them all as 'unreal' and simply logically true. This is because discussion of what 'might' have happened is discussion of what did in fact happen in a different possible world. So to use example 54) is to say that there is another possible world in which I caught the train and I was there to meet him; it just so happens that in the world I'm in I missed the train and wasn't there to meet him. Lewis introduces his study with the example:

58) If kangaroos had no tails, they would topple over.

He uses the symbol which has become conventional for counterfactual conditionals, and which distinguishes them from normal conditionals, '□→'. So if p is the proposition that kangaroos have no tails, and q is the proposition that kangaroos topple over, we can represent 58) as:

59) p□→q

Lewis suggests that the meaning of 58) above is: 'in any possible state of affairs in which kangaroos have no tails, and which resembles our actual state of affairs as much as kangaroos having no tails permits it to, the kangaroos topple over' (1). As we have seen, to say that something 'might have been' the case is to say that it actually is the case in some other possible world. So, Lewis is suggesting, we can decide on the truth-value of a counterfactual such as 58) by looking at the possible world, or set of worlds, in which the antecedent is true: the worlds in which kangaroos have no tails. However, it isn't just any of these worlds which are relevant. We need to consider those worlds which differ enough from our world to make the antecedent true, but which are in other respects similar to ours. There is a possible world in which kangaroos have no tails and they fall over. There is another possible world in which kangaroos have no tails, but this is compensated for by the fact that all animate objects are held up by big strings hanging down from clouds, so that kangaroos don't fall over. This is a possible world, but it's quite different from our world, certainly more different than the world in which the kangaroos just fall over. We can summarise the truth conditions for a counterfactual conditional as follows.

60) p□→q is true iff some world where p and q are the case is more similar to our world than any case where p and ~q are the case.

Substituting the propositions about kangaroos for p and q, we see that 60) makes 58) true; the world in which they fall over is more like the actual world than the world in which they don't. It also offers us a way of explaining why we want to reject 57) above. A world in which there were no clocks and everyone lived for ever would be less like our world than a world in which there were no clocks but people were still mortal.

Possible world semantics, and its applications to various 'problem' examples, gets much more complicated than the basics of the theory which we have considered here. For instance, the notion of 'similarity' between worlds has been discussed in much more detail than the loose definition we have used, and criteria have been suggested for calculating the 'relative closeness' of different possible worlds, and the degree of 'accessibility' which holds between them. Some introductions to this work, and some of the primary philosophical texts, are mentioned in the 'further reading' section at the end of this chapter. Before we leave the topic of possible world semantics, we should pause to take account of one particular approach to the study of language which developed within this framework: Montague Grammar.

Montague Grammar

Montague Grammar takes its name from the philosopher Richard Montague. His contribution to semantics, both of formalised and of natural languages, is a significant one, although he died at the early age of forty-one in 1971, eight years after becoming Professor of Philosophy at the University of California, Los Angeles. His aim was to produce a 'Universal Grammar'. Montague used this term to refer to a system of syntax and semantics capable of describing both formalised logical language and natural language. That is not to say that he wanted to 'purify' natural language or 'make it more logical'. But he did want to establish an account of language based on a formal theory consistent with logic, rather than on intuition and approximation. He saw the description of natural language as a legitimate field of study, but as one belonging to mathematics. In this sense, Montague Grammar is based on ideals that date back at least to Leibniz, and are also familiar to us from the work of Frege and of Russell.

An explicit statement of this position can be found in *Formal Philosophy*, a selection of Montague's papers published posthumously in 1974. Montague's own account of this view goes as follows:

> There is in my opinion no important theoretical difference between natural language and the artificial languages of logicians; indeed, I consider it possible to comprehend the syntax and semantics of both kinds of languages within a single natural and mathematically precise theory.
>
> (222)

However, he admits that it is possible that such a system is, in practice, unobtainable.

Montague Grammar, and the modal logic on which it depends, is notoriously difficult for students of language who don't have a good grasp of mathematics, chiefly because it is based on formal set theory. Montague's logic draws on the relationships between entities, predicates and beliefs within and across possible worlds. Like Donald Davidson, Montague saw the chief goal of studying any language as being to provide an account of the truth conditions for all the sentences of that language. In other words, he too was interested in producing an account of meaning based not just on truth-values, but on the individual propositions expressed by the sentences of a language. Unlike Davidson, however, Montague saw the truth conditions which his account was to provide as being necessarily defined over possible worlds. He claimed that it must be feasible to offer a definition of the conditions under which any given sentence will be true in any possible world.

In its various forms, then, possible world semantics offers an explanation of certain 'problem' examples. It also suggests a more general approach to the task of defining the meaning of a language in terms of the truth conditions of its sentences. In its incarnation in the work of Richard Montague, at least, it has been applied to natural, as well as formal languages, indicating that natural language can be recognised within this framework as a legitimate, and valid, topic of study.

In the next chapter we will consider some very different approaches to the study of natural language. These differ from a theory such as Montague's both in distinguishing sharply between natural and formal languages and, crucially, in rejecting the idea that the meaning of natural language can be described best, or at all, in terms of truth conditions. But first we will conclude this chapter by looking at the contribution which truth-based accounts of meaning have themselves made to present-day linguistics. Their influence can be most strongly felt in the area of formal semantics, where discussions of sentence-meaning often make reference to the notion of truth-conditionality.

Linguistic semantics

Throughout this chapter, we have been concerned with various attempts to explain the meanings of sentences in terms of those factors which serve to make them true or false. These accounts have all, in one way or another, offered explanations of how language relates to the world, and attempted to explain truth in terms of a relationship to reality. This same interest is apparent in the area of present-day linguistics which deals with literal- or sentence-meaning, namely semantics. There is, however, quite a clear distinction between philosophical and linguistic semantics. The individual works we have been concerned with in this chapter, disparate as they are in other ways, might all be said to be concerned with the nature of meaning itself, and with the questions of how meaning is possible and how it is best described. They are generally concerned not with offering a theory of meaning for any particular language, but with considering what such a theory would need to be like.

This type of approach is well exemplified by the ideas of Carnap, and in the theories put forward by Tarski and later Davidson. Such accounts imply that, in order to understand the problems surrounding the notion of meaning, it's necessary to consider the basic form which a theory of meaning for any particular language would take. It's not that this is necessarily thought to be achievable in practice, but that the process is said to illuminate the problems, and identify the essential concepts involved. As the philosopher Michael Dummett suggests at the start of his essay 'What is a theory of meaning? (I)' in his book *The Seas of Language*, published in 1993:

> According to one well-known view, the best method of formulating the philosophical problems surrounding the concept of meaning and related notions is by asking what form should be taken by what is called 'a theory of meaning' for any one entire language; that is, a detailed specification of the meanings of all the words and sentence-forming operations of the language, yielding a specification of the meaning of every expression and sentence of the language. It is not that the construction of a theory of meaning, in this sense, for any one language is viewed as a practical project; but it is thought that, when once we can enunciate the general principles in accordance with which such a construction should be carried out, we shall have arrived at a solution of the problems concerning meaning by which philosophers are perplexed.
>
> (1)

Linguistic semantics, on the other hand, might be described as being concerned with the practical construction of accounts of meaning for particular languages. Its aim is not so much to shed light on the types of problems involved in defining meaning, as to engage with those problems. Its methods tend to be more empirical than those of some philosophical approaches, in that the raw data of semantic accounts in linguistics generally come from the facts of the language in question. In the tradition of generative grammar, at least, semantics is largely concerned with the relationship between meaning and structure. Semantic analyses in this tradition are often used to demonstrate how sentences of a language relate to each other. Topics relevant to this are discussed in detail in some of the introductory works on semantics listed in the 'further reading' section at the end of this chapter. One such topic is the relationship between two sentences which 'mean the same', a relationship which is similar to that of synonymity, which we considered in Chapter 1 in relation to word-meaning. The following pair of examples might be said to be *paraphrases* of each other:

61) Bertrand Russell wrote *Human Knowledge*.
62) *Human Knowledge* was written by Bertrand Russell.

We might say that 61) and 62) have the same meaning because they describe the same event or state of affairs. The same set of factors would make them both true or both false; in our world we would want to label them both 'true'. Generative grammarians would claim that they are in fact both the same at the level of 'deep structure', the level at which meaning is determined. They would be able to explain to us how the passive sentence in 62) was derived from the same deep structure as its active counterpart in 61). To say that these two sentences mean the same because they are both true in exactly the same situations is, of course, to say that they have the same truth conditions. The same could be said for the following pair:

63) John Stuart Mill wrote *A System of Logic*.
64) It was John Stuart Mill who wrote *A System of Logic*.

In this case also, the two differ not in terms of their truth conditions, but in terms of their 'surface structure'. Example 64) contains what is known as a *cleft* construction, a construction of the general form 'it was x who ... ', while 63) is a *non-cleft*. Again, a generative grammarian could explain how 63) and 64) are both produced from the same deep structure using different grammatical rules. But to say that the two pairs of examples we have just considered are truth-conditionally equivalent is not, of course, to tell the whole story. We might not be able to distinguish between 61) and 62) in terms of the situation they describe, but that same situation certainly seems to be presented in different ways in the two examples. Similarly, the cleft and the non-cleft sentences may be identical in terms of the conditions which make them true, but they would seem to be appropriate to rather different contexts. For instance, while 63) presents a fact about the philosopher in question, 64) would seem appropriate only if the authorship of *A System of Logic* were a subject of disagreement, or at least under discussion.

We have seen some of the problems which an entirely extensional account of meaning, dependent on assigning the properties of 'true' and 'false' to each sentence, encounters. These were the problems which Davidson was confronting in supplementing an extensional account with an axiomatic system, so that sentences could be defined as corresponding to particular states of affairs, and not just to truth-values. But the above examples seem to suggest that any account which considers meaning in terms of truth conditions, or of the proposition expressed by a sentence, will also be missing some subtle but important aspects of meaning. One solution is to supplement a truth-conditional account of meaning with a presuppositional one. We saw at the end of Chapter 2 that one account of presupposition defines it in terms of sentence semantics. Such an account would explain that although 63) and 64) are truth-conditionally equivalent, they differ in terms of what is presupposed and what asserted. Principally, it is presupposed in 64) that *someone* wrote *A System of Logic*; what is 'at issue' is who this was.

Another account of those aspects of meaning which can't be explained in terms of truth conditions is to say that, since they seem to relate to contextual considerations of 'appropriateness', they must be explained as pragmatic in nature. The relationship, and also the appropriate divisions, between semantics and pragmatics, have been and continue to be the subject of much debate. A very general definition might specify that semantics is concerned with the study of meaning in isolation, and pragmatics with meaning in context. Another way of looking at this, as we saw in connection with discussions of presupposition in the last chapter, is to contrast linguistic meaning, the focus of semantics, with speaker meaning, the focus of pragmatics. The development of pragmatics as a separate discipline within linguistics, and its origins in twentieth-century philosophy, are the subjects of the next chapter.

Further reading

Truth conditions

Kant's ideas, and the distinction between *a priori* and synthetic knowledge, are discussed in Ayer (1971) *Language, Truth and Logic*, particularly in Chapter 4. A brief but clear account of Kant and his views on *a priori* knowledge is offered in Chapter 8 of Bertrand Russell's (1980) *The Problems of Philosophy*. Russell offers more discussion than we have had here of the notion and nature of 'things in themselves', and engages in a criticism of Kant's solution, and of the connection he draws between truth and thought.

Verification

Both of the books by Ayer mentioned in this section are succinct, clear and very readable. They were written with interested 'lay' people as well as professional philosophers in mind. In particular, Ayer's own introduction to the 1946 edition of *Language Truth and Logic*, and Chapter 2 of *The Central Questions of Philosophy* (1973) deal with the formulation and problems of the principle of verification. Verification, and the work of logical positivism in general, is considered in Devitt and Sterelny (1987) *Language and Reality*, Chapter 11.

Truth theories

Tarski's truth theory of meaning is set out in most of its detail in his (1944) article 'The semantic conception of truth and the foundations of semantics'. Davidson's version is summarised in his (1967) article 'Truth and meaning'; further discussion of the implications of a Tarski-style account, and Davidson's discussion of non-indicatives, can be found in his (1979) 'Moods and performatives'. The truth theories of meaning of Tarski and Davidson are discussed in R. Martin (1987) *The Meaning of Language*, Chapter 22. Martin relates Davidson's account to discussions of language and the mind, and of 'mentalese', which we will consider in Chapter 5. Evnine (1991) *Donald Davidson* is a book-length study of the work of Davidson, which presents his account of truth and meaning in the context of his philosophy as a whole. Chapter 5 in particular is relevant to those aspects of Davidson's work discussed here. Evnine considers the problems of trying to apply a theory developed for a formal language to natural language. He also offers an account of Tarski's theory.

Possible worlds

The connection between modality and possible worlds is discussed by R. Martin (1987) *The Meaning of Language*, Chapter 15, who relates modality and extensionality. Stainton (1996) *Philosophical Perspectives on Language* considers possible world semantics with particular reference to opaque modal contexts, in Chapter 4. McCawley (1981) *Everything that Linguists Have Always Wanted to Know about Logic* discusses modal logic in Chapter 10, looking in particular at different types of necessity. In Chapter 11 he goes on to consider the applications of possible worlds, looking in particular at Lewis' account of counterfactuals and notions of accessibility and the relative closeness of worlds. Both chapters are heavy going, but the early sections of each are quite accessible. McCawley also gives a detailed treatment of Montague Grammar, which is not discussed here in any detail, in Chapter 13. Cann (1993) *Formal Semantics* is written within the framework of Montague Grammar, and offers a good introduction to it.

Linguistic semantics

Useful introductions to linguistic semantics include Leech (1981) *Semantics*, and Hurford and Heasley (1983) *Semantics: A Course Book*. This includes an introduction to logic, and detailed discussion of word-meaning, topics introduced here in Chapters 2 and 1 respectively. Also useful is Hofmann (1993) *Realms of Meaning*. Kempson (1977) *Semantic Theory* is a more difficult read, but it includes discussion of some concepts from philosophical semantics, such as Tarski's conception of truth. She also looks at some topics which belong more obviously in linguistic semantics, such as the relationship between syntax and semantics, and the role of deep structure. Frawley (1992) *Linguistic Semantics* also offers an introduction to many of the topics considered in this chapter. In his introduction he outlines what he sees as some of the fundamental differences between philosophical and linguistic semantics. Frawley concentrates on method in explaining this difference; he sees philosophy as fundamentally deductive, linguistics as inductive and empirical. Lyons (1995) *Linguistic Semantics* is a comprehensive introduction to the subject. His earlier *Semantics* (1977) in two volumes, is a more detailed treatment, which includes discussion of the relationship between formal and linguistic semantics, and of the relationship between semantics and generative grammar. Katz (1972) *Semantic Theory* still ranks as one of the major attempts to combine semantics and generative grammar into a coherent description of natural language.

4 Speakers and hearers

Introduction

In our study of truth-conditional accounts of meaning in the last chapter, we encountered what could be summarised as two different categories of problem. The first category includes all those problems which are raised by individual theories of this kind, and which can best be resolved by modification, or development of those theories. Davidson's axiomatic account of meaning, for instance, was designed to address the problems that Tarski's truth theory encountered: namely that it could neither distinguish between different 'true' sentences, nor give a full description of an infinite language. The second category of problems for truth-conditional accounts, however, can't be resolved by any amount of 'repair work' to the accounts themselves. These are the problems raised by evidence that meaning is determined as much by how language is used as by semantic content. In response to problems of this type, various different approaches have been taken to the task of describing and explaining meaning in philosophy and, latterly, in linguistics.

The emphasis on language in use indicates that the philosophers and linguists engaged in these approaches have been concerned with language as an everyday means of communication and, therefore, with natural language. Many of the philosophers whose work we considered in Chapter 3 were interested in language as a formal system, as a type of logic, or as a mode of expression for scientific discovery. For the philosophers whose work we will be considering in this chapter, however, language is a system which, primarily, is used by human beings to interact with each other. The canonical use of language in such accounts is one where a *speaker* produces an *utterance*, in a particular *context*, which is interpreted by a *hearer*. None of these highlighted terms would have a place in a truth-conditional account of meaning. They emphasise the importance of a whole variety of factors which might be labelled *extra-linguistic*. That is to say that meaning is determined not just by the rules which explain a language, and relate it to the world, but also by a whole variety of factors which couldn't be described as a part of the language system.

As our first example of this type of account of meaning, we will start this chapter by looking at the work of Ludwig Wittgenstein. Wittgenstein is often seen as the founder of the philosophical interest in language use which began around the middle of the twentieth century. His philosophical development is an interesting one from our current perspective. In his early work, he was concerned with the formal properties of truth-conditional logic. Later in his career he moved away from this approach, concentrating instead on the variety of functions which language can be used to perform, and coining the phrase 'meaning is use'.

This slogan might remind us of the account of presupposition proposed by Peter Strawson, which we considered in Chapter 2. In his article 'On referring', Strawson emphasised the importance of use and context, suggesting that it is individual speakers who do things like referring and mentioning, not the language itself. This approach to the discussion of meaning in general, and referring expressions in particular, brought him into conflict with Bertrand Russell. The two philosophers disagreed about whether the use of everyday speech, and the attitudes and intentions of speakers, are relevant focuses of philosophical analysis. Strawson's position in this disagreement, as we saw, was representative of a group of philosophers working at Oxford in the middle of the twentieth century, engaged in the study of what became known as **ordinary language philosophy**.

Ordinary language philosophy is sometimes also referred to as *linguistic philosophy*, although we will use the former, more widespread term. Its most prominent proponents, apart from Strawson himself, included J. L. Austin, John Searle and Paul Grice, and it is their work which will be the main subject of this chapter. The term 'ordinary language philosophy' is not intended to imply, as is sometimes supposed, that they were interested in studying vernacular or casual, as opposed to standard or formal, uses of language. This is a much more recent development within linguistics. Rather, it refers to their interest in approaching philosophical problems by means of an analysis of the ordinary uses of the language in which they are expressed. This in turn led to an interest in natural language as a legitimate field of study in its own right. They rejected the idea that language could, or should, be explained solely in terms of logical relations. In particular, they rejected the idea that accounting for meaning was simply a matter of determining conditions for truth.

The following types of example have been used as evidence that any truth-conditional account of meaning must be inadequate for describing actual usage:

1) It is rather cold in here.
2) I bet you that it will snow before the end of the day.
3) I do wish you would shut the window.

These could all be described in formal linguistic terms as declarative sentences. It would therefore be possible to determine the circumstances which would make each of them true, and to present these circumstances, in the form of a series of truth conditions, as the meaning of each sentence. This might seem to work well enough for example 1); if we know the conditions which would make 1) true we might be able to claim that we know the meaning of 1).[1] But it doesn't work as well for the other two examples. We might be able to describe the state of affairs which would make 2) strictly 'true', but to offer this as an account of the meaning of 2) would somehow be to 'miss the point'. Such an account would miss the fact that 2) would most likely be used not to describe this state of affairs but to do something else entirely. It might be used actually to make the bet. Similarly, knowing what would make 3) true, the relevant state of 'wishing' which would have to be in place, doesn't explain how in many situations 3) would be understood as a request, or perhaps an order, to shut the window. In fact, in certain circumstances, we can imagine 1) also being understood as a request to shut the window, suggesting that a truth-conditional account of meaning may not always be appropriate even for such an apparently straightforward example.

The assumption that the primary use of language is to produce statements of facts, or descriptions of reality, is sometimes known as the *descriptive fallacy*. This term was first used by J. L. Austin, who suggested that, instead of concentrating on language as a means of description, it would be more useful to describe language as a means of 'doing things'. Later in this chapter we will look at his analysis of examples such as 1)–3) as being different types of actions, or *speech acts*, which speakers can carry out.

However, labelling different utterances as different types of action doesn't solve all the problems raised by truth-conditional accounts of meaning. Even restricting ourselves to examples in which some description of reality is made, we can think of many instances in which simply knowing the truth conditions doesn't seem adequate to the task of explaining meaning. Imagine that we have arranged to meet a friend at a certain time and, as is our custom, we show up just as expected. Our friend comments with approval:

4)   I can always rely on you to be on time.

We can explain this situation quite adequately in terms of truth. We can make sense of 4), we know what circumstances would make it true, and we can confirm that these circumstances are met.

But now imagine a different scenario. We make the same arrangement with our friend the following week but, because of a series of mishaps, arrive half an hour late. Our friend who, as luck would have it, has had to wait in the pouring rain, greets us with exactly the same remark, although delivered in a rather different tone of voice. A truth theory of meaning isn't much help here. In fact, all it can do is tell us that what our friend has said is false. But we can't help thinking that this somehow isn't the 'point', and that if we were to respond with a cheerful 'No, you can't, I'm half an hour late actually', we would only make things worse. The point, of course, is that although our friend has, literally, said that we are on time, that isn't quite what she meant. Rather, she was being sarcastic, and using a patently false statement to convey her displeasure.

Sarcasm offers one type of example in which what people 'say' and what they 'mean' can be two very different matters. But there are many other, more subtle examples to be found in which a similar process seems to be taking place. These are often most apparent when we look at an utterance in the context of the conversation in which it occurs, for instance by considering it as the response to a particular statement. Imagine the following exchange taking place in a crowded room:

5) *A* Mrs X is an old bag.
    B The weather has been quite delightful this summer, hasn't it?

The response which B makes is apparently about the weather, but in this context we'd probably want to say that she means something entirely different. Without further information, in particular without further details of the context, we aren't really in a position to be sure exactly what she meant, but her utterance might well be best taken as some sort of hint that it would be wise to select another topic of conversation hastily. Perhaps, unlike A, B is aware that a particular friend of Mrs X is within earshot. We know that there is probably a discrepancy between the literal and the implied meaning in this example, not because of any aspect of B's response in itself, or because of any linguistic rule, but because of the context in which it occurs. In other words, we know that B probably doesn't intend her utterance to be interpreted literally precisely because she is offering it as a response to A's unfortunate remark.

This example was originally suggested by another Oxford philosopher of ordinary language, Paul Grice, to illustrate what he saw as an important aspect of meaning in use: the distinction between what people 'say' and what they 'implicate'. He explained this example as involving a type of *conversational implicature*, an element of utterance meaning which can often be very different from the literal meaning of the sentence uttered. We will be looking at some more examples of conversational implicature later in this chapter, and considering the ways in which Grice explains them with reference to his *co-operative principle* of conversational interaction.

This brief introduction to Grice's work has raised two issues which make it particularly relevant to pragmatics, the branch of linguistics with which we will conclude this chapter. First, Grice's account is a conversational one. His example is presented with a short conversational context, and the act of interpreting an utterance such as B's in 5) above is one which must be performed by a conversational partner. This focus relates to the second part of the title for this chapter. Language use involves not just speakers who produce utterances, but also hearers, who are themselves part of the conversational context. For language to operate effectively as a means of communication, the role of the hearer is as central as that of the speaker. As we will see, the hearer's task of interpretation is an important focus in present-day pragmatics.

Second, Grice's distinction between literal and implicated meaning draws attention to the possibility that there are different types, or levels, of meaning, a possibility which has been much discussed, and also hotly disputed, in present-day linguistics. It suggests that while accounts of meaning based on linguistic analysis and on semantic rules may be able to tell us all we need to know about *sentence*-meaning, the meaning of any particular *utterance* of a sentence in context will depend on a whole host of other, non-linguistic factors. Semantics can tell us, at best, only part of what we need to know about utterance-meaning. Strawson sums up an important attitude of ordinary language philosophy when he claims, in 'On referring', that 'The context of *utterance* is of an importance which it is almost impossible to exaggerate' (230, emphasis added).

It is important to bear in mind, then, that not all the accounts we will be considering in this chapter need be seen as alternatives to semantic accounts, offered to replace inadequate, truth-conditional theories of meaning. Rather, some of them are best seen as complements to such accounts. They suggest that the meaning specified by linguistic rule is only part of the story, and that such rules need to be supplemented by a consideration of other, non-linguistic factors. But we will begin with a consideration of the work of Ludwig Wittgenstein who, as we shall see, came to believe that meaning could best, and perhaps only, be explained in terms of use.

Wittgenstein's philosophy of language

Ludwig Wittgenstein's writings touch on many of the topics we have been concerned with, but his work was by no means confined to the philosophy of language. He also wrote influentially on the philosophy of mathematics, of the mind, and on the nature of philosophical investigation itself. In 1922, the English edition of *Tractatus Logico-Philosophicus* (generally referred to by its abbreviated title, *Tractatus*) was published, in which he set out his views on logic and language. It was a remarkable first book in terms of its complexity and its subsequent importance, all the more so in that it was written while Wittgenstein fought in the trenches in the First World War in the Austrian army, and subsequently while he was detained in a prisoner of war camp.

Even setting aside his time in the army, Wittgenstein's career was an unusual and eclectic one. He was born in Vienna in 1889, and when he moved to England in 1908 he first studied engineering at Manchester, before moving to Cambridge and taking up philosophy. Then, after publishing *Tractatus*, Wittgenstein abruptly left Cambridge and turned his attention to various other occupations, including time as a schoolteacher and as a gardener. This move is sometimes interpreted as a grandiose statement to the effect that he had said all he had to say on the subject. But after several years Wittgenstein did return to philosophy, and to Cambridge, where he continued work on the themes he had begun in *Tractatus*, although his later work differed in many respects from his earlier. He became a professor of philosophy in 1939, but immediately left to serve as a medical orderly in the Second World War, which meant that in effect he took up the post in 1945, just two years before he retired and six years before his death.

Tractatus was the only book which Wittgenstein published during his lifetime. His other works, all published posthumously, include the account of his later philosophy known as *Philosophical Investigations* published in 1953, and various collected notes and lectures. The style of much of his writing is sometimes described as enigmatic or 'aphoristic', in that he writes in a series of statements or assertions, often leaving the reader to fill in the connections between them. In *Tractatus*, he numbered these statements, starting each on a new line. As with classical writers, it is the custom to refer to the work by means of these numbers, rather than by page number in any specific edition.

Wittgenstein's original philosophical interest, growing out of his studies in engineering, was in the philosophy of mathematics. His early influences include Bertrand Russell, whose pupil he was during his brief studies at Cambridge before the First World War. In turn, Russell was himself influenced by *Tractatus*, and particularly by the claim that offering an account of thought involves offering an account of language, a claim which became crucial in the subsequent development of analytic philosophy. Wittgenstein's early work also had an impact on the Vienna Circle, who read *Tractatus* at several of their meetings, some of which Wittgenstein himself is known to have attended. Again, his emphasis on the centrality of language was perhaps the most influential part of his work. We have already seen that, in the logical positivism of the Vienna Circle, discussion of problems, or 'pseudo-problems', of philosophy often focus on the language in which they are expressed. Wittgenstein's later work was no less important. It can be seen as the precursor of the growing interest, in the middle of the twentieth century, in studying how language is actually used, rather than focusing on specific logical structures, or idealised 'perfect' languages.

Tractatus starts with the characteristically bold and challenging statement that 'The world is the totality of facts, not of things' (1.1). The world in which we live is characterised not, or at least not solely, by the objects which it contains; it is characterised by the ways in which these objects are constituted and related. The facts, of course, determine what true statements can be made about the world. We can see from this that Wittgenstein begins essentially with a correspondence account of truth and meaning; the facts of the world determine what is true. He explicitly states that: 'To understand a proposition means to know what is the case if it is true' (4.024).

For Wittgenstein, a proposition is the presentation of a thought. He therefore equates his task in studying language with that of studying thought; language is essentially the expression of thought. The thoughts which are expressed by the propositions of 'factual language', language used to convey information, he describes as 'pictures'. Now of course only those pictures which represent, or correspond with, reality, can be described as 'true', but all pictures at least represent a possible state of affairs. Here we can see a connection between Wittgenstein's account of language and the idea of 'possible worlds', which was developed later in the century. Indeed, it has been suggested that possible world semantics can be seen as a generalisation of Wittgenstein's framework, in which the specific notion of 'possible worlds' is added to his notions of things and truth-values.[2]

Wittgenstein's own treatment of possible states of affairs is a very specific one. For him, all possible states of affairs are contained within the objects of the actual world. Possible states may differ to varying degrees from our own, but all have a common form determined by the objects. Within this constriction, we can think of a number of different states of affairs, and 'What is thinkable is also possible' (3.02). What is thinkable can be expressed in a proposition. The 'perceptible sign' of that proposition, in other words a spoken or written sentence, is 'a projection of the possible state of affairs'. His account, then, is a truth-conditional one, in which meaning is defined in terms of the situation which would make a proposition, and therefore the sentence which expresses it, true. But it is an account concerned with understanding the regularities of natural language, rather than with constructing an ideal one. The process of logical analysis is one of discovering the logical form of a sentence, whatever grammatical form it may take.

One way of looking at the difference between Wittgenstein's ideas in *Tractatus* and those in his later work, particularly in *Philosophical Investigations*, is in terms of his account of language, or rather his view of what an account of language entails. In particular, in the later work he dispenses with the idea that speech or writing consists primarily in producing 'perceptible signs' of propositions. *Tractatus* offers a uniform account of the nature of language, defined in terms of propositions, and its role in expressing thought. In his later work, Wittgenstein explicitly rejects the possibility of giving a general account of propositions, or indeed of language. Instead of being a unified phenomenon, language is seen as a collection of activities which are all different. Wittgenstein famously refers to these activities as 'language games'; just as there are many different types of game, all of which can be characterised as 'games' but all of which are different, so there are many different types of use of language, all of which can equally validly be described as 'language'. Wittgenstein explains that: 'Here the term "language-*game*" is meant to bring into prominence the fact that the *speaking* of language is part of an activity, or of a form of life' (23, original emphasis).[3]

There are 'countless' different language games, because there are countless, and ever changing, ways in which people use language. Wittgenstein suggests just a few of these games, which include, for instance, 'giving orders', 'reporting an event', 'making up a story', 'making a joke' and 'translating from one language to another'. The nature of the language game can be ascertained only by observing use; there is nothing 'hidden beneath the surface' to be discovered by analysis. The task of the philosopher, therefore, is to observe and describe these language games, not to subject certain, selected, structures to logical analysis. Wittgenstein comments on the philosophical tradition, including his own earlier work:

> It is interesting to compare the multiplicity of the tools in language and of the ways they are used, the multiplicity of kinds of word and sentence, with what logicians have said about the structure of language. (Including the author of *the Tractatus Logico-Philosophicus.*)
>
> (23)

Wittgenstein also presents in his later work a markedly different account of the role of names, or the relationship between words and objects, the issue which we considered in Chapter 1. In *Tractatus* he seems to envisage a straightforward denotational relationship between words and objects. He specifies that: 'The name means the object. The object is its meaning' (3.203). In *Philosophical Investigations*, however, he rejects the idea that there can be any straightforward relationship between words and objects. Individual words can't be associated with any one meaning, but rather should be thought of as tools which can be used for a variety of purposes, and which are best defined in relation to those purposes. Therefore, 'for a large class of cases – though not for all – in which we employ the word "meaning" it can be defined thus: the meaning of a word is its use in the language' (43). There are a number of different ways in which any one word may be used. If we consider these different uses as a way of identifying meaning, we will find that there isn't 'something that is common to *all*, but similarities, relationships, and a whole series of them at that' (66). For this reason, it's best to consider any given word as having not one, fixed meaning, but 'a family of meanings' (77), which are related by a series of 'family resemblances'. Just as different members of a family may not all share even one characteristic in common, but may be said to display a certain network of similarities, so the meanings of a word may be identifiable as a set, but not defined by any one feature.

In his later work, then, Wittgenstein emphasises the importance of language as it is actually used. Until this point, philosophy, including his own, had largely ignored many types of language use. Such straightforward uses as asking questions and issuing commands had largely been dismissed from philosophical study because they couldn't be explained in truth-conditional terms. Wittgenstein also rejects the idea that any word or any sentence has an identifiable meaning, an idea fundamental to the work of philosophers such as Frege. Rather, he sees words and sentences as being characterised by the individual and often very different uses they can be put to. Finally, we should pay attention to a statement in *Philosophical Investigations* about the philosophical method itself. Wittgenstein remarks that: 'When I talk about language (words, sentences, etc.) I must speak the language of every day' (120). He sees 'every day' language use as appropriate not just as a topic of study, but as a means for expressing that study. This was to be a central tenet in the development of ordinary language philosophy in the years immediately following Wittgenstein's death.

Ordinary language philosophy

One of the most influential figures in this and in other areas of British philosophy of the time was Gilbert Ryle. Born in 1900, Ryle spent his academic career at Oxford, becoming Professor of Philosophy. In 1953 he published an article called 'Ordinary language' which can in many ways be seen as setting the agenda for the approach to the philosophy of language taken in Oxford in the middle part of the twentieth century. As such, it perhaps made possible the development of the ideas we will be looking at in this chapter, which have in turn been important to the development of modern linguistics. Ryle points out that, in emphasising the importance of ordinary language, philosophers were, at least in part, appealing to a consideration of the 'stock' uses of words, as opposed to any unusual or 'non-standard' uses. Philosophy was to treat the way in which speakers ordinarily use language as a valid area of study. But in addition it was to treat the words used in philosophy as having their 'ordinary' or 'stock' meanings.[4] Ryle suggests that ideally it shouldn't be necessary to explain such ordinary uses of words although, he comments wryly:

> in philosophical debates one is sometimes required to do it, since one's fellow-philosophers are at such pains to pretend that they cannot think what its stock use is – a difficulty which, of course, they forget all about when they are teaching children or foreigners how to use it, and when they are consulting dictionaries.
>
> (110)

In 'Ordinary language', Ryle emphasises what was to be another central tenet of his school of philosophy, the idea that it is the use of a word which should be considered in any discussion, not the word itself. He rejects the idea that words in themselves 'have' meanings, that some entity, a meaning, is associated with each word. Rather, the meaning, or value, of a word is determined only by how it can be used. In a later article published in 1957, 'The theory of meaning', he argues that it is ridiculous to say that the man, Hillary, is the meaning of the phrase *the first man to stand on the top of Mt Everest*. He argues that this is impossible; 'meanings are not born and do not die and they never wear boots' (134). In this paper he acknowledges the obvious debt which these ideas owe to Wittgenstein, and particularly to *Philosophical Investigations*. In this book, Ryle claims, Wittgenstein realised that: 'the use of an expression, or the concept it expresses, is the role it is employed to perform, not any thing or person or event for which it might be supposed to stand' (144).

This account is clearly at odds with some of those we considered in earlier chapters. Remember, however, that philosophers such as Frege, Russell and Carnap were principally concerned with the philosophy of mathematics, and attempted to explain language in terms of the logical regularities they found in that subject. Such earlier philosophers were not, of course, unaware that language was used in less precise ways, but they regarded such uses as peripheral, or 'imperfect', and therefore not suitable focuses of study. In Chapter 3 we saw how Carnap was eager to produce a 'perfect' language which would obey logical rules in a way in which ordinary language would not. And in 'On referring', Strawson attacks what he sees as Russell's misplaced attempts to 'purify language'. As part of our consideration of 'conversational implicature' later in this chapter, we will look at some of the specific problems which natural language presents for accounts based on mathematical logic.

The ordinary language approach to philosophy flourished for a decade or more at Oxford, and has been very important in the subsequent development of various branches of philosophy and linguistics in Britain and America. But it was not universally accepted. Bertrand Russell, for instance, was still very much a major figure in British philosophy in the 1950s, and was not at all impressed by this new movement. He had been an enthusiastic champion of Wittgenstein's early work, being instrumental in getting *Tractatus* published in English. But he made little secret of his disappointment in Wittgenstein's later work, seeing *Philosophical Investigations*, in particular, as an abandonment of his earlier rigour in favour of dismissing complicated matters of logic as 'pseudo problems'. Russell continued to produce work which was concerned mainly with mathematical and logical problems of meaning and knowledge, and only secondarily with language. We saw in Chapter 2, in his response to Strawson, that he was highly critical of 'linguistic' approaches to such matters.

The philosophers working on ordinary language at Oxford in the middle part of the twentieth century all shared the idea which Russell found so objectionable: that natural language, together with its use in everyday situations, was a legitimate field of study in its own right. This idea derived from their emphasis on the 'everyday' uses of words as the appropriate tools for clarifying, and possibly solving, the philosophical problems which are expressed using them. This is not to say that there is only one line of argument which can be identified as representing ordinary language philosophy, or that its proponents were all in agreement on every matter. Rather, ordinary language philosophy represents a particular framework within which many different topics were discussed. The two topics which have been most influential in linguistics, and which will therefore be the focus of our attention in the remainder of this chapter, are *speech acts* and *implicature*. The work which we shall be considering can all be seen as belonging within the framework of ordinary language philosophy, despite the many differences in emphasis and interpretation which we shall encounter.

Speech acts

In the introduction to this chapter we considered the 'descriptive fallacy', identified by Austin, a leading philosopher of ordinary language. Austin's full name was John Langshaw Austin, and he is generally referred to in philosophical discussion as 'J. L. Austin', to avoid confusion with another, earlier, John Austin, who wrote on moral and legal philosophy in the early nineteenth century. J. L. Austin established a reputation for his work at Oxford after the Second World War, and became Professor of Moral Philosophy there in 1952, eight years before his death at the age of forty-nine. In his work, he made particular claims about the ways in which, or the purposes for which, people use language. It is interesting that even Strawson, who as we have seen, insisted in 'On referring' on the significance of context and the inapplicability of mathematical logic to natural language, seemed to take it for granted in this same paper that 'One of the main purposes for which we use language is the purpose of stating facts about things and persons and events' (229). Austin's claim in identifying the 'descriptive fallacy' was that, on the contrary, stating facts could account for only a very few of the many uses of language.

Little of Austin's influential work in this area was published during his lifetime; his ideas were made public almost entirely through his lectures and talks. In 1955 he gave the annual William James lectures at Harvard University, and after his death his notes from these were edited and published in 1962 as a book, *How to Do Things with Words*. The title is a succinct statement of his main theme. Austin was interested in the many things which people do with language, such as asking questions, issuing orders, making requests and offering invitations. An account of meaning interested only in truth and falsity could have little to say about these.

How to Do Things with Words begins with a clear statement of the importance of these non-truth-conditional uses of language to any account of meaning. On the first page Austin also introduces another of his central observations: that these different uses are not necessarily, or even usually, distinguished by grammatical form. Consider the following, all of which could, in appropriate circumstances, be interpreted as orders to open a window:

6) Open the window.
7) Could you open the window?
8) I'd be grateful if you would open the window.
9) Shall we let in some fresh air?
10) It's getting rather stuffy in here.

A grammarian would notice that only 6) is an imperative, the grammatical form conventionally associated with giving orders; 7) and 9) are interrogatives, usually assumed to be used to ask questions; 8) and 10) are declaratives, and as such might be expected to be used to make statements of fact. But they can all be used to do the same thing: to ask someone to open a window. Austin drew a distinction between the *meaning* of an expression and its *function*. The meaning he saw as roughly equivalent to the conventional meaning of the sentence, including the appropriate sense and reference. The function, on the other hand, was entirely dependent on the situation in which the expression was used and, crucially, the intention with which it was used. Whether or not examples such as 6)–10) have the function of issuing an order will depend at least, although not exclusively, on whether the speaker intends them to have this function. As we will see in the next section, the success of these examples as orders depends on that intention of the speaker being recognised.

The uses of language which Austin discussed came to be known as 'speech acts'. This was an expression which Austin himself used only in connection with the later part of his Harvard lectures, which we will consider below. However, it sums up one of his central observations. Speech can be analysed from the point of view not just of what information it communicates, but of what acts it performs. Austin originally considered the possibility of distinguishing a particular type of such acts, which he labelled **performatives**. In his later work he came to see that such acts were not as clearly distinguished as he had thought, and he eventually abandoned the idea. But we will look first at the characteristics and properties of performatives, because they illustrate the nature of Austin's insights, and are a significant stage in the development of his ideas.

Performatives

The 'performative hypothesis', as this stage in Austin's thought came to be labelled, holds that performatives can be clearly distinguished from those uses of language which are intended simply to convey information. Austin called these latter uses **constatives**. It is appropriate to ask of constatives whether they are true or false, but the same can't be asked of performatives. Instead, they are either appropriate or inappropriate in a particular context. In Austin's terms they can be either 'happy' or 'unhappy'. 'Happy' speech acts are sometimes known as *felicitous*, and the factors which are necessary to make them so are known as *felicity conditions*.

Austin noticed that, by the very act of saying certain words, in the appropriate context and with the appropriate intentions, speakers can perform the very act they are apparently describing.[5] His most famous examples are 'ritualised performatives' of the following kind:

11) I name this ship the Black Pig.
12) I sentence you to five years hard labour.
13) I will. [*in the context of a wedding ceremony*]

The use of these expressions can in itself bring about certain states of affairs: ships can be named, convicts sentenced, couples married. Austin originally suggested that certain grammatical properties are necessary to performatives, namely that they must always be in the first person, and that they can only be in the simple, not the progressive, present tense. So while 11)–13) can all be used to perform actions, 14)–15) can only be used to describe what action is being performed.

14) I am naming this ship the Black Pig.
15) He sentences you to five years hard labour.

Now, uttering expressions such as 11)–13) does not, of course, always bring about any particular situation. They must be uttered by someone with a specific authority to perform that action, while in the appropriate circumstances. As Austin noticed, an example like 11) wouldn't work if uttered by a protestor who had just grabbed the champagne bottle out of the hand of the invited dignitary, and 13) wouldn't work if uttered by someone who was already married. The identity of the speaker and the details of the situation make up the felicity conditions for the performative. To utter 13) happily you need at least, under English law, to be unmarried, to be in the presence of another unmarried person of opposite sex whom you intend to marry, and to be in the presence of a registrar or priest and two witnesses.

There are many performatives which have a less limited use than those in 11)–13). Austin originally considered the possibility of going through a dictionary and listing all the verbs which could be used performatively. Here are just a few examples:

16) I bet you £5 that John will be late for the lecture again.
17) I promise not to plagiarise your essay.
18) I dare you to stand up and sing the national anthem backwards.
19) I warn you not to come here again.

On this account, the verb *warn* can be classified as performative because you can warn someone just by uttering 19). The verb *insult*, however, is not be a performative verb because you can't effectively insult someone by saying 'I insult you'. Although the circumstances in which these speech acts can be performed are less restricted, there are nevertheless certain felicity conditions attached to their use. So you can't actually bring about a bet by uttering 16) unless the person you are addressing takes you up on it. Similarly, you don't genuinely promise if you utter 17) insincerely. Again, the notion of intention is significant here; 17) only works as a promise if the speaker intends to use it to promise, and if the hearer recognises and accepts that intention.

As mentioned above, in the course of the lectures which were published in *How to Do Things with Words*, Austin found problems with, and finally abandoned, the performative hypothesis, although many of its insights remain significant to his work and to later work on speech acts. The various problems which Austin identified can be related to his own distinction between truth conditions and felicity conditions. Considering the types of logical relations which can exist between statements, he noticed that there are more ways in which a constative can be inappropriate, or in Austin's term 'outrageous', than simply being false. For instance, making a statement implies belief in that statement. To say 'the cat is on the mat' when you don't believe that the cat is on the mat is insincere, and therefore unhappy in the same way that an insincere promise is unhappy. Similarly, Austin considered presupposition. To say 'all Jack's children are bald' when Jack in fact has no children is not false. We saw in Chapter 2 that it suffers from what has been described as 'presupposition failure'. Austin defined this as a type of unhappiness, similar to that which arises when 'I name this ship ... ' is uttered without the appropriate institutional setting.

Conversely, Austin noticed that to say that a performative utterance such as 'I apologise' is happy is to make a series of claims about truth, most noticeably that 'the statement that I am apologising is true' and that 'the statement that certain [felicity] conditions obtain must be true' (53). There are other examples of performatives for which it seems appropriate to speak even more directly of truth and falsity. For instance, a performative such as 'I warn you that the bull is about to charge', uttered in a context where the bull is not about to charge, wouldn't be described as a failure to warn, but as a false or mistaken warning. Austin also drew attention to a class of performatives which begin 'I state that ... '. These can be used to make statements of fact, and as such can be said to be true or false. Austin claimed that it is false to say 'I state that John is running' if John is not in fact running.

This particular claim was later criticised by John Searle in his 1968 article 'Austin on locutionary and illocutionary acts'. Searle argues that Austin is here confusing 'statement-objects' with 'statement-acts'. In the example above, the statement-object is the 'thing stated': the proposition that John is running. The statement-act is the stating itself: the act of uttering 'I state that John is running'. Statement-objects, then, are propositions and can therefore be true or false, whereas statement-acts are individual acts of stating, and as such can't have truth-values. Nevertheless, Austin's realisation that constatives could in fact be discussed in terms of felicity or infelicity, and performatives in terms of truth or falsity, is generally taken to validate his claim that the distinction couldn't be maintained. He developed a different way of thinking about speech acts, which depended not on a distinction between constatives and performatives, but on identifying three levels of acts which are performed when an utterance is produced. These he called the **locutionary**, the **illocutionary** and the **perlocutionary** acts.

Illocutionary force

In his later work, Austin returned to his critique of the 'descriptive fallacy'. He explained that philosophers have in general been concerned only with the act *of* saying something, ignoring the much more significant act performed *in* saying something. These acts he labelled locutionary and illocutionary, respectively. The locutionary act is closely related to what Austin described as 'meaning' in his earlier work. It is the act of uttering a sequence of words, together with their literal meaning, including the appropriate sense and reference. At the level of the illocutionary act, the intention of the speaker becomes relevant. To know what illocutionary act has been performed we need to know what it is that the speaker intends to achieve or bring about by producing this utterance. This is sometimes known as the *illocutionary force* of an utterance. Finally, the perlocutionary act depends not just on the speaker but on the hearer. It is concerned with the result or consequence of the utterance having been produced. In Austin's terms, it is what we bring about *by* saying something.

Austin illustrates these distinctions with a discussion of the possible uses of an utterance of 'shoot her'. Examples 20), 21) and 22) respectively, represent some of the possible locutionary, illocutionary and perlocutionary acts involved.

20) He said to me 'Shoot her!' meaning by 'shoot' shoot and referring by 'her' to *her*.
21) He urged (or advised, ordered, etc.) me to shoot her.

22) He persuaded me to shoot her.

The perlocutionary act in 22) is one which coincides with the speaker's intention, but Austin noted that this needn't always be the case. The hearer may 'miss the point' and fail to respond as expected. Or he may understand the intention but fail to comply with it, for instance by producing a further utterance, such as one objecting to the fact that the first utterance was performed. Austin described illocutionary acts as being defined by convention, in that they are related to the form of words used. Perlocutionary acts, on the other hand, he saw as unpredictable and context-dependent.

Austin saw the notion of illocutionary force as a 'general theory' of meaning, which could explain the problems he had identified for the distinction between constatives and performatives. Both types of utterance can be said to have illocutionary force, since 'to state is every bit as much to perform an illocutionary act as, say, to warn or to pronounce' (134). To say 'I state that he did not do it', in which the illocutionary force of stating is explicitly identified, is, Austin claims, to perform the same act as using the 'primary' form, 'he did not do it'.

Searle on speech acts

In the last lecture in *How to Do Things with Words*, Austin set out to classify different types of utterance, according to their illocutionary force. It was this task which was subsequently taken up by John Searle although, as we will see, he suggested various modifications to Austin's account. Searle was well placed to evaluate and develop Austin's ideas. As a student at Oxford he was taught by both Austin and Strawson during the 1950s. He completed a D.Phil. thesis on sense and reference in 1959, and later became Professor of Philosophy at the University of California at Berkeley. He can be seen as an important figure in linking the predominantly English-based work of the philosophers of ordinary language in the middle part of the twentieth century, with work on the philosophy of mind and in the growing discipline of linguistics in America in the later part of that century. In the preface to *Speech Acts*, a book published in 1969, he records his thanks to both J. L. Austin and Noam Chomsky.

In *Speech Acts*, and in various published articles on the same topic, Searle develops Austin's work by enumerating the different classes of illocutionary act, by elaborating the nature of the felicity conditions for these classes, and by relating the account of speech acts to wider issues in the philosophy of language. His discussion of some of these issues begins to sound like the questions which were later to be asked in pragmatics. For instance, near the beginning of *Speech Acts* he asks: 'What is the relation between what I mean when I say something and what it means whether anyone says it or not?' (3). This book also includes some particularly blunt expressions of what Searle saw as the essential relationship between meaning and use. For instance, borrowing the by-then popular comparison between languages and games, he suggests that studying language without use is like studying the rules of baseball without considering it as a game.

The work for which Searle is probably best known, at least in linguistics, is his account of indirect speech acts (often abbreviated to ISAs). In his 1975 article of that name, Searle describes ISAs as 'cases in which one illocutionary act can be performed indirectly by way of performing another' (60). He is considering examples such as the following, common enough in ordinary language, but potentially problematic for an account of speech acts in terms of the illocutionary act performed:

23) Can you pass the jam?
24) I'd be grateful if you would keep quiet.
25) Would you be willing to help me?

In these examples, it isn't possible to define a single illocutionary act, even if we are aware of the speaker's intentions. Although 23) can be understood as an enquiry about the hearer's abilities, it can also be understood, and is in fact most likely to be intended, as a request. Searle defined this most likely intention as the *primary illocution* of the utterance, which is derived from the *secondary illocution*, in this case that of question, with reference to the felicity conditions for each act. In the case of questions, one of the felicity conditions which Searle identifies is that the speaker must be genuinely ignorant as to the answer. In most cases in which 23) is used it will be unlikely that the speaker really can't assess whether the hearer is able to pass the jam. However, the hearer's ability to pass the jam is one of the felicity conditions for making a request that he do so.[6] Example 23) will therefore be interpreted not as a question but as a request.

Searle describes the primary illocutionary force as 'conventional'. However, he argues that it isn't appropriate to describe examples such as 23) as having the single illocutionary force of 'request', or to argue that they 'have an imperative force as part of their meaning' (67). It would be quite acceptable for the hearer to respond to both primary and secondary illocutionary acts, for instance by saying 'yes' and passing the jam. It is significant that, while it would be possible to respond to just the secondary, derived illocutionary force, by passing the jam in silence, it would seem inappropriate to respond only to the primary force. In other words, it would seem at least sarcastic, and probably be interpreted as deliberate rudeness, simply to answer 'yes'.

Similar explanations can be found for 24) and 25). An utterance of 24) is unlikely to fulfil the felicity condition for an assertion, namely that it conveys information which is new to the hearer; it is therefore likely to be interpreted as a request for silence. And 25) is likely to be understood not as a simple question, but as an indirect request for help. Searle notices, almost in passing, that 'In directives, politeness is the chief motivation for indirectness' (64), a point which was to be taken up later in pragmatics, as we will see at the end of this chapter.

In looking at speech acts, we have been referring to the importance of speaker intention in defining meaning, and in determining the effect of an utterance. This concept is an important one in ordinary language philosophy, and also in present day linguistics, and it's worth taking some time to consider how it fits into the broader philosophical framework. In doing so, we will look at some important work in this area by Paul Grice, whose account of 'conversational implicature', also developed within ordinary language philosophy, will be our next main topic.

Meaning and intention

Two basic beliefs about language have been more or less implicit in the work of many of the writers we have considered, from classical times right up to the twentieth century. The first of these beliefs is that the significance of words is arbitrary and conventional. The second is that, when it is used as a means of communication, language operates in much the same way as any other arbitrary code; a thought in the speaker's mind is encoded into language, which is then decoded by the hearer, so that the thought ends up in his mind. The communication will be successful to the extent that the thought in the mind of the speaker to begin with and the thought in the mind of the hearer to finish with are the same.

The first of these beliefs was put forward by many of the philosophers interested in meaning whom we have studied in earlier chapters, for instance Plato, Locke and Mill. It was challenged by Leibniz, who attempted to provide reasons for the forms which words take. But it's generally agreed that it isn't appropriate to ask 'why' a particular word has a particular meaning. One of the best known statements of this is the one offered by the Swiss linguist Ferdinand de Saussure, who is regarded as one of the founders of Structuralism, and whose work we will consider in context in the final chapter. In his 1915 *Cours de Linguistique Générale* (translated into English as *Course in General Linguistics* in 1960), he discusses the relationship between a 'signifier', for our purposes a word, and the 'signified', the concept which forms its meaning. Saussure notes that it's generally accepted that 'the bond between the signifier and the signified is arbitrary' (67), and goes on to advance in support the fact that different languages have different words for the same concept:

> The idea of 'sister' is not linked by any inner relationship to the succession of sounds *s-ö-r* which serves as its signifier in French; that it could be represented equally by just any other sequence is proved by differences among languages and by the very existence of different

languages: the signified 'ox' has as its signifier *b-ö-f* on one side of the border and *o-k-s (Ochs)* on the other.

(67–8)

The second basic belief in a sense follows from this; if language consists of a series of 'signs' which arbitrarily stand for ideas, then it must be possible to 'encode' a thought by translating it into a series of signs. In most discussions these signs are identified as sounds, which, when received by a speaker of the same language can be 'decoded' back into the same thought.

More recent philosophers and linguists have retained the 'arbitrary sign' belief but rejected the 'code', or at least the 'simple code' model of communication. This approach can be found in the work of Paul Grice. Grice was a member of the group of ordinary language philosophers, although he himself was uneasy about the suggestion that this represented a single school of thought. He was active in Oxford at the same time as Austin and, like Searle, he later became Professor of Philosophy at the University of California, Berkeley. He continued writing on various areas of philosophy almost until his death in 1988.

Grice is now best known for his work on 'conversational implicature', which we will look at next. But in 1957, ten years before he delivered the series of lectures in which this work was outlined, he published an article called simply 'Meaning'. Grice begins this by comparing some of the ways in which the word *mean* is used in ordinary language. Here are some of his examples:

26) Those spots mean measles.
27) Those three rings on the bell (of the bus) mean that the bus is full.
28) That remark 'Smith couldn't get on without his trouble and strife', meant that Smith found his wife indispensable.

Grice observes that there are two different types of 'meaning' involved here, one represented by 26), and the other by 27) and 28). The first type he describes as 'natural meaning'. The spots correspond to measles because of their physical nature; they are symptoms of the disease. It is not the case that anyone means anything *by* the spots. And further, if 26) is true then we are necessarily faced with a case of measles. Examples 27) and 28), however, represent what is sometimes known as 'conventional meaning'. The three rings, and the quoted utterance, have the meaning ascribed to them not because of their physical nature, but because of their place in a pre-arranged system. In the case of the three rings this system is a very simple one, a code agreed between the conductor and the driver. In 28), however, the system is a very complicated one. The meaning of the utterance relies on the individual meanings of all the words it contains; in effect it relies on the English language. In these cases someone (the bus conductor, the producer of the original remark) means something by the rings and the utterance. And it's possible for 27) and 28) to be true in themselves while these 'meanings' are incorrect. The bus may still have room on it but the conductor incorrectly believes it to be full; Smith and his wife may have been separated for many years, but the speaker being reported was trying to hide this fact.

Grice proposes to call the type of meaning represented by 27) and 28) 'non-natural meaning', or 'meaning$_{NN}$' for short. In such cases it's appropriate to say that someone (A) meant something by an utterance (x). Grice therefore introduces a notion of intention to this type of meaning; the speaker produces an utterance with a particular intention in mind, whether to inform (as is generally the case with declaratives) or to produce a result (as with imperatives). But it isn't just the speaker's intention which is important, but also the recognition of this intention by the hearer. Grice suggests that if he leaves something prominent in a room for his wife to find, for instance a piece of china broken by his daughter, he may well do so with the intention of imparting some information to his wife, for instance that a particular accident has taken place. However, his wife will understand this information whether or not she recognises this as an act of communication; the broken pieces are in themselves a natural indication that an accident has taken place. This won't be a case of meaning$_{NN}$ because the intention, although present, wasn't necessary to the communication. Grice offers the definition that to say A meant$_{NN}$ something by x is to say that 'A uttered x with the intention of inducing a belief by means of recognition of this intention' (219).[7]

The same distinction between natural and non-natural meaning can be made with respect to communication intended to cause a particular action on the part of another, rather than simply to impart information. Grice compares the case of 'a policemen who stops a car by standing in its way' with that of 'a policeman who stops a car by waving' (220). In both cases the policeman intends to make the car stop, but only in the second case is it necessary for the driver to recognise this intention in order for the communication to be successful. In the first case the act of standing in the road is in itself sufficient to stop the car. Only the second case is an example of meaning$_{NN}$. With this type of meaning, 'to ask what A meant is to ask for a specification of the intended effect' (220).

Grice's elaboration of the role of intention in utterance production and comprehension had an important influence on his own later work, and on much of the work which was to be produced in this area in linguistics. For instance, it explains one way in which an account of communication which is dependent only on speaker and hearer sharing a common code, is inadequate to explain what goes on in instances of language use. The hearer needs to be able not just to 'decode' the speaker's utterance, but also to be able to assess the intention with which she produced it. This, together with other types of information derived from context, needs to be added to what can be understood from encoded meaning. In other words, the 'code' model of communication needs to be complemented by an 'inferential' model. In the next section, we will consider how Grice's approach to meaning informed his own account of language use, and in particular how he explained these additional, 'inferential' aspects of meaning.

Conversational implicature

Like Austin, Grice presented some of his most influential ideas about language when he was invited to give the William James lectures at Harvard. Grice's lectures were given in 1967, and were entitled 'Logic and conversation'. Some of the ideas presented there were published in an article of the same name in 1975, and the lectures were later published, together with selections from Grice's other writings, in *Studies in the Way of Words* in 1989.

'Logic and conversation' begins with a discussion of the differences between the logical operators and their apparent counterparts in natural language. Grice rejects the 'formalist' approach to this problem: the claim that natural language is imperfect and that only an idealised form of language is worth studying. He also rejects the 'informalist' account: the claim that natural language should be studied in its unsimplified, illogical form. Grice's reason for rejecting both approaches is that their basic premise is flawed, and that natural language expressions don't diverge from their logical counterparts as much as is supposed in either. He suggests that the differences in interpretation can be explained not in terms of the actual meanings of the natural language expressions, but in terms of the use to which they are generally put. Significantly, he claims that this mistaken assumption 'arises from inadequate attention to the nature and importance of the conditions governing conversation' (24). Before we consider Grice's suggestion as to what these conditions are, we will look at some of the apparent discrepancies between expressions of logic and of natural language. In so doing, we will be referring back to our investigation of the operators of propositional logic in Chapter 2.

Natural language and logic

It isn't hard to understand why those interested in the logic of mathematics might be tempted to relate this interest to language. There are a number of words and expressions in natural language which appear to have equivalents in logic. The most obvious and frequently cited of these is the word *and*. If asked to define the meaning of *and*, we might begin by suggesting that, like logical co-ordination, it joins together two propositions, expressed by the two conjuncts. And if we were inclined to define meaning in terms of truth, we might go on to say that its meaning is truth-functional. Joining two true conjuncts gives a true statement, while joining one false and one true, or two false conjuncts, gives a false one. This is the standard definition for logical co-ordination, the one which appears in truth tables. It can be illustrated with examples such as the following:

29) Wellington won the Battle of Waterloo and 1968 was a leap year.
30) William the Conqueror invaded England in 1066 and Henry VIII had seven wives.
31) Henry VIII had seven wives and William the Conqueror invaded England in 1066.
32) Napoleon won the Battle of Waterloo and 1979 was a leap year.

Assuming that we can agree on our facts, we can probably agree that 29) is true, because it is the co-ordination of two true conjuncts, whereas 30), 31) and 32) are all false because they each contain at least one false conjunct. Notice from a comparison of 30) and 31) that for such an account of *and* the order of the conjuncts is not significant; it doesn't affect what we want to say about truth and falsity. It is also significant that *all* we are saying about 29) is that it is true; we haven't made any claims about it sounding in any sense 'natural': the sort of thing we might imagine saying, or that we might be able to think of an appropriate context for. This is precisely the problem with applying such logical definitions to expressions in natural language. Although true, 29) sounds rather 'odd', because we can't find any significant link between the two conjuncts. In other words, although we know what the sentence means, we can't imagine what anyone might 'mean' by saying it. In contrast, 33) seems much more natural:

33) The Lone Ranger jumped onto his horse and rode off into the sunset.

We can imagine saying 33), because we can see a connection between the two conjuncts. But notice that something else has changed too. Now it *does* seem to matter which order the conjuncts are in; the '?' in front of 34) is a conventional way of showing that it sounds distinctly 'odd' even though, if both events did in fact happen, it should be no different in truth-value from 33).

34) ?The Lone Ranger rode off into the sunset and jumped onto his horse.[8]

This oddity arises because *and* in this case seems to mean more than just its logical equivalent. It seems to mean that the events described both took place *plus* they took place in the order in which they are presented.

It's not just the order of events which we seem to be able to understand from uses of the word *and*. Examples 35) and 36) illustrate two further uses, both of which seem perfectly natural, and also seem to have some 'extra' meaning attached.

35) The inebriated lecturer fell off the platform and she had to be taken to hospital.
36) John walked into the room and he turned on the television.

Again, we would probably understand that the two events described in 35) occurred in the order presented, but there is also a notion of 'causality' associated with this use of *and*. We understand not just that the events took place in the order presented, but that the second event occurred as a result of the first. Similarly, in interpreting 36) it could be claimed that as well as ordering there is an 'identity of place'; we understand that John turned on the television while he was in the room.

Notice that the various paraphrases for *and*, whether it be 'and then', 'and as a result', or 'and in that place', all *include* simple co-ordination. It is almost impossible to paraphrase any of these meanings of *and* without starting 'and ... '. So all the uses of *and* share this as part of their meaning, but they all have different, extra meanings as well. Before we consider how we might account for all these variations, we will look at two further aspects of natural language which might appear to have logical equivalents, but which present problems similar to those we have encountered with *and*. These are disjunction and negation.

Consider the word *or*. You might want to claim that at least you know what this means and, crucially, how it differs from *and*. If the following sign were displayed in a cafeteria, you might reasonably expect to be challenged for helping yourself to both soup and a pudding.

37) Lunch includes soup or a pudding.

However, there is another use of *or* which does seem to allow for both the apparent alternatives, and this too is usually easily interpreted. If it were the case that you were over sixty-five and also on a low income, you would be unlikely to be deterred from asking for a concession if you read the following notice:

38) Concessions are available to those who are over 65 or are on a low income.

To gloss this use of *or* we would probably say that the appropriate conditions are met if at least one of the alternatives is the case. And this is close to the logical relationship of 'disjunction', the relationship to which natural language *or* is sometimes compared. Remember that in the truth table for disjunction, the expression as a whole is false only if both disjuncts are false. In all other cases it is true. This relates to what is sometimes described as 'inclusive or'. In contrast, uses of *or* such as that in 37) are known as 'exclusive or'. Equating *or* with logical disjunction doesn't allow us to explain such uses.

There is one further problem presented by words such as *and* and *or*. The extra, non-logical meanings associated with various uses of them are *defeasible*. That is, it's possible to use the expression and then to deny the non-logical meaning. In contrast, you can't use the expression and then deny part of its logical meaning without saying something which is nonsensical, or contradictory. Example 39) below is quite acceptable, while 40) is just a contradiction.

39) I took off my shoes and got into bed, but not in that order.
40) ! I took off my shoes and got into bed, but I didn't do both those things.[9]

The same seems to hold for the different meanings of *or*. You can deny the 'exclusive' sense of *or*, as in 41), but it doesn't work to try denying the 'logical disjunction' sense, as in 42).

41) You can have cream or ice cream with your pudding – in fact you can have both.
42) ! You can have cream or ice cream with your pudding – in fact you can't have either.

Similar problems are posed by negation. In the case of logical negation, we might say that if a statement is true then its negation must be false, and vice-versa. There are various expressions in natural language which might be thought of as corresponding to logical negation, the most obvious being *not*, as well as *it is not the case that*, *it is not true that*, and the prefix *un-* on adjectives. If 43) is true then 44) must be false, and the same applies to 45) and 46).

43) Frederick lives in Canterbury.
44) Frederick does not live in Canterbury.
45) Tabatha is happy.
46) Tabatha is unhappy.

Now, if these expressions were simply equivalent to logical negation, we should find that using two such expressions would cancel each other out, giving us the equivalent of a simple positive statement, just as we are taught in mathematics that 'two minuses equal a plus'. However, if we were to hear or read example 47), we wouldn't be inclined to think that it was simply equivalent to 48):

47) I found your lecture not unhelpful.

48) I found your lecture helpful.

We need to be able to explain why these two don't seem to mean the same: why, in short, 47) seems to be a rather more 'reserved' form of praise than 48).

There are further problems for an account of meaning in natural language dependent on logical relations of truth and falsity, this time ones which don't depend on the supposed equivalence between logical functions and individual words. Tautologies are expressions which, logic dictates, are necessarily true because of their internal properties. A statement of identity between two objects which are the same might be said to be necessarily true, as would a mathematical equation be which stated that '$x = x$'. But yet again the situation in natural language seems to be rather more complicated than a logical definition allows. Consider Grice's example of a logical tautology:

49) War is war.

Logically this is a necessary truth, and if meaning were defined in terms of truth relations there should be nothing more which we could say about it. But we can imagine a situation in which someone might use this expression to make suggestions with which we might want to disagree. For instance, we might want to argue that, even during wartime, certain rules must apply, or certain human rights must be upheld.

Something similar can be said about contradictions. It is possible to find examples in natural language use in which a statement which is necessarily false can nevertheless be used to make a significant comment, something with which you might want to agree. Most people would agree that 50) and 51) are both perfectly acceptable, and can be used meaningfully, even though they are logically contradictory.

50) I'm not his girlfriend – he's my boyfriend!
51) I'm sorry to be leaving and I'm not sorry to be leaving.

Remember that Grice maintained that natural language can be seen as closely related to its logical counterparts, provided that sufficient attention is paid to the conventions of conversational exchange, the context in which natural language is most frequently used. He therefore set himself the task of outlining these conventions, in such a way that they would be able to explain the apparent divergences between logic and natural language. It is his version of these conventions which we now need to investigate.

The co-operative principle

It is Grice's interest in the regularities of conversation which forms the basis of his account of meaning in use. In 'Logic and conversation' he defines conversation as an essentially interactive and co-operative process. He sums up the conditions which govern it in his 'co-operative principle', which he states as follows:

52) 'Make your conversational contribution such as is required, at the stage at which it occurs, by the accepted purpose or direction of the talk exchange in which you are engaged.'

Unfortunately this principle is sometimes read as a 'rule' for proper conversational behaviour, and Grice is sometimes criticised for trying to regulate something which should be a free and creative process. But it's clear from 'Logic and conversation', and from other writings, that he doesn't see himself as laying down rules for correct behaviour, or as trying to impose order on conversational practice. Rather, he is attempting to account for how people actually behave, to explain how conversation works. The co-operative principle is intended to be *descriptive*, describing what people do when they engage in conversation, rather than *prescriptive*, laying down laws for how they ought to behave.

In explaining conversation, Grice is drawing on his interest in the relationship between intention and meaning. His account of conversation is based on the assumption, now commonplace in pragmatics, that linguistic interaction is generally successful because speakers intend to communicate, and because hearers recognise this intention. People in general behave co-operatively in conversation because in general they want to be understood. The co-operative principle is a norm of successful conversational behaviour, but its full significance to interpretation only emerges when it is apparently not being followed.

Grice identifies four main areas in which conversational partners co-operate, and presents these as four maxims of conversation. These maxims together describe how speakers follow the co-operative principle, and they are themselves divided up into further submaxims. The four main maxims relate to quantity, quality, relation and manner, and we will briefly consider these four categories before examining their effects on meaning in conversation.

The maxim of *quantity* is concerned with the amount of information which is supplied in any conversational contribution. It is subdivided into two submaxims, which Grice expresses as follows:

53) 'Make your contribution as informative as is required (for the current purposes of the exchange).'
54) 'Do not make your contribution more informative than is required.'

These two submaxims describe the delicate balance which makes a contribution appropriate. It isn't co-operative to withhold (relevant) information, but nor is it co-operative to provide an excess of (irrelevant) information. It is significant that it's almost impossible to explain the maxim of quantity without making some reference to relevance which, as we will see, is defined by a separate maxim. The distinctions and relationships between the maxims are one of the acknowledged problems with Grice's account; he mentions it himself, and it has frequently been discussed in commentaries on his work.

The maxim of *quality* is also concerned with the information provided by a speaker, this time with the quality, or veracity, of that information. Again, Grice suggests two submaxims:

55) 'Do not say what you believe to be false.'
56) 'Do not say that for which you lack adequate evidence.'

It is uncooperative to provide information which you don't yourself believe, or which you have no particularly concrete reason to believe.

The maxim of *relation* is the least defined and, by Grice's own admission, the most problematic of the maxims. He defines it simply as follows:

57) 'Be relevant.'

Grice admitted that more work needed to be done to elaborate this, work to which he himself never returned.

The maxim of *manner*, unlike the other three maxims, relates not to the information conveyed in a conversational contribution, but to how it is conveyed. Grice offers four separate submaxims relating to manner:

58) 'Avoid obscurity of expression.'
59) 'Avoid ambiguity.'
60) 'Be brief.'
61) 'Be orderly.'

He suggests that 'one might need others' (27).

These four maxims, then, can be seen as describing the form of fully co-operative, fully communicative conversation. They also, significantly, offer an explanation of how it is that literal meaning so often differs from the meaning intended by a speaker. To describe this additional, intended meaning, Grice suggests the term 'implicature', and he proposes to investigate the distinction between 'what is said' and 'what is implicated by the saying of what is said'. In doing so, Grice is acknowledging a similar distinction to that of which Austin was aware when he discussed the difference between meaning and function. But Grice goes further than Austin; as well as identifying various differences between linguistic- and speaker-meaning, he attempts to provide an explicit account of the principles which account for these differences. His aim is to show how what is implicated is derived, as a result of co-operation between speaker and hearer, from what is said.

Grice sees his 'what is said' as a somewhat elaborate form of literal meaning. He describes what is said as being 'closely related to the conventional meaning of the words (the sentence) uttered' (25), but as including, at least, reference assignment and any necessary disambiguation. It is from this that 'what is implicated' is derived. Grice allows that 'in some cases the conventional meaning of the words used will determine what is implicated' (25). He illustrates this point with the following example:

62) He is an English man; he is, therefore, brave.

Grice claims that all that is strictly *said* here is that the subject possesses the properties both of being English and of being brave. The idea that the two are causally linked, that bravery follows from Englishness, is an implicature. Example 62) would therefore not be strictly false if this causal relation did not hold, although it would be a misleading way of presenting the two properties. Grice labels this type of phenomenon *conventional implicature*. However, it is *conversational implicatures* which are dependent on the maxims of conversation, and on which we will concentrate here. We shall begin by returning to some of the examples we considered earlier, which seemed to illustrate a mismatch between formal logic and natural language. We shall look at how Grice's account might explain these.

We have seen that Grice describes the discrepancies between logic and natural language as apparent rather than real. So for him the word *and* in examples such as 63) and 64) literally means simply that the two events took place. This is 'what is said'.

63) The Lone Ranger jumped onto his horse and rode off into the sunset.
64) The inebriated lecturer fell off the platform and she had to be taken to hospital.

However, in presenting the information in this way, the speaker implicates some additional meaning. Specifically, if the hearer assumes that the speaker is being co-operative, he will assume that the orders in which the events are explained to him are in some way significant, and therefore that there is a link of sequence in 63) and of sequence and probably also causality in 64). It would be inappropriate and misleading, although not strictly false, for a speaker to produce an utterance of 64) to describe two events which were completely unrelated. We could say that these implicatures follow from an assumption that the maxim of manner is being observed, and particularly the submaxim to 'be orderly'.

Similarly, we could say that the inclusive meaning of *or* is what is actually *said* in the following:

65) Lunch includes soup or a pudding.

Strictly speaking, it wouldn't be false to use this in a situation in which you could have both soup and pudding. However, if the speaker were in a position to give this additional information she ought, following the maxim of quantity, to do so. The hearer assumes that the speaker is providing all the information she is able to, and therefore that the use of *or* here can be taken to implicate an exclusive meaning.

In each of the examples we have considered so far, the implicature arises from the use of a particular word, and from the hearer's knowledge of the literal meaning of this word together with his assumption that the speaker is behaving co-operatively. Such examples are not dependent on any particular context of utterance, and are described by Grice as *generalised conversational implicatures*. As we saw earlier, such aspects of meaning can be cancelled without contradiction, for instance in 66):

66) You can have cream or ice cream with your pudding – in fact you can have both.

Grice distinguished this type of implicature from those which he described as *particularised conversational implicatures*. These are dependent on context, and are therefore particular to a specific use; removed from that context the words are not in any way associated with the implicatures. Grice's examples of this are 67) and 68):

67) *(A is standing by an obviously immobilized car)*
    A   I am out of petrol.
    B   There is a garage round the corner.

Here, A would be justified in assuming that the garage mentioned by B sells petrol. B wouldn't be following the maxim of relation if her remark about the garage were not related in this way to A's situation.

68) *A*   Smith doesn't seem to have a girlfriend these days.
    B   He has been paying a lot of visits to New York lately.

Again, the maxim of relation is involved here. All that B actually says is that Smith has been going to New York a lot, but she implicates that Smith may have a girlfriend there. If no such implicature were intended, B's remark would be uncooperative, because irrelevant, as a response to A's leading comment.[10]

In these examples, the co-operative principle can be used to explain how a response to a question or comment can be interpreted as relevant. But Grice doesn't assume that the picture is always this simple, or that all conversational exchanges are as straightforward as these examples. He also considers examples in which it is less clear that a particular speaker is being fully co-operative. These too, he argues, can be explained by means of the co-operative principle, but only if it is assumed that speakers may sometimes choose to 'flout' the maxims in the process of conversation.

Flouting the maxims

In 'Logic and conversation', Grice allows that speakers sometimes produce conversational contributions which appear to be extremely uncooperative. He considers how it is that hearers nevertheless manage to interpret these as contributions to the current conversation. Such examples are explained in terms of the hearer's continued assumption that the speaker is being co-operative, despite appearances to the contrary. Grice describes examples where conversational maxims are blatantly disregarded, with no apparent intention to deceive, as examples of 'flouting' a maxim. The speaker might be said to be exploiting a particular maxim for communicative effect. Grice notes that 'This situation is one that characteristically gives rise to a conversational implicature' (30). Below are some of Grice's examples of this phenomenon. In each case the maxim is infringed only at the level of what is *said*. At the level of what is *implicated* these can be interpreted as co-operative contributions.

69) War is war.

Remember that we discussed this earlier as an example of a blatant tautology, which can nevertheless be used to convey significant ideas. In Grice's account, such examples are 'totally noninformative' at the level of what is said, failing to impart any information. As such, they clearly flout the first submaxim of quantity. However, if the hearer maintains the assumption that the speaker is being co-operative, he will assume that some information *is* provided at the level of what is implicated. Exactly what this information is will of course depend on context. It could be that the speaker is suggesting that, once a state of war has been declared, no particular rules can be said to apply. Or she may be suggesting that the relationship between two people under discussion is a very hostile one, and that this explains their behaviour.

There are certain other 'figures of speech' which Grice explains in terms of the distinction between 'what is said' and 'what is implicated', notably *irony* and *metaphor*. His examples of these two phenomena are as follows:

70) [*In a situation where X has betrayed a secret of the speaker.*]
    X is a fine friend.
71) You are the gin in my Martini.

At the level of what is said we could say that both these examples are simply false. They are said in apparent disregard of the maxim of quality. But on the assumption that the speaker isn't simply stating falsehoods uncooperatively, these examples can be reanalysed as conveying something significant, and something possibly true, at the level of what is implicated. In the case of the ironic 70), Grice suggests that the 'most obviously related proposition' is the contradiction of what is said, and this is taken to be what is implicated. This is not the case for metaphors such as 71), where the contradiction of what is said is an uninformative truism. Rather, the speaker is taken to be implicating that there are certain features of gin in Martini which can be attributed to the subject.

Remember the example of the abrupt change of topic, used to indicate that what had just been said was in some way inappropriate. Grice explains this as an example of a flouting of the maxim of relation, a maxim which he suggests is perhaps not flouted as commonly as the others are. He asks us to consider the exchange, repeated here, as taking place 'at a genteel tea party' (35).

72) *A*   Mrs X is an old bag.
    B   The weather has been quite delightful this summer, hasn't it?

B produces a response which is clearly and blatantly not relevant to what A has just said. On the assumption that B is being co-operative, and not merely producing random comments, A understands that B is implicating, although not of course saying, that this is an unsuitable comment.

Conversational implicatures which arise from an apparent disregard for the maxim of manner are, of course, dependent on the form of expression which the speaker chooses. Grice in fact suggests that this distinguishes them from other implicatures, because it means that they can be 'detached'; they won't, or won't necessarily, arise if the speaker rephrases her conversational contribution. To illustrate this type of implicature, we can return to another of the problematic examples which we considered earlier in this chapter, that of double negation. Remember we saw that, if negation in natural language were to correspond exactly to logical negation, 73) should be indistinguishable from 74) in terms of meaning. Yet someone who said 73) would not be taken to have paid the same compliment as someone who said 74).

73) I found your lecture not unhelpful.
74) I found your lecture helpful.

By choosing 73) rather than the simpler, and logically equivalent 74), the speaker must, if she is being co-operative, be intending some particular
o be associated with this mode of expression. Specifically, she is
y flouting the submaxim of manner which states 'be brief'; 74) is,

quite simply, a shorter form of expression than 73). She is taken to implicate that the briefer, and therefore apparently more co-operative 74) is not appropriate in the context. Therefore she is taken to implicate, although not strictly to say, that the lecture was not entirely helpful.

The two papers in which Grice develops his account of conversational implicature, 'Logic and conversation' and 'Further notes on logic and conversation', both read as 'work in progress'. He acknowledges that some of his definitions need clarification, for instance that of 'what is said', and that further thought needs to be given to issues such as the relationships between the various maxims. This was work to which he never really returned, although as we will see in the next section, it has been taken up by others. However, Grice's work has been hugely influential, with its focus on conversation as an interactive, negotiated task, and its attempt to characterise a limited number of principles to explain a wide variety of communicative effects. This influence can be seen particularly in linguistic pragmatics, which we will consider briefly to conclude this chapter.

Pragmatics

The philosophical accounts of meaning we have considered in this chapter differ in a number of important ways. But they are all based on the idea that what is communicated between speaker and hearer can be fully explained only with reference to context, an idea which has been fundamental in the development of pragmatics. Pragmatics is sometimes defined as being the study of 'language in use' or 'language in context'. It is concerned centrally with meaning as something which is communicated between users of a language, and only indirectly with meaning as something which is specified by linguistic rule.

Pragmatics is often contrasted with semantics, the study of purely linguistic meaning. Semantics is sometimes described as being concerned with the meaning of sentences, entities which have no physical form but are defined by the grammar of the language in question. Pragmatics, on the other hand, is concerned with utterances, specific uses of sentences in speech or writing on particular occasions. This distinction can clearly be related to Strawson's discussion of the difference between a 'sentence' and a 'use of a sentence', and Austin's argument that certain conditions of context must be in place for an act, or use of language, to be 'happy'.

Austin's work in this area has had a profound and continuing influence on pragmatics. There are still linguists working within a broadly 'speech act' framework, in which utterances are discussed in terms of their illocutionary force. In particular, there has been a lot of interest in the notion of indirect speech acts. The discussion of these has been developed, along lines suggested by Searle, in terms of 'politeness'. In *politeness theory*, indirectness is described as a means of indicating deference and minimising imposition, or of balancing the demands of 'face' of the participants in a conversation. The use of direct and indirect forms of address has been studied as one way in which the balance of power is established, maintained or challenged in various types of institutional and informal discourse. The concept of speech acts has also been employed in studies of language acquisition. It has been suggested, for instance, that an understanding of some of the different functions of speech acts is essential to the acquisition of language, and must in fact be attained by a child before grammatical competence can develop.

There has been one notable attempt in linguistics to tackle the problem, of which Austin was aware, of the variety of grammatical forms which performatives can take. Remember that Austin was eventually forced to abandon the notion that it would be possible to draw up a list of performative verbs, when he realised that many utterances, including declarations of fact, could be seen as 'implicit performatives'. As well as an explicit performative such as 75), a 'hint' such as 76), and even a statement such as 77) could be described as performative.

75) I bet you that Newcastle will win the FA cup.
76) I wouldn't trouble the vice chancellor right now if I were you.
77) The train now at platform three is for Dover Priory.

Austin noticed that it would be possible to paraphrase an implicit performative such as 76) as 'I (hereby) warn you not to trouble the vice chancellor right now', and a statement such as 77) as 'I (hereby) inform you that the train now at platform three is for Dover Priory'. Austin himself merely noted the discrepancies which are possible between the form of an utterance and the speech act it can be used to perform. However, within the framework of generative semantics in the 1970s, an attempt was made to explain implicit performatives at the level of deep structure. Using the conventional abbreviations 'Vp' for 'verb phrase' and 'S' for sentence, the 'performative analysis', or 'performative hypothesis', stipulated that every sentence shared the following form at the 'highest' level of deep structure:

78) I (hereby) Vp you (that) S.

In other words, the 'underlying' form of 76) and 77) would be 79) and 80), respectively:

79) I (hereby) warn you (that) you don't trouble the vice chancellor right now.
80) I (hereby) tell you (that) the train now on platform three is for Dover Priory.

In a final transformation before surface structure, these 'performative' parts could then be (optionally) deleted, explaining how 76) and 77) could be performative in meaning without being performative in form. Generative semanticists supported this analysis with complex syntactic arguments, claiming that it captured a number of important generalisations which couldn't otherwise be explained. It also fitted in with their general approach to meaning, which was that all aspects of 'surface' meaning should be explained in terms of grammatical structure at some level, and therefore be linguistic, or semantic in nature. Their claim was that illocutionary force, rather than being dependent on context and on individual speakers, could be explained in terms of semantics. However, in the late 1970s and 1980s, the growing interest in pragmatics as separate from but related to semantics, led to accounts of this type, based entirely on form, being largely abandoned in favour of those which concentrate on the interaction of form and context.

Linguists have also drawn on Grice's distinction between what is said and what is implicated, and his idea that there should be certain principles to connect the two. 'Gricean pragmatics' has been used as a framework for investigating the language of literature, of the courtroom, and of jokes, among many other applications. Grice's basic, rather sketchy account of conversational implicature has been developed by linguists in various ways. For instance, Laurence Horn has suggested that the maxim of quantity can explain why it is that various terms in English, which can be arranged semantically on 'scales of informativeness', seem to implicate the denial of other terms on the same scale. Stephen Levinson has suggested that Grice's maxims can be reduced to a distinction between so-called 'Q' and 'I' maxims.

Perhaps the most significant new work in this area since 'Logic and conversation' has been the development of 'relevance theory' by Dan Sperber and Deirdre Wilson, and others. Proponents of relevance theory see themselves as building on Grice's insights about communication, while abandoning the notion that there are certain 'maxims' which speakers 'follow'. They reassess Grice's problematic maxim of relation as a general principle of human cognition, the 'principle of relevance'. Human beings, they claim, are naturally inclined to search for the most relevant interpretation of any stimulus they are presented with. As a result speakers construct, and hearers interpret, utterances in such a way as to maximise their relevance in their particular context. Sperber and Wilson are explicit in their claim that their account of communication depends on the interaction of 'code' with 'inference'.

However, some linguists working in the area of language use have criticised the very nature of the approaches taken by Austin and by Grice. Their criticisms have largely been aimed at the manner in which the philosophers describe and explain communicative processes, and raise some interesting questions about what it is we are looking for in a theory of language use. Basically, it has been argued that Austin and Grice both concentrate exclusively on short, constructed examples of one or two 'utterances'. Their work doesn't take account of, and is in fact inadequate to explain, what goes on in real exchanges involving actual language users. Speech act theory in particular has been seen as unable to explain longer stretches of discourse. It has been pointed out that several turns in the conversation may make up a single speech act. Austin is criticised for writing, despite his insistence on the significance of context, as if utterances were produced more or less in isolation. Similarly, Grice has been criticised for concentrating on short exchanges, and for providing only a brief statement, or a single preceding utterance, as context.

Linguists working with real language data, for instance with recordings and transcriptions of actually occurring conversations, have suggested that the context of any utterance will almost always be too complex to analyse or describe fully. There are two distinct responses to the work of Austin and Grice in the light of this conclusion. One is to accept their accounts as simplifications which are necessary in order to be able to say anything systematic about language use. This approach, adopted in 'discourse analysis', is rather like that of the scientist who, as we saw in Chapter 3 from Carnap's analogy, studies controlled experiments in order to try to understand the natural world. The alternative approach is to reject accounts such as Austin's and Grice's as unjustifiable simplifications, which can tell us nothing about language use in the 'real world'. 'Conversational analysis', which follows this school of thought, describes language use as a series of interactional sequences, which can only be analysed as a whole.

Such approaches suggest rather different answers to the question of what is required from an account of language use, although they both use real language data as their benchmark for testing such accounts. The first suggests that a theory of language use is valid to the extent that it adequately models natural language exchanges, given a suitably restricted range of contextual factors. The second suggests that the most successful approach is one which explains the ways in which actual, individual exchanges are structured and sequenced. Yet another answer to the question is that put forward by psycholinguists working on language processing. Grice prefigured later work in linguistics by emphasising the importance of the hearer's interpretation to the construction of meaning. More recent work has focused on this interpretation as a series of cognitive processes, which can tell us something about the ways in which language is interpreted, and also perhaps something about how the mind works. This relates to a growing interest, in linguistics and in other areas of study, in the nature and operation of the mind. The study of the mind, and in particular of how it relates to language, is the subject of the next chapter.

Further reading

Wittgenstein

A good selection from Wittgenstein's writings, including extracts from both *Tractatus* and the later work, can be found in Kenny (1994) *The Wittgenstein Reader*. Many writers have offered interpretations of Wittgenstein's work. One of these is the Oxford philosopher Michael Dummett, who has discussed and developed Wittgenstein's work in his writing. A number of his papers are collected in his (1993) book *The Seas of Language* (the title itself is a quotation from *Philosophical Investigations*). In particular, he discusses the later Wittgenstein's notion of 'language games' in the essay 'Language and truth'. In 'What does the appeal to use do for the theory of meaning?', he considers some of the ways in which Wittgenstein agrees with, and differs from, Frege.

Wittgenstein's apparent insistence in his later work, that meaning can be explained only in terms of use, prefigures a debate in linguistics as to whether anything at all can be said about meaning away from context. This issue is not discussed here, but see for instance Harris (1996a) *The Language Connection: Philosophy and Linguistics*.

Ordinary language philosophy

The two articles by Gilbert Ryle referred to here are both very readable. As suggested, 'Ordinary language' can be seen almost as a manifesto for this particular school of philosophy. It consists of a series of definitions of key terms such as *ordinary*, *use*, *usage*, etc. 'The theory of meaning' presents a survey of the philosophical background, looking particularly at Mill, Frege and Wittgenstein. Both of these articles by Ryle are reprinted in Caton (1963) *Philosophy and Ordinary Language*, a useful collection of essays in the field, including some less well-known ones. References to Ryle's essays in this chapter are to this edition.

Paul Grice's account and defence of ordinary language philosophy, 'Postwar Oxford philosophy' was written in 1958 and appears in his (1989) *Studies in the Way of Words*. A contemporary critique of the whole approach to philosophy is Ernest Gellner (1979) *Words and Things*. Subtitled *An Examination of, and an Attack on, Linguistic Philosophy*, this amounts at times to a polemical criticism, particularly of the work of Wittgenstein and Austin. It is supported in a foreword by Bertrand Russell.

Speech acts

Austin's 1955 Harvard lectures were published posthumously as *How to do Things with Words* (1962). This is readable and lively, and accessible even as an introduction to the subject. The essentials of his account of performatives, and of his realisation that they could not be clearly distinguished from statements, are in his paper 'Performative utterances' (1961). Searle's critique and development of Austin's ideas, and the wider implications he sees in them for the philosophy of language, are set out in *Speech Acts* (1969). The main points of his account are also presented in 'What is a speech act?' (1965) and 'Indirect speech acts' (1975). Another interesting commentary on Austin's work, which reconsiders performatives in the light of work on grammatical transformations, and therefore ties in with later work on the performative hypothesis, is Vendler (1972) *Res Cogitans*.

Meaning and intention

Clark (1987) *Principles of Semiotics* is a succinct survey of work on natural and non-natural meaning. In particular, Chapter 2 traces its origins in classical philosophy's discussion of 'signs'. This account also fills in some of the gaps we have left, by looking at the philosophical tradition of the Middle Ages, and continues up to the behaviourism of the twentieth century, which we will consider in the final chapter. Chapter 4 is concerned with the role of signs in communication, and includes a discussion of Grice's work.

Conversational implicature

The discrepancy between logic and natural language is discussed in Allwood *et al.* (1979) *Logic in Linguistics* and, in greater detail in McCawley (1981) *Everything that Linguists Have Always Wanted to Know about Logic*. In his chapter on 'Speech acts and implicatures', McCawley explains how Grice's co-operative principle attempts to account for these discrepancies. Most of the salient points of Grice's account of conversational implicature are set out succinctly in his article 'Logic and conversation' (1975). They are developed in 'Further notes on logic and conversation' (1978). There is a great deal of explanatory and critical work available on this subject. Much of this has been produced by linguists working in pragmatics, and it is therefore listed in the next section.

Pragmatics

There are a large number of introductory books on pragmatics available, most of which include some discussion of the work of Austin, Searle, and Grice, and their contributions to linguistics. Some of the most popular with students of linguistics are: Lyons (1981) *Language, Meaning and Context*, Leech (1983) *Principles of Pragmatics*, Levinson (1983) *Pragmatics* and Thomas (1995) *Meaning in Interaction*.

Bates (1976) *Language and Context: The Acquisition of Pragmatics*, suggests that the acquisition of speech acts is necessarily prior to that of grammar. The 'performative hypothesis' is proposed in a number of works from the 1970s, notably Sadock's (1974) *Towards a Linguistic Theory of Speech Acts*. The main arguments from this, and a refutation of them, are offered in Chapter 5 of Levinson's (1983) *Pragmatics*. The major work on the development of the study of indirect speech acts into an account of politeness in conversational interaction is Brown and Levinson's (1978) article 'Universals in language useage: politeness phenomena'.

Larry Horn's development of Gricean implicatures of quantity into scalar implicatures has not been published in book form; it appeared in his (1972) Ph.D. thesis 'On the semantic properties of the logical operators in English'. The fundamental aspects of this are discussed in Chapter 3 of Levinson (1983) *Pragmatics*. Horn's study of the interaction of negation with this type of implicature is in his article 'Metalinguistic negation and pragmatic ambiguity' (1985), an extended version of which appears in his (1989) *A Natural History of Negation*.

Sperber and Wilson's critique of Grice, and their alternative account of communication in terms of a single principle of relevance, is set out in *Relevance* (1995). A useful commentary on this is Blakemore (1994) *Understanding Utterances*.

There is a huge literature on the empirical study of real language data. Good introductory texts include Brown and Yule (1989) *Discourse Analysis* and Schiffrin (1984) *Approaches to Discourse*. Both include discussion of the different methods of pragmatics, discourse analysis and conversational analysis. The latter work offers a detailed analysis of some naturally occurring language data using Gricean implicature, and thereby highlights some of the problems which such data pose.

5 Language and mind

Introduction

In turning our attention to the relationship between language and mind we are, in one sense, embarking on a whole new topic. We will be comparing accounts which describe language as a type of knowledge with those which describe it as a type of behaviour, and we will be looking at what these accounts suggest about how language is learnt, used and understood. In another sense, however, we have been concerned with language and mind all along. So, for instance, in Chapter 1 when we looked at what has been said about the relationship between words and objects, we considered the idea that words stand not for objects themselves but for 'mental images' of the objects in the mind. And in Chapter 4 we examined accounts of communication which depend on the 'intention' in the mind of the speaker, and the recognition of that intention by the hearer. The discussion of many aspects of language sooner or later involves a discussion of the mind or of mental processes, because language is so intimately bound up with the way we understand, describe, and affect the world around us.

We will be concentrating on two main issues here.[1] Principally, we will be looking at the ways in which descriptions of language have either depended on, or alternatively ruled out, the relevance of properties of the human mind. In other words we will be comparing work which sees language as solely, or at least most importantly, a mental phenomenon, with work which excludes all reference to the mind from the description of language. The second main issue concerns the nature of the processes involved in the acquisition of language by children. As we will see, this is closely related to the more general issue of the relationship between language and mind. In essence, it centres on questions of whether children go through a process of acquiring certain types of knowledge, or of learning certain forms of behaviour.

We will begin with the Swiss linguist Ferdinand de Saussure, whose work we considered briefly in Chapter 4. We have already seen that Saussure described the relationship between an object and its name as *arbitrary* and *conventional*, and in this chapter we will look in more detail at Saussure's definitions of objects and names. We will also consider what he said about the relationships between words. Briefly, he argued that these relationships are, in contrast, not arbitrary but highly structured, and that it is these structures which make up the language we speak. Saussure claimed that we need to learn a language before we can entertain fully developed thoughts. So our language determines the way our ideas about the world are structured, whether or not we express these ideas to other people. We will see that some later linguists argued that speakers of different languages actually perceive the world around them differently. The words and forms of expression we learn determine, but also limit, the ways in which we can describe the things and events we see to other people, and also to ourselves.

Our investigations will then bring us back to a topic which we considered in the first chapter: the innate properties of the human mind. We have seen that discussion of what can be said to be innate in the human mind dates right back to classical times. The discussion centres on the question of how much of our understanding, and indeed knowledge, is inherited, and how much must be learnt from our environment. To describe something as innate is to claim that it is an essential property of human nature; to describe something as learnt is to claim that it is dependent on experience. Remember that Plato's account of Ideal Forms, which are known before any experience of actual objects, can be seen as an early model of innate knowledge. Aristotle, on the other hand, took the view that knowledge of the world is derived directly from the impressions we receive from our senses.

These two approaches lead to very different accounts of what we are 'born with'. One consequence of **innatism** is that a newborn child must be described as having certain types of knowledge (for Plato, knowledge of the Ideal Forms) already in place. In contrast, Aristotle's version is often taken to imply that the mind of the newborn child is a *tabula rasa*. This Latin phrase translates as 'blank tablet' or 'clean slate'; the child is born without knowledge, which must be 'written' into its mind by experience. Both of these theories of mind have featured in more recent discussions of how it is that children learn, or acquire, the language being spoken around them. We will look at some very different accounts of the process of language acquisition, and consider how they stem from these two pictures of the newborn mind.

We saw in Chapter 1 that the ideas of both Plato and Aristotle reappeared in the work of philosophers of later centuries. Plato's interest in innate knowledge is reflected in the work of rationalists such as Leibniz. Rationalists argued that data from the senses is not enough to give knowledge of the world; there must be a certain disposition of mind which determines the form of knowledge which can be acquired. In a later century, Kant claimed that certain types of knowledge are *a priori*; they don't derive from, but rather precede, experience. On the other hand, Aristotle's influence can be seen in particular in the work of empiricists such as Locke and Berkeley. We have seen that, while Locke allowed that some basic cognitive capacity must be innate, he maintained that all knowledge must be derived from experience.

The term *empiricist* has also been applied, in a slightly different but related sense, to an approach to the study of language which developed in the early and middle part of the twentieth century. Although much criticised, this approach has been very influential, and is still current in various forms. It is also generally acknowledged, even by those who disagree with it, as having been very important in the process of establishing linguistics as a separate branch of academic study. Interest in innate properties of the mind certainly didn't die out, and indeed it was a revival of these ideas which led to the development of an important alternative to empiricism in the middle of the twentieth century. We will be considering this revival later. But before that we will return to Saussure, and look at how his ideas influenced the study of language earlier in the century.

Signs and structures

Ferdinand de Saussure was one of the first people to base an academic career on the study of language for its own sake. Born in Switzerland in 1857, he became a professor at the University of Geneva in 1906. His interests included the detailed description of individual languages, as well as the history and nature of language itself. His work was extremely influential in the subsequent development of linguistics, but he published very little during his lifetime. After his death in 1913, a number of his students compiled some of the lectures he had given at Geneva from their notes and from his own drafts. These were published as *Cours de Linguistique Générale* in 1916, which was translated into English and published as *Course in General Linguistics* in 1960.

In these lectures, Saussure rejects the extensional account of meaning: the idea, which we considered in Chapter 1, that language consists of a series of names referring directly to objects. He argues that language can be said to consist of a series of 'signs' in which two different entities are united, but that 'the linguistic sign unites, not a thing and a name, but a concept and a sound-image' (66). Saussure stresses that both these entities, and the link between them, exist primarily in the mind of the speakers of the language. The 'concept', like the 'ideas' in ideational accounts of meaning, can be thought of as a mental image of some actual object (Saussure's examples are of the concepts of 'horse' and 'tree'). The 'sound-image' is not the actual sounds formed when you pronounce the words associated with these things, but the 'psychological imprint of the sound' (66). This is something you are aware of if you just recite the words silently to yourself. The study of language, then, is the study of one aspect of the human mind: a series of mental sound images, and the concepts we have learnt to associate with them.

Saussure adopts the terms *signified* for a concept and *signifier* for the sound-image associated with it. These two together form a *sign*, the basic linguistic unit. Remember that we saw in Chapter 4 that Saussure describes the relationship between signifier and signified, the relationship which forms a sign of the language, as arbitrary. There is no rational or natural link between the two parts of the sign; they are united only by the conventions of individual languages, and differ without limit between languages. But the relationship within the sign isn't the only type of relationship which the linguist needs to take into account. There are also a whole series of relationships *between* the signs of a language. These are central to the nature not just of the language as a whole, but of each individual sign, since each sign is significant only in how it relates to and, crucially, differs from, the other signs in the language. In Saussure's own words, signs function 'not through their intrinsic value, but through their relative position' (118); to function efficiently a sign must be recognisably distinct from all other signs in the system.

Language for Saussure, then, is a mental structure. But this is only part of his definition. No account of language is complete, he argues, without reference to its function in a society; 'language never exists apart from the social fact ... its social nature is one of its inner characteristics' (77). Language becomes a means of communication for the individual when a sound-image, related within a sign to a concept, is realised in actual sound. The sound must then be received by another speaker of the same language, who is able to recognise the sound image and therefore to arrive at the same mental concept. So Saussure presents a model of communication of a type we considered in Chapter 4; it is dependent on the encoding and decoding of ideas. He calls the psychological component of communication, the system of signs, the 'language' (Saussure's original French term, widely used in this special sense, is *langue*). This is shared by a community of speakers because they have all acquired, 'not exactly of course, but approximately' (13) the same set of relationships between signified and signifier. The system which constitutes the *langue* is contrasted with the process of producing sounds in order to communicate, which Saussure labels 'speaking' (or *parole*) and which 'is always individual' (13). Speaking, then, can only be performed by individuals, deliberately and with purpose. Language, on the other hand, 'is not complete in any speaker; it exists perfectly only within a collectivity' (14). A language is dependent on the community of speakers who share it.

Saussure saw language as differing in complexity, but not in basic nature, from all sorts of other systems of signs shared by groups of people. He was interested in the study of human use of signs in general, or the discipline of *semiology*, as he labelled it. The method he suggested for the study of all systems of signs, like that for language, was one of looking for the structural relationships between the signs. His approach was therefore labelled *structuralism*, a term which came to be applied to a major school of thought of the twentieth century. Saussure's general interest in semiology had some important consequences for his view of language which, as we will see later in this chapter, distinguish it from some alternative views from later in the same century. In particular, Saussure described languages as not sharing any particular characteristics, other than their level of complexity, which are not also present in other social systems. As a result they can differ from each other almost without limit.

One aspect of structuralism which became particularly significant in linguistics derived from the idea that the significance, or value, of every sign, is dependent on its place in the general structure. Put simply, the meaning of an individual word depends primarily not on something external to the language system, but on the system itself. The system determines the values of its signs, so the individual 'concepts' which form part of these signs are brought into being by the language. In this way, thought itself is actually dependent on language. People have access to certain concepts, and therefore see the world in certain ways, because of the structure of the language they have learnt. Saussure argues that the concepts with which we are familiar can't actually exist independently of, or prior to, our language: 'if words stood for pre-existing concepts, they would all have exact equivalents in meaning from one language to the next; but this is not true' (116). This idea was subsequently taken up by a number of American linguists, most notably Edward Sapir and Benjamin Lee Whorf.

Linguistic determinism

Structuralism is sometimes described as having developed in two directions, very different from each other in focus and method, but both drawing on Saussure's ideas. In Europe, interest broadened from the study of systems of signs to the study of their use, the 'texts' they are used to create, and the effects which these texts have. *Semiotics*, as it became known, was concerned largely with the analysis and criticism of literary texts, but also more generally with structures of the world and of society. In America, the focus was more narrowly linguistic. This tradition was also, confusingly, labelled *semiotics*, a term coined independently by Charles Morris, whose work we considered in the introduction to this book. It was concerned with the detailed study of the structures of individual languages: their systems of syntax, phonology and meanings. Modern linguistics can be seen as developing, at least in part, from this branch of structuralism.

This 'American' semiotics of the middle part of the twentieth century included Leonard Bloomfield's empirical studies of language, which we will consider in the next section. It also included the theory developed by Sapir and Whorf which became known as *linguistic determinism*. This can basically be seen as a development of Saussure's ideas about the relationship between language and thought. Remember that Saussure argued that languages differ in terms both of the signifiers they contain and also of the ideas signified. Since the actual concepts which are available for speakers to encode and communicate are determined by the particular language they speak, thought itself must be dependent on language. The theory of linguistic determinism states that the way in which an individual thinks, and indeed perceives the world, is dependent on his or her language; we learn to see the world in a certain way as part of the process of learning our language.

Edward Sapir was born in 1884 and held posts at the University of Chicago, and then at Yale, where he became Professor of Anthropology in 1931. His anthropological interests were chiefly focused on Native American tribes; he studied their cultures, their traditions and, principally, their languages. He was impressed by the evidence that, although the languages he studied often differed in many significant ways from each other, and from English, all showed similar levels of complexity and powers of expression. This observation may not seem particularly remarkable now, but at the time in which Sapir was writing (his major work, the book *Language*, was published in 1921) it was a significant claim to make. Sapir is following the custom of his time when he writes of 'the language of the savage' (22), and he doesn't hesitate to suggest that more sophistication and civilisation is to be found in a 'higher culture'. But he goes on to argue that such differences in culture aren't reflected in the complexity of the language: 'both simple and complex types of language of an indefinite number of varieties may be found spoken at any desired level of cultural advance' (219).

For Sapir, then, differences in culture are not reflected in differences in language. He does, however, maintain that human languages differ in remarkable ways, in terms of the concepts they contain and therefore the thoughts they can be used to express. Like Saussure before him, he argues that knowledge of a language, including the particular concepts it can be used to signify, is a necessary prerequisite to thought. In support of this, he argues that the introduction, or at least the full understanding, of a new concept is dependent on there being a word to express it:

> The birth of a new concept is invariably foreshadowed by a more or less strained or extended use of old linguistic material. ... As soon as the word is at hand, we instinctively feel, with something of a sigh of relief, that the concept is ours for the handling.

> (17)

Sapir's ideas about the relationship between language and thought were of particular interest to his student Benjamin Lee Whorf. When Whorf enrolled on the course in 'American Indian linguistics' which Sapir set up on arriving at Yale, he was already deeply engaged in research of his own in this area. His linguistic work was, and remained, entirely a matter of his own interest, pursued as an end in itself. He never sought academic positions or titles, and in fact turned down a number of university posts offered to him. All the time that he was researching and publishing his prolific and highly original work in linguistics, he was working full-time as an inspector for a fire insurance company. Indeed, there is some suggestion that the exhaustion caused by this 'double life' may have contributed to his early death in 1941 at the age of forty-four.² Whorf published a number of articles during his lifetime, but his work is now best known from *Language, Thought and Reality*, a selection of his writings published posthumously in 1956.

Sapir encouraged Whorf to study the Native American language Hopi, and this work was to prove particularly important in the development of his ideas. Whorf noticed that the means available for talking about events in Hopi seemed to be completely different from those in English. In particular, 'the Hopi language is seen to contain no words, grammatical forms, constructions or expressions that refer directly to what we call "time"' (57). This, he argues, doesn't reflect a weakness in the language, but rather illustrates the point that 'it is possible to have descriptions of the universe, all equally valid, that do not contain our familiar contrasts of time and space' (58). Instead of these contrasts, Hopi has an alternative distinction between *manifested* (roughly: all that is or has been accessible to the senses) and *manifesting* (roughly: the mental, including the future), a distinction which allows for a rich and complex description of reality, without the need for grammatical forms such as verb tenses.

Whorf also looked at the ways in which different languages divide up the world by means of vocabulary. Famously, he noted that English has one word, *snow*, which does the same job as a number of different words in Eskimo:

> To an Eskimo, this all-inclusive word would be almost unthinkable; he would say that falling snow, slushy snow, and so on, are sensuously and operationally different, different things to contend with; he uses different words for them and for other kinds of snow.
>
> (216)

Whorf's contention is that differences between languages of these types actually result in different ways of perceiving and understanding the world. Speakers of Hopi think about events differently from speakers of English because the language they have learnt describes them differently. Similarly, Eskimos perceive what we would think of as various types of snow as completely separate entities, because they have learnt to call them by different names. It may be that we would fail altogether to see some of the distinct types of entity obvious to the Eskimo, because we have not learnt to label them differently. The general theory became known as the 'principle of linguistic relativity', or sometimes the 'Sapir–Whorf hypothesis'. It is based on a concept of linguistic determinism; the language people speak is said to determine how they see the world around them. In structuralist terms, the structure of a language (including the relationships between its signs) limits the ways in which its speakers understand reality as structured. Language is an important focus of study precisely because it can explain worldviews and systems of belief. Whorf sums this up by claiming that the real concern of linguistics is 'to light up the thick darkness of the language, and thereby of much of the thought, the culture, and the outlook upon life of a given community' (73).

The Sapir–Whorf hypothesis explains the structure of mind as being, at least in part, dependent on the structure of language. The language we learn determines the way we think about the world and therefore, to some extent, the way our minds work. Their hypothesis is also an account which, like Saussure's, highlights the differences between individual languages. As such it hasn't fitted well with some more recent developments in linguistics which, as we shall see later in this chapter, have emphasised the basic and remarkable similarities between languages. In addition, some doubt has been cast on the validity of Whorf's more specific claims. For instance, his assessment of the Hopi concept of time has been shown to be unfounded. And it has been suggested that he significantly overestimated the number of words for 'snow' in Eskimo, while at the same time overlooking the variety of expression also found in English (think of *sleet, blizzard, avalanche, slush,* etc.). Nevertheless, the Sapir–Whorf hypothesis was in its time an important development in linguistics, and has remained influential in work on the connection between language and thought. In the next section we turn our attention to another branch of mid-twentieth-century linguistics, again one which had its origins in Saussure's structuralism, but this time one which emphasised the observable phenomena of language use over any putative relationship between language and the mind.

Empiricism

Philosophers such as Locke and Berkeley became known as 'empiricists' because they emphasised the importance of experience, and of the evidence of the senses. They explained all knowledge as derived not from inborn understanding, but in response to what we might call the 'data' available to the individual. The 'empiricist' approach to the study of language which developed in the twentieth century also emphasised the evidence offered by data. Data of actual language use was held to be the only legitimate focus of attention in the study of language. These new empiricists, as we will see, rejected metaphysical speculation about 'mental states', and even about abstract 'meaning', in favour of concentrating on the observable phenomena of language use: spoken and written utterances. One pioneer of this new style of empiricism was the American linguist and professor at the University of Chicago, Leonard Bloomfield.

Bloomfield

As we have seen, Sapir and Whorf argued that if we describe a language we are inevitably describing something of the minds of the people who speak it. Leonard Bloomfield, however, maintained that in describing language we can't claim to be saying anything at all about mind. Throughout his career, he was keen to promote the scientific study of language as a field of enquiry in its own right. By 'scientific' he meant that, like any natural science, the study of language should be based on rigorous observation and analysis. At the start of his book *Language*, published in 1933, he laments that: 'The effects of language are remarkable, and include much of what distinguishes man from the animals, but language has no place in our educational program or in the speculation of our philosophers' (3). The contemporary tradition of language teaching was *prescriptive*, with an emphasis on providing rules and correct models of how language should be used. Bloomfield's aim was to promote the teaching of what is now known as *descriptive* linguistics, in which linguists record and describe language as it is actually used.

Bloomfield sets out his agenda for the scientific study of language succinctly when he claims that: 'The only useful generalizations about language are inductive generalizations' (20). By this he means that the only legitimate method is to observe language data and draw conclusions from these observations. The **inductive** scientific method is one which looks at a range of the available empirical evidence, and arrives at general conclusions which are licensed by these. In contrast, the **deductive** method takes a general idea, or hypothesis, as its starting point, and looks to the data to either confirm or falsify this. As we will see later, both methods have been, and continue to be, used in linguistics.

Bloomfield, then, allows only generalisations directly licensed by observation of language data and of human behaviour. Such generalisations can only be about language and behaviour; it's not legitimate to use such data as evidence for mental states, which aren't accessible to empirical study. Bloomfield explicitly rejects the **mentalistic** approach to language, an approach which maintains that a full account of the data can be given only if reference is made to the 'underlying' facts of mind. In Bloomfield's own terms, a mentalistic account of language would explain it in terms of 'the interference of some non-physical factor, a *spirit* or *will* or *mind* … that is present in every human being (32, original emphasis).

In contrast, Bloomfield advocates a *materialistic* account of human behaviour, including linguistic behaviour.[3] Such an account describes the observable facts of behaviour, and explains them without reference to mental states. So, for instance, he offers a materialistic account of the meaning of an expression when he claims that it is made up of 'the situation in which the speaker utters it and the response which it calls forth in the hearer' (139). In discussing semantics, Bloomfield argues, it isn't legitimate to talk about 'underlying meaning' or 'linguistic knowledge'. Rather, the linguist must collect information from many observations of utterances which share a phonetic form, and generalise from these observations to the characteristic contexts and consequences of that form. To take a very simple example, if the linguist observes the word *apple* being uttered on a number of different occasions, each time in the presence of a piece of fruit which 'presents certain relatively definable characteristics' (141), the linguist may conclude that *apple* is the name of that class of fruit in the language under observation.

In developing this account of meaning, Bloomfield was in fact applying the contemporary school of thought known as **behaviourism** to the study of language. This had developed in American psychology some twenty years before the publication of *Language*, although its implications for linguistics are now perhaps best known from the 1957 book *Verbal Behaviour* by the American psychologist B. F. Skinner. Behaviourism was both empirical and materialistic in spirit. Its method of psychological investigation was to observe individual instances of behaviour. The explanations it offered for these were not in terms of mental states but of the physical conditions which caused the behaviour, and the results which followed from it. Behaviour could be seen in terms of a series of *responses* to observable *stimuli*. Certain responses lead to further stimuli which serve to *reinforce* the response, with the consequence that the organism is more inclined to produce that same response the next time the stimuli is presented. The term *organism* is an important one in this context. Behaviourism didn't rely on any exclusively human characteristics in its explanations, and in fact became notorious for extrapolating from the behaviour of animals in controlled experiments to that of human beings in social settings.

Bloomfield's account of language is behaviourist because he explains the meaning of linguistic expressions in terms of the situations, or stimuli, which characteristically cause them to be uttered. The meaning of *water* is defined by the fact that it is characteristically uttered when someone is thirsty. If an utterance is suitably reinforced (if the speaker is handed a glass of water) the speaker will be likely to produce a phonetically similar utterance the next time. This, of course, has important implications for the way in which language is learnt, implications which Bloomfield outlines as follows. The child begins by producing sounds in imitation of the adults around. If the adults recognise a sound as being similar to one of their speech sounds they reward the child (for instance by handing over a doll in response to 'da'). This reward serves to reinforce the child's behaviour, making it more likely to be repeated in the future. In this way, 'the child's speech is perfected by its results' (30). The implications of behaviourism for language, its relationship to the mind, and the way it is learnt by children, were also considered, and were more fully developed, by the philosopher Willard Van Orman Quine.

/uine, as he is generally referred to, is an empiricist in his general
ical outlook, not just in his approach to language. He became
: of Philosophy at Harvard University in 1948, and published
ely during his long career there. But before that, in the early
1... he spent time in Europe and was heavily influenced by the philosophy of the Vienna Circle, especially that of Rudolph Carnap. In his early
work he developed what has become known as a 'scepticism' about
meaning. He argued that there are no meanings which words or expressions in some sense 'have' independently of any occasion of use. This idea
isn't new to us; we have already encountered versions of it in the later
work of Wittgenstein, and in Bloomfield. And it is consistent with Quine's
empirical approach; the best way to establish what a word or sentence
means is to observe as many instances as possible of how it is used.

Quine's scepticism about meaning is apparent in 'Two dogmas of
empiricism', an article first published in 1951, and included in his 1961
book *From a Logical Point of View*. In this, he concedes that linguistic
expressions are 'meaningful', in that they may be used to refer to objects,
and may be judged to be synonymous or not with other expressions. But,
he claims, it simply isn't necessary to posit a notion of 'meaning', which
we might think of as being equivalent to Frege's 'sense', to explain this.
Quine rejects the idea of meaning as something which exists in the mind in
between a word and an object; 'meanings themselves, as obscure interme-
diary entities, may well be abandoned' (22). We could summarise this
position by saying that he allows that linguistic expressions may have
extensional, but not intensional, meanings.

As well as a sceptical and extensional approach to meaning, Quine adopts
a form of **holism** in his early work. A holistic account, as the name suggests, is
one which explains any complex entity as a whole. It stipulates that the
significance of the whole is more than merely the sum of its parts, and that it's
not possible fully to explain the nature of any individual part without looking
at the whole to which it belongs. So according to Quine's 'semantic holism',
any expression within a language system can only be fully explained, or
defined, in relation to the other expressions in that system. We can recognise
in it something similar to Saussure's account of *langue*, the language system.
Remember that Saussure explained the significance, or value, of every sign in
the language as being interrelated with, and dependent on, that of every other
sign in the same system. This structuralist account of meaning is in keeping
with Quine's scepticism about meaning in general. Meaning isn't 'determinate', or assigned to any linguistic expression by virtue of its form. Rather, it
is dependent on the use of the expression and on the use of every other expression in the language. This approach has profound consequences for the
nature of language, and for the relationship between language and mind,
which we can consider in relation to some of Quine's later work.

In 1960, Quine published a book called *Word and Object*, which he dedicated to Rudolph Carnap, and in which he set out his approach to semantics. As we might expect, the approach is thoroughly empirical in nature; it combines the extensional and holistic outlook developed in his earlier work with a behaviourist account of language of the type proposed by Bloomfield and by Skinner. This mixture is nowhere more apparent than in Quine's discussion of *radical translation*.

Quine asks his reader to engage in the following mental exercise, in the interest of discovering something of the nature of language, and of its relationships to the speaker and the speaker's perception of the world. Imagine that you find yourself among a remote tribe of people, whose language you are interested in understanding, but with whom you have no obvious way of communicating. Your task is to observe the natives' behaviour, until you are able to supply a translation in your own language for every word or sentence in theirs. You are engaged in 'radical' translation because you can't rely on any similarity between the tribe's language and yours, as you might with a group of people speaking French or Spanish. You have no reason to believe that any words in their language will sound similar to words in English, that they will use gestures and body language in the same way as you do, or even that they will share your perception of the world.

Quine's description of the processes you would need to go through is lengthy and complex. We will consider just the very beginning of it, and then skip to the conclusions which he draws from it. The whole process is described in detail in *Word and Object*, and is discussed in some of the works listed in the 'further reading' section of this chapter. In your task as field linguist, you are most likely to begin by trying to find translations for words which are 'keyed to present events that are conspicuous to the linguist and his informant' (29). Out walking with a native one day, you both see a rabbit, and the native says 'Gavagai'. You speculate that this can be translated into English as 'Rabbit'.[4] But of course you can't yet be sure about this; the native might have been referring to the colour of the rabbit, or the way it was moving, or just using a word equivalent to 'animal'.

Your next move might be to experiment, in order to discover what other objects will lead the native to assent to 'Gavagai'. You utter 'Gavagai?', in what you hope will be recognised as a tone of enquiry, in the presence of various rabitty and non-rabitty objects, and note what response you get. You can't rely on gesture or facial expression (for all you know, shaking the head may mean 'yes' for these people), but you notice that sometimes when you say 'Gavagai?' you get the response 'Evet', and sometimes you get the response 'Yok'. This might seem like some sort of progress, but you quickly spot another problem. You may speculate that these two can be translated as 'Yes' and 'No', but you have no way of knowing which is which. Eliciting an 'Evet' in the presence of a rabbit is no guarantee that you can translate it as 'Yes', since this would rely on your own, uncon-firmed speculation that 'Gavagai' can be translated as 'Rabbit'.

In fact, your task of radical translation becomes harder the longer you stay with the tribe, as you realise that every hypothesis you form about meaning is related to, and has potential effects for, your translation of every other word or sentence you encounter. We can clearly recognise in this Quine's 'semantic holism'; our decisions about the meaning of each expression of the language we are studying depend on those we make about all other expressions. But Quine draws a further, related conclusion from this, which has important implications for the relationship between language and mind.

If you persevere long enough, you may eventually come up with transla-tions for every expression, which are consistent with each other and together give you a picture of the language you are studying. Suppose that you then meet another linguist who, unknown to you, has also been staying with the tribe and has also just compiled an account of the language by radical translation. You compare notes, and find that, although both of you have reached systems of translation which are coherent and which allow you to converse freely with the natives, the systems of translation which you have developed differ markedly from each other. Here you have two options. Either you could each insist on the superiority of your own system, and attempt to discover who has made the 'right' translation. Or you could find this situation perfectly satisfactory; you both have systems which work, so there is no reason to believe that one must be 'right' and the other 'wrong', or even that one must be better than the other.

Quine suggests the second of these responses. The fact that you have each come up with a different system of translation is an almost inevitable consequence of what Quine calls the 'principle of indeterminacy of transla-tion' (27). As we have already seen, he argues that words don't have determinate meaning. Now he suggests that there is no single, determinate, way of explaining the semantics of a language, or of translating it into another language. All that needs to be explained by an adequate account of any language is what can be observed by someone interested in the behaviour of its speakers. Any two accounts which are both successful in explaining this behaviour can be seen as 'empirically equivalent' (78), a claim which, Quine notes, is in conflict with 'the almost universal belief that the objective references of terms in radically different languages can be objectively compared' (79). Quine is reiterating his claim that meaning is not something which words and expressions can be said to 'have' in any concrete sense. Rather, it's necessary to make subjective, empirical deci-sions about how each expression is used. The correct process of translation is not one of matching up expressions from the two languages which 'have the same meaning', but of observing similarities in verbal responses to various stimuli.

This is, of course, a behaviourist account. Language is seen as a series of observable responses to stimuli; the linguist's task is to predict accurately what utterances will be promoted by what stimuli, for instance by the appearance of a rabbit. It is also behaviourist in that it sees the observable behaviour as *all* there is to language; there is nothing 'underlying' the behaviour which needs to be explained. If you and your fellow linguist have both deduced explanations of the behaviour you have observed, you have both produced satisfactory accounts of the language, because the behaviour is all there is to explain. This has important implications for the nature of language, and for what it means to 'know' a language, which we shall consider later in this chapter.

The moral about the nature of language which Quine draws from the exercise of radical translation has implications, too, for the child's task in learning a first language. Remember that in *Language*, Bloomfield described a process of stimulus, response and reinforcement which gradually leads to the child's use of language becoming more and more like that of the adults around. Similarly, in a chapter of *Word and Object* called 'The ontogenesis of reference', Quine describes a process whereby a child initially produces random utterances, which are 'selectively reinforced'. Subsequently, 'the creature tends to repeat the rewarded act when stimuli recur that chanced to be present at the original performance' (81). For Quine, what we call a 'language' is defined as a series of tendencies to reinforce certain types of verbal behaviour in a group of people. Language therefore is centrally defined in terms of the practices of a community; he begins *Word and Object* with a clear statement to this effect:

> Language is a social art. In acquiring it we have to depend entirely on intersubjectively available cues as to what to say and when. Hence there is no justification for collating linguistic meanings, unless in terms of men's dispositions to respond overtly to socially observable stimulations.
>
> (ix)

For Quine, a language exists only in the practices of those who use it, and acquiring the language involves a gradual process of observing those practices. In a sense then, the task of children in acquiring a language is very similar to that of the field linguists we have just considered; they too have no preconceived ideas about what sounds might relate to what objects, but must deduce this from observation. Just like the field linguists, children will arrive at a satisfactory version of the language insofar as they are able to produce the appropriate behaviour in the appropriate situation, and eventually to reinforce the appropriate behaviour in others. There is nothing 'beyond' the dispositions to behaviour which they need to acquire. It was these aspects of Quine's account of language acquisition, and their implications for the relationship between language and mind, which were the focus of a critique of *Word and Object* by the philosopher and linguist Noam Chomsky. We will look at this next, since it illustrates many of the fundamentals of what came to be known as the 'Chomskyan revolution'.

The Innateness Hypothesis

In 1969, when Chomsky published his response to *Word and Object*, it would hardly have come as a surprise that he didn't take a very favourable view of Quine's linguistics. If Quine is best described as an empirical philosopher, belonging to the tradition of Locke and Berkeley, then Chomsky can be classified as a rationalist, drawing on the work of Leibniz, of Kant, and ultimately of Plato. Since the late 1950s, Chomsky had been publishing books and articles which had established his reputation as an innovative thinker about the language and the mind. Among linguists, he had attracted admirers and critics in perhaps equal numbers, but his impact on linguistics was such that no one had been able to ignore him.

Noam Chomsky was born in Philadelphia in 1928. At the age of twenty-seven he took up a research post at the Massachusetts Institute of Technology, where he eventually became a professor. Chomsky's contribution to linguistics has been wide-ranging and profound, and we will be assessing only part of it here. However, linguistics is just one of the subjects in which he has distinguished himself, and may not be the one for which he is best known. Probably more people are aware of his writings in politics and current affairs. He has been a staunch campaigner for human rights and critic of American foreign policy, and indeed spent some time in jail after protesting against the Vietnam War in the 1960s.[5]

Chomsky's 1969 response to *Word and Object* was an article entitled 'Quine's empirical assumptions'. In this, he criticises both the details of Quine's account of language acquisition, and the very nature of the account itself. His criticisms of the details are largely related to ways in which he finds the account unworkable, or unable to explain the apparent facts of language acquisition. The reasons why he opposes the nature of Quine's account in general will become apparent as we investigate the mentalist and innatist, as opposed to empirical and behaviourist, account which Chomsky proposes.

Chomsky's main argument against any purely empirical account of language acquisition can be summarised as follows. Consider the knowledge children must build up in order to be able to use a language; it is very complex, and very specific. Then consider the type of evidence which is available to developing children; it is fragmentary and unreliable, a random collection of utterances including some which a grammarian would class as 'errors'. Put these two together and, Chomsky argues, you can't help but reach the conclusion that the available data aren't sufficient to account for the derived knowledge. This observation led him to discuss the 'poverty of input' available in the process of language acquisition. In particular, the number of sentences which speakers of a language are capable of understanding or using is infinite, but in acquiring that language they will actually encounter only a very small number of them. If learning a language involved simply the process of being conditioned to respond in appropriate ways, it could only ever result in a finite number of 'set responses' to sentences encountered many times before.

In his criticism of Quine, then, Chomsky would appear to have set himself the task of explaining how children reach the stage where they can understand, and use, an infinity of sentences, very few of which they will ever have encountered before. He had, in fact, been developing just such an explanation over a number of years, in various publications. We have already seen that Chomsky can be placed in the rationalist tradition, the school of thought which explains the ways in which we perceive and understand the world in terms of innate properties of the human mind. His account of language acquisition has become known as the '**Innateness Hypothesis**'. It is also sometimes described as being **nativist**, a general term applied to theories which rely on innate or inborn ideas or knowledge.

Chomsky's Innateness Hypothesis (commonly abbreviated to IH) is based on the claim that there is a specialised and independent 'language faculty'. This is a mental capacity, common to all human beings, which allows us to acquire and use language, and which serves no other purpose. It is the specialised nature of the language faculty, and the claim that it causes the natural and effortless development of language, which make the IH distinctive. For Quine, to speak of 'acquiring' a language is just an alternative way of speaking about 'learning' it; we learn language using mental capacities similar to those we use to learn a vast number of other skills. But for Chomsky the two are not equivalent. Children 'acquire' language as they develop, but they don't 'learn' it as they might, for instance, learn to ride a bicycle or use a knife and fork.

The idea that there is a mental faculty employed in acquiring language, whatever individual human language that might be, is not original to Chomsky. As he himself acknowledges in his 1966 book *Cartesian Linguistics*, it was one focus of seventeenth-century rationalist philosophy. There was a general interest within this tradition in the contribution made by the human mind to the type of knowledge it can acquire. This in turn led to an interest in discovering innate principles of mind, including those relating to language. As Chomsky explains, 'By attributing such principles to the mind, as an innate property, it became possible to account for the quite obvious fact that the speaker of a language knows a great deal that he has not learned' (60). However, Chomsky applied this idea to the observable problems of language acquisition, and suggested a definite form for this faculty, as we will see later in this chapter.

Chomsky's proposal has important implications for the nature of language, which we will explore later, and also, of course, for the human mind. This, in fact, was Chomsky's main focus of interest in developing the IH. Although he is well known for his work on language acquisition, he hasn't spent much time on the actual developmental stages children go through.[6] Rather, his interest lies in considering what the human mind must be like, given the languages it is able to acquire and use. The mind of an adult who has successfully acquired a language can be considered as having reached a certain 'steady state'; Chomsky's interest is in considering this and, by extension, the 'initial state' of the human mind, or the properties which must be innate to it in order for the steady state to be obtainable. In his own words, the task he has set himself is to 'devise a hypothesis about initial structure rich enough to account for the fact that a specific grammar is acquired, under given conditions of access to data'.[7]

This quotation reveals something of Chomsky's general philosophical method, an issue which he addresses directly in 'Quine's empirical assumptions'. There, he responds to Quine's criticism that, in positing the IH, he was going beyond what was strictly licensed by experience, and discussing the existence of mental entities for which he had no concrete evidence. Chomsky argues that this method is in fact the one which must be adopted if interesting philosophical discussion is to be possible. Serious hypotheses, he argues, will always 'go beyond' the empirical evidence available: 'If they did not, they would be without interest' (66). In other words, whereas Bloomfield advocated a strictly inductive method in linguistics, Chomsky's method is a deductive one of forming hypotheses. The role of the data of language is to test out these hypotheses; the data might support the hypotheses or alternatively cause them to be amended, or even abandoned. The process of hypothesis formation, he argues, allows linguists to do more than describe and analyse; it allows them to use the evidence which is available to inspection, such as the observable data of language use, to think about phenomena which are not available, such as the underlying mental states and processes.

As we have seen, one of Chomsky's main arguments in favour of an innate language faculty is the comparison between the complex language system and the apparently inadequate evidence on which it is built. He claims that, despite the poverty of the input, children acquire language rapidly, without much apparent effort, and in an order and time scale which is remarkably standard across all human languages. It is further claimed that there is little evidence of differences in order and speed of acquisition between children of widely differing intelligence. So children can't be using general intelligence and cognitive capacities to 'figure out' the language. Rather, Chomsky describes the knowledge of a language as 'growing' in the mind in an appropriate environment, at the appropriate stage of development.[8]

Any account of language which is based on innate properties of mind relies on an assumption of the *universality* of language. At its most basic, this universality is reflected in the fact that all human beings, regardless of race or geographical location, have language, a property shared by no other species.[9] Despite huge differences between cultures in terms of social arrangements, beliefs and customs, no mute human tribe has ever been found and, as Edward Sapir pointed out in the 1920s, all human languages are alike in terms of complexity and power of expression.

However, stronger claims of universality have been made. We have seen that Saussure and Bloomfield, for instance, describe human languages as capable of differing from each other without limit. Chomsky, on the other hand, argues that there are regularities, or 'language universals'; all human languages share certain general rules about what word classes and what structures are, and are not, possible. It's important to bear in mind that, in talking about language universals, linguists such as Chomsky aren't concerned with the individual words, or the vocabulary lists we might find ourselves learning as part of a foreign language class. In discussing language, Chomsky is concerned with grammar, with the rules of sentence formation. There is no suggestion that there is innate knowledge of the actual words of any language. After all, a newborn child is equally well equipped to learn any human language. Rather, language universals are said to exist among the general grammatical rules which determine how languages are structured.

The existence of language universals is a controversial claim, as we will see, but one necessary to the IH. If there were no restraints on what forms human languages could take, there could be no single faculty specifically tailored to acquiring any language. If the language faculty is innate, it must be universal, just as the physical organs of the human body are universal. Before we consider the nature of the innate 'language faculty' which Chomsky claims is able to account for such universals, we will look fairly briefly at some of the arguments which philosophical contemporaries of Chomsky have used against its very existence. We will consider some of the separate arguments put forward by linguists in the final section of this chapter.[10]

Anti-nativism

Philosophical opposition to Chomsky's ideas came from a number of sides, not just from the behaviourist tradition represented by Quine. Two names particularly associated with this opposition are those of Hilary Putnam, a near-contemporary of Chomsky, and Nelson Goodman, twenty years older. Both American philosophers were awarded professorships at Harvard; Goodman in 1967 and Putnam in 1976. Putnam's objections to the IH are summed up in an article entitled 'The "Innateness Hypothesis" and explanatory models in linguistics', first published in 1967. He summarises what he sees as the main claims made in the IH, characterising it as '*essentially* and *irreparably* vague' (293, original emphasis).[11] Most of his criticisms, however, are based around the central notion that the IH is simply not necessary to account for the facts of language acquisition and use; for the IH to be worth serious consideration, it must not just be compatible with the relevant linguistic facts, but actually offer the only way of explaining at least some of them, something for which Putnam finds no evidence.

In support of his claims, Putnam speculates about the probable properties of a 'Martian' language used by beings with human-like intelligence. He argues that any such language would have to have a grammar – it would have to be 'built up by recursive rules from a limited stock of basic forms' – or else it couldn't be 'practically infinite' (294). We would have to say that the Martians shared some general cognitive capacity with humans, but not that they also shared an innate language faculty. Any organism capable of using language must, to some extent, possess innate mental capacities:

> How could something with *no* innate intellectual equipment *learn* anything? *To be sure*, human "innate intellectual equipment" is relevant to language learning; if this means that such parameters as memory span and memory capacity play a crucial role. But what rank Behaviorist is supposed to have ever denied *this*?
>
> (295, original emphasis)

This raises an important issue in relation to the competing theories of language and mind we are considering. It is sometimes tempting to construe the debate as a straightforward opposition between 'innatist' and 'non-innatist' accounts, that is, between seeing language acquisition as determined entirely by 'human nature' on the one hand, and by 'experience' on the other. However, both types of account depend to some extent on both nature and experience; they just place different emphasis on their relative importance. For an innatist such as Chomsky, the right sort of experience, or input, is necessary, but only in order to trigger the natural process of language development. For philosophers such as Putnam, and indeed Quine, experience is of primary importance, and is acted on by very general innate learning principles. As we have seen, these are general enough to be applied to language as well as other skills and behaviours.

Putnam is equally sceptical about the claim that the IH is justified by 'universal' word classes such as noun, verb and adjective. He suggests that such apparent similarities can be more simply explained by the fact that all languages include means for identifying objects, and for saying things about those objects. He argues that many of the 'universal' features of human language could equally well, and more simply, be explained by all languages being 'descended from a single original language' (296). Putnam further suggests that the apparent ease and rapidity with which children learn their first language is no great surprise if you consider the amount of time they have at their disposal to observe and study it. It turns out to be no more remarkable than that people should be able to learn to solve difficult problems, or to play chess. Chomsky, he argues, is ignoring the real issue: the much more significant question of how it is that human beings learn in general. Thus, 'invoking "Innateness" only postpones the problem of learning; it does not solve it' (298).

Nelson Goodman has also raised questions about the necessity of an innate language faculty. In his book *Of Mind and Other Matters*, published in 1984 but drawing on work from earlier decades, he sets out succinctly some of the reasons why he finds claims about language universals dubious. He argues that any collection of languages, or indeed of any type of system, will, coincidentally, have certain features in common. The claim that the features which have been identified as common to all languages are natural 'language universals' can't be supported; it is 'a gratuitous one immune to feasible experimental test' (16). He introduces a further argument against the existence of language universals, which goes as follows: 'The linguistic universals usually cited, such as subject-predicate form, seem to be features of translations into our language rather than of the language translated' (16). In other words, Goodman is suggesting that linguists are able to claim that there are regularities which hold across all languages only because they have been able to 'impose' certain features on to languages which may be radically different from their own, usually from English. The existence of so-called 'language universals', he argues, is neither as remarkable nor as widespread as Chomsky claims.

The language faculty

As we have seen, the innatist hypothesis is strikingly different from other, contemporary explanations of language and the processes by which it is learnt. If we compare Chomsky's account of an innate language faculty with Quine's behaviourist model of stimulus, response and reinforcement, and with Putnam's interest in general cognitive capacity and learning mechanisms, we might find ourselves wondering how the three philosophers could be writing about the same phenomenon. And perhaps there is a sense in which they are not. That is, their views on language, and therefore on the processes involved in acquiring language, are so different, that they aren't even trying to account for the same set of facts. In comparing Chomsky's theory with those of his contemporaries, we aren't just considering which best accounts for the facts of language; we are looking at completely different versions of those facts.

In drawing on the philosophical tradition concerned with innate properties of the mind, Chomsky was committed to a mentalist account of language. In other words, a full description of language for him would involve an account not just of the observable behaviours associated with it, but also of the mental process 'behind' these. Remember that for Quine the 'indeterminacy of translation' was evidence that there is no objective truth, or underlying rules, to be discovered in studying language, and therefore that no single description of any language could be said to be the 'right' one. All that the linguist could, or indeed should, do was to observe and explain the linguistic practices of a community of speakers. For Chomsky, on the other hand, language is not just governed by a set of underlying rules; it actually consists of those rules. The child's task in acquiring a language is not one of learning the correct dispositions to behave, but of mastering the rules of the language. The linguist's task is not one of describing the behaviour of a group, but of accurately modelling the knowledge of each individual.

Chomsky's beliefs about the nature of this knowledge are significant in his response to Putnam's criticisms. Putnam argued that, given the nature of communication and of intelligence, it's no great surprise that languages exhibit certain similarities. It would be more useful to explain these in terms of general learning processes than of specific innate capacity. Chomsky's reply to these criticisms first appeared in 1969 as part of a long article, but were published in 1981 as an extract entitled 'Reply to Putnam'. This begins with a statement to the effect that Putnam's arguments are based on an incorrect view of language:

> Specifically, he enormously underestimates, and in part misdescribes, the richness of structure, the particular and detailed properties of grammatical form and organisation that must be accounted for by a 'language acquisition model', that are acquired by the normal speaker-hearer and that appear to be uniform among speakers and also across languages.
>
> (300)

Chomsky emphasises the significance of the way in which sentences in natural languages are formed, something which he suggests Putnam either overlooks or is unaware of. Phrase structure rules generate base structures on which transformational rules operate to give surface structures. These processes can be traced, and indeed show remarkable similarities, across all natural languages. The nature of these processes, or structure-dependent operations, are 'of a peculiar sort that have never been studied outside of linguistics, in particular not in any branch of mathematics with which I am familiar' (302). Linguistic knowledge, then, is of a very complex, very specific type, and could hardly be seen as arising naturally and unsurprisingly from general cognitive capacity. The relevant mental state of a speaker who has acquired a language is best described as a full generative grammar for the language. In devising a suitable generative grammar, the linguist is therefore modelling part of the human mind.

As we have seen, the initial state of the human mind must be complex enough to enable any child to acquire any human language, but specific enough to be compatible only with the form common to all such languages. Chomsky conceives of it as containing a series of rules, or *principles*, which are shared by all languages. The child's task in acquiring a language, then, is to discover certain properties which are unique to the language in question. To aid this process, the initial state also contains a number of variables, or *parameters*, which will be given different values depending on the language to which the child is exposed. These allow for the 'fine tuning' which determines that the child acquires one particular language. In this way, Chomsky offers a solution to the logical problem of language acquisition. The data available to children wouldn't be adequate if they had to learn everything about the language from scratch. But it *is* sufficient to allow them to carry out the task of determining how certain parameters, of which they have innate knowledge, are set for the language in question.

The principles and parameters, then, make up the innate initial state. They are compatible with every human language, and explain the ease of acquisition for any individual language. Chomsky describes them as the **Universal Grammar**. His main interest, as we have seen, is not in the process of language development, but in the final or steady state of the adult mind: in the question of what it is that people 'know' when they have successfully been through these processes. We will conclude our investigation of the Innateness Hypothesis with this question.

Knowledge and use of language

We have seen that mentalist and empirical accounts view language, and therefore the task of explaining language, very differently. As a result they differ in terms of the scope of what they attempt to explain. So, unlike an empirical account such as Quine's, Chomsky's mentalist account doesn't attempt to explain completely the observable behaviour of language use. Chomsky is quite explicit, in much of his work, that his aim is not to account for everything which goes on in communication: that he is concerned only with those mental phenomena, the generative rules of grammar, which for him make up human language. These contribute to the observable phenomena of language used in communication, but are only one type of a number of disparate factors involved.

You may have spotted a problem in the last paragraph, centring on the term *language* itself. For an empiricist, *language* refers simply to what you can observe actual speakers and hearers doing. But Chomsky claims that, whatever the observable behaviour may be, language is actually something in the *mind* of the speakers and hearers. This presents a problem of terminology, which arises from trying to use the same term to refer to both the observable and the mental phenomena, and explains why Chomsky found it necessary to come up with two new terms.

In his early work, Chomsky distinguishes between *competence* and *performance*. Competence is the set of knowledge which forms the steady state of the speaker. It is modelled by a generative grammar, capable of producing all and only the grammatical sentences of the language.

Performance, on the other hand, is made up of the much more diverse phenomena which actually occur in language use. It is dependent on competence, but also draws on a range of other personal and contextual factors. For instance, in *Aspects of the Theory of Syntax*, published in 1965, Chomsky argues that 'To study linguistic performance, we must consider the interaction of a variety of factors, of which the underlying competence of the speaker-hearer is only one' (4). The other relevant factors include phenomena as diverse as memory, tiredness and emotional state.[12]

In later work, for instance in *Knowledge of Language*, published in 1986, Chomsky introduces the distinction between **I-language** and **E-language**. The *I-*, or *Internalised-language* is the state of mind of the speaker, which has always been his main focus of interest. The *E-*, or *Externalised-language* is the observable behaviour. He describes the change of emphasis brought about by generative grammar:

> the shift in focus was from the study of E-language to the study of I-language, from the study of language regarded as an externalised object to the study of the system of knowledge of language attained and internally represented in the mind/brain.
>
> (24)

Chomsky goes so far as to claim that, in generative grammar, the concept of E-language 'appears to play no role in the theory of language' (26). His claim is that language is an internal state of mind which only secondarily, and almost coincidentally, is used in producing a type of behaviour which serves in communication. This particularly extreme view has attracted a lot of criticism, but it isn't one which he seems to adhere to, or to express so controversially, in some of his other writings. In any case, we can see how different Chomsky's approach is from accounts such as those offered by Quine, or indeed by Saussure, in which language is dependent on its use in communication. Generative grammar attempts to model, and so explain, what it is that speakers know when they 'know a language'. It doesn't attempt to model what happens when those speakers proceed to communicate with each other.

In both philosophy and linguistics, work has continued, within broadly 'innatist' and 'non-innatist' traditions, on the relationship between language and the mind. The American philosopher Jerry Fodor, for instance, can perhaps be seen as going to the opposite extreme from Sapir and Whorf, who argued that modes of thought are dependent on, and acquired with, individual languages. He has proposed not just an innate language faculty, but an innate language or *mentalese*, which is the medium of thought, and is therefore necessarily prior to the acquisition of any particular language. The connection between language and mind has, more generally, remained a central topic in the various directions in which linguistics has developed and continues to develop, and we will conclude with a brief look at some of these.

Empiricist and mentalist linguistics

The relationship between language and mind has continued to be an enduring topic of interest in linguistics. This has inevitably meant that some linguists have been working in areas closely related to psychology. The intersection of interests between linguistics and psychology has become the focus of the branch of modern linguistics known as *psycholinguistics*. This can broadly be defined as the study of what goes on in people's minds when they produce and interpret spoken and written language: when language is stored and accessed, processed and interpreted.

Mental processes are, of course, difficult to observe and record for the purposes of analysis. Language processing in particular tends to take place so quickly and with so little conscious effort that it is impossible to study it by asking speakers what they are 'doing' when they use language. Researchers in this area of psycholinguistics have therefore devised various experiments and other forms of observation to serve as indirect evidence of the processes involved. For instance, they have studied 'slips of the tongue', arguing that the mistakes in word choice which people make in speech can illuminate the ways in which words are arranged and stored in the 'mental lexicon'. It is, of course, possible to see the influence of mentalist approaches to language in this type of study, concerned as it is with the mental processes 'behind' the observable data of language use.

The different approaches to the study of language offered by empiricism and mentalism are to be found in discussions of other topics in psycholinguistics, and indeed in linguistics in general. The empirical linguistic method is particularly apparent in the area of conversation analysis which, as we saw at the end of the last chapter, emphasises the observation and analysis of actual data of language use. Empiricism is also the framework for the discipline of *corpus linguistics*, which emerged with the growth in capacity and availability of computers. Large samples of language data are collected in machine-readable format for analysis by computer, often statistical analysis. The emphasis is on the authenticity of 'real life' data, as opposed to the data of 'invented sentences' and intuition. It has been claimed that a corpus should ideally be sufficiently large to be fully *representative* of the language; it should contain, in the form of examples, everything which the linguist could need to know about the language.

Not surprisingly, Chomsky has been an opponent of the methods and claims of corpus linguistics since its origins in the late 1950s and early 1960s. His mentalist approach entails that the facts about a language can never be contained in a list of examples, however large. In his own more recent terms, all this could ever give you is some examples of E-language. The actual facts of language, the I-language, exist only in the minds of individual speakers, and can be accessed only by means of those minds. Everything you need to know about a language is present in the mind of a speaker, and can be accessed either by questioning informants, or even by a process of intuition on the part of the linguist. A corpus won't add anything to this, and may in fact contain examples which don't belong to the language under investigation. It may contain slips and other 'performance errors'.

As we have seen, in drawing a distinction between the 'real' facts of language and the distractions of performance, Chomsky sees the task of linguistic theory as being to account for just part of what goes on in communication. Some more recent approaches, in contrast, have seen the task of the linguist as one of explaining communication in all its aspects. Linguists working within this framework seek to do away with what they see as the artificial distinction between 'linguistic' and 'contextual'. In other words, they don't recognise the existence of linguistic knowledge which can be distinguished from the observable behaviour of language use. One such account has become known as *integrationist* linguistics, developed by the Oxford linguist Roy Harris, and others. This attempts to integrate all aspects of communication into one account; meaning is not something which individual parts of language 'have', it is something which only exists, and can only be analysed, in terms of what individual speakers do in particular circumstances, and what effects this has.

Chomsky's rigorously mentalist approach to linguistics, then, is no more widely accepted now than it was when it was first offered as a challenge to empiricism and behaviourism. However, its influence is still strong in some areas of linguistics. For instance, psycholinguists have built on his work on the nature of linguistic knowledge and on language acquisition. In particular, clinical linguists, interested in language disorders and the evidence they offer about the nature of language, have studied patients with specific mental impairments, whether present from birth or resulting from stroke or other trauma. The findings of some of these studies have been claimed as evidence that linguistic ability is quite separate from many other cognitive capacities, including other types of cognition used in communication. This has in turn been offered in support of a mentalist account of language; the apparent independence of linguistic ability can only be explained by the existence of a particular, separate mental faculty concerned with language.

Work within the mentalist tradition in the area of language acquisition has branched out from the early emphasis on syntax and its relationship to Universal Grammar; it now includes studies of children's development in phonology, semantics and morphology, with an interest in assessing whether innate universal principles can be found in these areas. It has been claimed that, in general, deliberate correcting of grammar doesn't take place, and isn't effective when it does; the child will produce the correct forms and structures only when developmentally ready to do so. The suggestion that there is no 'negative evidence' available to the child – that the child is in general not told what is incorrect – has been used to argue that language isn't, and can't be, taught.

Other approaches to language acquisition have concentrated on the social and interactional nature of language use rather than on the complexity of the mental states involved. As a result, they have emphasised the place of language in the child's general development, focusing, for instance, on how the child develops both 'core linguistic' and more general 'pragmatic' abilities. Linguists in this field argue that children acquire not a series of more or less abstract mental structures, but a rich system for communication with those around them. In particular, the linguist Catherine Snow has challenged Chomsky's central claim about the poverty of input. Remember that Chomsky argues that there must be an innate language faculty because children could never arrive at the complex knowledge of a language just on the basis of the fragmentary evidence they receive. Snow has argued that, on the contrary, adults tend to adopt a particular style of talking when they are interacting with children which makes it easy for them to learn the language. This style, which has become known as 'Child Directed Speech' (CDS for short) is simplified to meet the child's level, and is slow and careful and full of repetitions. Snow claims that evidence from an empirical study of how adults speak to children is enough to remove the apparent mystery behind the process of language acquisition.[13]

We have looked at ideas about the relationship between language and mind put forward in the work of some twentieth-century philosophers, and seen how they have contributed to the development of linguistics as a separate academic discipline. These ideas formed part of a growing interest within philosophy in studying language in its own right. As we know, philosophers from earlier centuries who discussed language were rarely interested in it for its own sake. Their work on language developed out of interests in areas such as knowledge, science, or logic. During the twentieth century, however, some philosophers began to concentrate on the best ways to describe and explain languages, as well as the ways in which language in general could be related to other types of human activity. This is not to say that linguistics originated just in this branch of philosophy, or indeed just in philosophy at all. As we have seen, work which proved important in the development of linguistics came not just from philosophy but also from psychology, anthropology, and other disciplines.

Writers from all these different backgrounds have confronted questions of how language relates to mind, of whether it influences or is influenced by thought, of the extent to which people can be said to 'share' a language. Some have seen language principally as a type of behaviour, geared towards communication; others have seen it as a type of knowledge, existing primarily as a mental state in the individual. But they have all been interested in the study of language because of the potential answers it offers to such questions, and therefore the insights it affords into human nature itself. Interest in these questions was fundamental in the establishment of linguistics during the twentieth century, and they remain some of the most difficult, but intriguing focuses of enquiry for present-day linguists.

Further reading

Signs and structures

Saussure's *Course in General Linguistics* (1960) is a wide-ranging discussion of many of the issues which were to become central to modern linguistics. He deals with the notion of the linguistic sign in Part I, 'General principles'. Whorf's version of linguistic relativity is set out in the papers in *Language, Thought and Reality* (1956). The introduction to this, by John B. Carroll, gives a sketch of Whorf's unusual career, and draws interesting parallels between his professional work and his interest in linguistics. Linguistic relativity in general, and the Sapir–Whorf hypothesis in particular, is discussed in Chapter 10 of Devitt and Sterelny (1987) *Language and Reality*. Some of the criticisms we have considered, including specific rejections of Whorf's claims, are summarised in Pinker (1995) *The Language Instinct*, Chapter 3.

Empiricism

The two major empirical works on language which we have considered in this chapter are Bloomfield (1935) *Language* and Quine (1960) *Word and Object*. We also made reference to Skinner (1957) *Verbal Behavior*. The most famous critique of Skinner's work on language is Chomsky (1959) 'A review of B. F. Skinner's *Verbal Behavior*'. Here Chomsky criticises behaviourism as speculative and unscientific, and takes issue with the idea that animal experiments are unproblematically applicable to human behaviour. He also introduces some of the ideas that were to prove central to his own account, such as the ease and regularity with which children acquire language, the ability of speakers of a language to construct and interpret novel sentences, and the complex and structured nature of language. Quine's work doesn't make particularly easy reading, but has been the subject of many more accessible commentaries. R. Martin (1987) *The Meaning of Language* includes a discussion of Quine's 'radical translation' in Chapter 6. Radical translation is also discussed, and contrasted with Chomsky's theories of innateness, in Stainton (1996) *Philosophical Perspectives on Language*, Chapter 8.

The Innateness Hypothesis

Chomsky developed the theory which has become known as the Innateness

Hypothesis over several decades and many different publications. In 1966 he published *Cartesian Linguistics*, which outlines the essentials of an account of language acquisition in terms of innate properties of the mind, and traces its history in rationalist schools of thought. His interest in studying the human mind, and in hypothesising from the evidence of the steady state to the probable form of the initial state, is set out in his (1980) *Rules and Representations*, particularly Chapter 5. He offers a detailed account of what he calls 'Plato's problem', the logical problem of language acquisition in his (1986) *Knowledge of Language*, Chapter 3. In this book he also gathers together his ideas about I-language and E-language, which are presented in Chapter 2. *Aspects of the Theory of Syntax* (1965) contains a detailed account of the nature and function of the language faculty.

Much has been written about the impact of Chomsky's work on ideas about the nature of language and the processes by which it is acquired. Devitt and Sterelny (1987) *Language and Reality*, Chapter 8, discuss Chomsky's account of linguistic competence, and its relationship to his theories of innateness. Pinker (1995) *The Language Instinct* is a popular and accessible introduction to the innateness hypothesis and its implications, although his views and approach differ in places from Chomsky's.

Jerry Fodor's ideas about an innate 'language of thought' which is necessarily prior to the acquisition of any natural language, together with some discussion of Chomsky's work, can be found in his (1976) book *The Language of Thought*.

Empirical and mentalist linguistics

A popular and very readable introduction to psycholinguistics in general, with particular emphasis on language acquisition, is Aitchison (1989) *The Articulate Mammal*. The storage, retrieval and recognition of words are discussed in another of Aitchison's books, her (1987) *Words in the Mind*. Of particular interest is Chapter 2, in which she discusses the evidence presented by slips of the tongue and other sources.

Many textbooks and introductions to linguistics include outlines of the consequences of Chomsky's linguistics, even if they are not credited to Chomsky, or directly linked to his work. See, for instance, the first chapters of R. Martin (1987) *The Meaning of Language*, and O'Grady *et al.* (1997) *Contemporary Linguistics*. Smith and Wilson's (1990) *Modern Linguistics* is entirely devoted, as the subtitle explains, to 'the results of Chomsky's revolution'.

A good introduction to corpus linguistics, which discusses the empiricist approach to language which underpins it, is McEnery and Wilson (1996) *Corpus Linguistics*. Chapter 1 in particular discusses the framework within which corpus linguistics developed, and distinguishes it from the mentalist approach to linguistics.

Harris' 'integrationist' account of language, and his critiques of many of the philosophers we have considered here, can be found in his (1996a) *The Language Connection* and (1996b) *Signs, Language and Communication*.

An extended study of one case of cognitive impairment, presented in support of an innatist account of linguistic knowledge, is Smith and Tsimpli (1995) *The Mind of a Savant*.

Goodluck (1991) *Language Acquisition* is a fairly technical but accessible introduction to the subject from an innatist perspective. In contrast, as mentioned in the 'further reading' section of the last chapter, Bates (1976) *Language and Context* considers the relationship between the development of language and the development of the child's pragmatic abilities, including the appropriate use of speech acts. Fletcher and Garman (1986) *Language Acquisition* is a useful collection of essays, including work on a number of different topics and from a number of points of view. In this, Catherine Snow's article 'Conversations with children', describes and illustrates CDS, and assesses the challenge it poses to the Innateness Hypothesis.

Glossary

The first occurrence of these terms is highlighted in **bold** type in the main text.

Analytic An analytic sentence is logically a necessary truth because the predicate is contained within the concept of the subject; it is true by virtue of its intrinsic properties, regardless of context. Often contrasted with **synthetic** sentences.

A posteriori A description of knowledge which is derived from, and logically follows, experience of the senses: knowledge which is empirical. Often contrasted with *a priori* knowledge.

A priori A description of knowledge which is not derived from experience, but is independent of and prior to observation of reality. Usually discussed in opposition to *a posteriori* knowledge.

Behaviourism A psychological school of thought which concentrates on describing and explaining observable behaviour rather than postulating unobservable mental states. Applied to language study, behaviourism entails that the meaning of any individual utterance can be defined only in terms of the effects it has, and that language learning must be achieved in terms of a series of stimuli, responses and reinforcements. Often contrasted with **mentalism**.

Conditional A logical expression equivalent to 'if p, then q', which is true except when p is true and q false. Expressed in propositional logic as p→q.

Conjunction A term of logic for the joining together of two propositions, symbolised as p∧q in the form p&q. The propositions p and q are in this context described as *conjuncts*. Logical conjunction is truth-functional; joining two true conjuncts gives a true statement, while joining one false and one true, or two false conjuncts, gives a false one.

Connotation The connotation of a word or phrase is the set of properties which determine what is referred to; it is dependent not on external reality but on the individual word or words. Often contrasted with **denotation**.

Constative Type of speech act identified by J. L. Austin. An utterance used to make a statement of fact, which can be judged to be either 'true' or 'false'. Often contrasted with **performative** speech acts.

Contingent A sentence is logically contingent if it is neither necessarily false nor necessarily true, but depends on the nature of external reality to be assigned a truth-value. A contingently false sentence could be true in different circumstances; a contingently true sentence could be false.

Contradiction Two expressions, one of which entails a proposition p and the other of which entails the negation of p are said to be contradictory, because they cannot both be true or both false. A single expression can be described as a contradiction, or as self-contradictory, if it entails both p and the negation of p, and is therefore necessarily false.

Correspondence According to a correspondence theory of truth, a statement is true just in case it corresponds to reality, or to the way the world actually is.

Deductive The method of scientific investigation which starts from a general hypothesis, and uses the available data to confirm, to modify or completely to falsify this. It is often contrasted with the **inductive** method; both are used in modern linguistics.

Denotation The denotation of a word or phrase is the object or objects to which it refers. The term is often restricted to the relationship between a singular term (generally a proper name or definite description) and its referent. It can be contrasted with the **connotation**.

Disjunction A term of logic similar to natural language *or*, which links two propositions, described in this context as *disjuncts*, in the form pVq. The expression as a whole is false only if both disjuncts are false; in all other cases it is true.

E-Language A term used in the later work of Chomsky to describe the observable performance of spoken and written utterances. It is contrasted with **I-Language**, the real focus of interest in the study of linguistic knowledge.

Empirical Empirical knowledge is that based on experience, or on evidence of the world provided by the senses. An empirical mode of study is one which involves perception and analysis of data.

Entailment If proposition p entails proposition q, then q can be said to 'follow logically' from p, a relationship which is generally represented as p→q. If p is true then q must be true, but if p is false we can say nothing about the truth value of q.

Extension The extension of a referring expression is the object or property referred to. The extension of 'the present Prime Minister of Britain' is the actual person who currently holds that office. Extensionality is sometimes also applied to sentences; the extension of a sentence is simply its truth-value. Often contrasted with **intension**.

Holism The idea that any complex whole consists of more than the sum of its parts, and therefore that no single part can be fully explained without reference to the whole to which it belongs. *Semantic holism* claims that no individual expression of a language can be defined in isolation; its meaning depends on the meaning of every other expression in the language.

Ideal Form A concept from the philosophy of Plato. Words properly refer to ideal or perfect versions, whether of objects ('man', 'dog') or of qualities ('justice', 'beauty'). Actual objects and qualities which we encounter in the world are 'named after' these ideals because they share certain properties with them, although they can never attain the same level of perfection. Platonic ideal forms are real but abstract.

Ideational Theory An account of meaning which claims that, since we can have direct access only to our ideas of objects, and not to the objects themselves, our words must refer to our ideas. Such accounts can be traced back to the work of Aristotle, and are found in, for instance, the work of John Locke.

Iff Used in logic, an abbreviation for the relationship 'if and only if'.

I-Language A term in the later work of Chomsky to describe the mental state which forms the speaker's linguistic competence, or knowledge of a language. Contrasted with **E-Language**.

Illocutionary act The second of the three acts identified in the later work of J. L. Austin as making up a speech act. At this level it is necessary to take account of the intention of the speaker in producing the utterance, or the illocutionary 'force' of the utterance.

Inductive The scientific method, used for instance in empirical linguistics, which involves observing the available empirical evidence, and considering what general conclusions are licensed by these. Contrasted with the **deductive** method.

Innateness Hypothesis The term 'innatist' is applied to any account of the mind from Plato onwards which posits certain innate, or genetically inherited, mental faculties or forms of knowledge. The particular hypothesis was developed by Chomsky and others in the mid-twentieth century; its central claim is that there is a unique faculty which governs the acquisition and knowledge of language.

Intension The intension of a word or phrase is the set of properties which determine its correct application. While the **extension** of 'the tallest man in the world' is whichever individual fits that description at any given time, its intension is the property of being the tallest man in the world. When the term is applied to sentences, the intension is said to be the thought or proposition expressed, rather than the actual truth-value.

Locutionary act The first of the three levels of act which constitute the definition of speech acts in the later work of J. L. Austin. The act of uttering a sequence of words, together with an identification of what they literally mean, including the appropriate sense and reference.

Logical positivism A branch of positivist philosophy which developed in

Europe in the early part of the twentieth century, and is particularly associated with the philosophers of the Vienna Circle. Like positivism generally, it is an essentially **empirical** approach. The propositions which it describes as meaningful are those which express **analytic** truths, those of logic and mathematics, and those which can be subject to a process of **verification**. All other propositions, notably those of metaphysics, religion and aesthetics, are treated as senseless, or meaningless.

Mentalism The school of thought which stipulates that a complete account of any observable behaviour must include reference to the underlying mental processes. Mentalist accounts of language have concentrated on understanding and explaining a speaker's knowledge of, or competence in, a language, rather than the actual performance of individual utterances.

Metaphysics A term applied to any form of study which goes beyond the description of material reality, and considers the existence of non-physical entities, or reality which lies outside of normal sensory experience. The validity of metaphysics as a type of philosophical investigation has been challenged by, among others, empiricists and logical positivists.

Modality In logic, expressions containing modality are concerned with statements of necessity and possibility. Necessary propositions ($\Box$p), possible propositions ($\Diamond$p) and actual propositions (p) can be defined in terms of each other and of negation.

Nativism Another name (besides **innatism**) for the theory that some forms of knowledge or of thought are innate, and hence that not all knowledge and understanding is derived directly from experience.

Negation A logical operator, similar to the use of 'not' in ordinary language, which maps a true proposition on to a false one and vice versa. The logical symbol for the negation of p is ~p.

Opaque contexts Also described as intensional contexts. Formulae in which substitution of one expression by another with which it is extensionally equivalent does not necessarily result in the truth-value of the whole remaining unchanged. Modal sentences and propositional attitudes are types of opaque context.

Ordinary language philosophy A school of thought which flourished in Oxford in the mid-twentieth century. The philosophers involved were all interested in natural language, and particularly in language use, as a legitimate field of study in its own right. They rejected the idea that linguistic meaning could be adequately defined in terms of logical relations, and of truth-conditional semantics.

Performative A type of speech act identified by J. L. Austin in an early phase of his work in this area. The very act of uttering a performative can, in appropriate circumstances, count as a performance of the act apparently being described, and bring about certain states of affairs.

Performatives aren't appropriately labelled 'true' or 'false', but can only be 'felicitous' or 'infelicitous'.

Perlocutionary act The last of the three acts identified by J. L. Austin as making up a speech act. It is concerned with the result or consequence of the utterance having been produced; in Austin's terms, it is what the speaker brings about by saying something.

Possible worlds A concept introduced into formal semantics to deal with various problems of reference, and used in one definition of **modality**. Possible world semantics recognises that things could be other than they in fact are, and posits a series of worlds, or states of affairs, other than what is actually the case.

Presupposition Originally used in work by Frege and Strawson to describe a logical relationship between propositions, the term has since been used in linguistics to describe, variously, relationships between sentences, words, utterances and speakers. In the case of logical presupposition between two propositions, where p presupposes q, the truth of q is generally taken to be a necessary condition for the truth or falsity of p. If q is false, p is said to be neither true nor false, making this relationship inconsistent with classical, two-valued logic.

Proposition Most commonly in recent philosophy of language, this term is used to refer to a non-linguistic unit of meaning. A proposition can be the object of thought, belief, etc. It is the **intension** of a declarative sentence.

Propositional attitude A sentence describing someone's believing, desiring, doubting, etc., that a certain proposition is the case, is described as being concerned with a propositional attitude. Such sentences are one type of **opaque context**.

Quantifier In logic, an operator used to make statements over sets of entities. The most common quantifiers are the existential and universal quantifiers. The existential quantifier is represented by the symbol $\exists$. ($\exists x$) can be read as 'there is at least one entity x'. The universal quantifier is represented by $\forall$. ($\forall x$), can be read as 'for all entities x', 'of every x'.

Scepticism The belief that no knowledge can be certain and that we can at best make judgements of probability. The view was particularly associated with the empirical approach to knowledge; we have access only to our sense experience and can't be sure that this relates to any external reality.

Synthetic A description of a sentence in which the predicate is logically independent of the subject. The truth or falsity of such sentences can therefore only be ascertained with reference to external reality. Contrasted with **analytic**.

Tautology A statement which will always have the truth-value of 'true'; a necessary truth.

Truth condition The semantics of a sentence are often equated with its truth conditions. These specify the state of affairs which would have to hold for the sentence to be true.

Truth-function Any logical connective which combines two or more propositions to form a compound proposition, in which the truth of the compound is dependent on the truth of the simple propositions, is said to be truth-functional. The connectives involved are known as *operators*.

T-sentence A sentence stating the truth-conditions for a sentence in any language being studied ('object language') and having the form: 'The sentence S is true in L iff P'. Tarski claimed that you would have an adequate account of truth for a language (L) if you could stipulate a T-sentence for each sentence in L.

Universal Grammar A series of rules which account for linguistic universals, and thereby place constraints on the form which a language can take. In the work of Chomsky and others, Universal Grammar (UG) is said to explain the striking similarities between all human languages. It is said to be innate in all human minds, and to explain the ease and the universal regularity of language acquisition.

Verification A methodology adopted by the **logical positivists** for identifying meaningful propositions. To be meaningful, any proposition which is not either **analytic** or belonging to mathematics or logic must be capable of being verified; there must be a process by which its truth can be assessed by means of empirical observation.

Notes

1 Words and things

1 As we shall see, not all philosophers have accepted that proper names such as these have intensions at all, but we will assume for the time being that they can be treated just the same as descriptions, such as *the chap in the Conservative club*.

2 It is traditional to give references to Plato's work not by page number in the particular edition used, but by means of the page number to the 1587 edition published in Paris. In this, the pages were further divided into five parts, indicated by lowercase letters. In most modern editions the page numbering and lettering are given, providing a uniform way of referring to Plato's work. The edition used here is Jowett (1964).

3 Again, there are special conventions for referring uniformly to Aristotle's works, rather than relying on the individual edition used. The method used here is perhaps the simplest of these conventions. Works such as *de Interpretatione* are divided into short chapters, and the number of the chapter is given as the reference. The edition used here is Barnes (1984).

4 References to *An Essay Concerning Human Understanding* are given by book, chapter and numbered paragraph.

5 Reference to *Principles of Human Knowledge* is by paragraph number. The introduction and the main text are numbered separately.

6 Leibniz wrote all his books either in Latin or, as in this case, in French.

7 At the time in which Mill was writing, of course, the word *man* was used uncontroversially in the generic sense of 'member of the human race' or 'person'. It is striking for a modern reader to find Mill using *Mary* as an example of an individual 'man', but it may have been a deliberately inclusive gesture on his part. Mill has been described as an early feminist, and argued in print that men and women should have equal freedoms.

8 More recently, for instance in Martinich (1996), Frege's article has appeared as 'On sense and denotation'. This is quite a helpful terminology, making it clear that *Bedeutung* corresponds to something like what we have been describing as *denotation*, but its use is not widespread in discussions of Frege's work.

9 Frege, or his translator, is here using the term *designate* in the way in which we have been using *denote*. Some writers distinguish between *designate* for a singular term and *denote* for a general term, but it is also common practice to use *denote* for both, as we are doing here.

10 The three pairs of terms are not in fact exactly equivalent, but we need not worry here about the precise differences between them. These are discussed in detail in Carnap (1957) esp. 124–9.

11 The rather neutral term 'convey' is used here deliberately; we are postponing discussion of the nature of this relationship to the next chapter. Russell sees it as a relation of *entailment*; others, such as Peter Strawson, have described it as one of *presupposition*.

12 Like Frege and Russell before him, Kripke defines his own particular use of the term 'name'. He specifies that he is using it just for 'proper names': *John, Hull, England*, etc.

13 Page references are to the reprinted article in Martinich (1996).

14 Note that in this case contexts involving direct quotation would not be appropriate tests; if Gus said 'I'm a bit of a lad', then it is certainly not true that Gus said 'I'm a bit of a boy', but this tells us nothing about the meanings of *lad* and *boy*. Propositional attitudes provide a more satisfactory test.

2 Propositions and logic

1 For present purposes, we shall ignore the problem that it may in fact never be possible to produce an exact translation from one language to another.

2 We might claim that we can imagine saying this, or hearing it said, in such a way that we would want to argue that it was true, or at least not necessarily false. For instance, in a particular context it might be used to mean something like 'Alice is only ten but behaves like an adult'. This is something will return to in Chapter 4.

3 It is customary to cite just the property being ascribed by the predicate ('three bedrooms', 'rotten') as the instantiation of the variable. 'Grammatical' words such as *has, is*, etc., tend to be omitted on the grounds that they are required simply by the grammar of the language and don't add anything to the logical structure of the proposition.

4 There is a complication which we needn't worry too much about here. It's not actually the case, of course, that every entity has a father, although it is certainly the case that every entity which is human has a father. To be accurate we should perhaps add this to our logical formula, by introducing the predicate 'H' for 'human' and specifying that if an entity is human then it has a father: $(\forall y) (Hy \rightarrow ((\exists x) (Fxy)))$.

5 In Frege's example the presupposition is actually one of existence in the past. Most examples of existential presuppositions which have been discussed in the literature involve present existence. The distinction is due to the tense of the verb, not to anything concerning the name itself, and so need not concern us here.

6 Page references are to Grice (1989).

7 For a fairly extensive list of these, see Levinson (1983) 181–4.

3 Truth and reality

1 The terms 'the world' and 'reality' are here being used interchangeably. This reflects general philosophical and linguistic usage. Scepticism of the type we considered in Chapter 1 aside, it is generally assumed that what we can see around us makes up the world in which we live, and counts as what we know of reality. Similarly, the term 'universe' is often used in the same way.

2 That is not, of course, to say that and example like 2) can't be used successfully to convey an idea which is not necessarily false. A member of the bank's executive board might use 2) to suggest, for instance, that Braeburn-Twinsett's recent domestic problems have made him unfit to continue in his job, because he is no longer able to concentrate sufficiently. This isn't a fact about the semantic, truth-conditional meaning of the sentence, but about the specific significance of

an utterance of it in context. We will consider approaches which have been suggested to this type of problem in the next chapter.

3 In saying this, we have to assume that any situation in which we consider the truth-value of 6) is one in which the words *thirty-four* and *twenty* mean the same as we understand them to mean. It is of course possible that in some science fiction world these words might mean 'eighteen' and 'ninety-five' respectively. In that case, to say 6) would be to say something false, but we wouldn't be making a judgement of truth-value about the same proposition.

4 The word *correspond* is perhaps not as self-explanatory as it may at first seem. Indeed, one of the criticisms which has been levelled at this type of account is that it is by no means clear what it would mean for a proposition to correspond with a state of affairs.

5 It is customary to give references to the original version of the *Critique of Pure Reason*, whatever individual translation is used. Page numbers are prefaced with 'A' for the first edition and 'B' for the second edition. In this particular case, the passage quoted appears in the second but not in the first edition.

6 It is in fact this doctrine which gained them the name 'logical positivists'. They were distinguished from the positivists of the nineteenth century by their inclusion of mathematical and logical statements as meaningful.

7 Page references are to the reprinted version of Tarski's article in Martinich (1996).

8 Page references are to 'Truth and meaning', in Martinich (1996).

9 There is, of course, an important distinction to be drawn between sentence types and the uses to which they can be put. As just one example, declaratives don't always state facts; they can be used to give orders, issue threats, elicit information and many other uses. This distinction is one of which Davidson is aware, and which he in fact draws in 'Moods and performances'. For the time being we will use interrogatives and imperatives as our examples of language used to do something other than state facts, but we will focus on this important distinction in the next chapter.

10 Of course, even this seemingly innocuous definition is itself controversial, because of the sort of objections which have been put forward, which we considered in Chapter 1, to the idea that we can ever be confident about the nature of 'how things actually are', apart from our own perception of it.

11 Leibniz's own account therefore implies that, as we considered above, the term 'world' can in this context be used interchangeably with 'universe'.

12 Lewis argues in *Counterfactuals* that this type of difference between worlds would never in fact be possible. Translating Lewis' argument to our present case, we might say that it would be impossible for two worlds to differ *just* in the colour of snow; blue snow would also imply a different type of water from that which we have, or perhaps different laws of physics. We need not worry too much about this here.

4 Speakers and hearers

1 In coming up with a truth-conditional account of 1), we would have to confront the problem presented by *here*. Its meaning, the actual place referred to, is entirely dependent on context. This is an example of what is known as *deixis*: an expression which serves to 'point at', or single out, some aspect of context. Deixis has been extensively studied in linguistics, and is another factor which has been used to argue against the adequacy of a purely truth-conditional account of meaning, but isn't something we will be looking at here.

2 See, for instance, Richmond Thomason's introduction to Richard Montague's *Formal Philosophy*, 41.

3 Reference to *Philosophical Investigations* is by paragraph number.
4 The examples of words which Ryle gives include *cause, infinitesimal* and *remorse.*
5 Throughout this chapter, we will be adopting the convention which has now become fairly standard practice in pragmatics, of referring to the speaker of any example as *she* and the hearer as *he.* This system has the advantage of avoiding the type of confusion which can occur when one generic pronoun is used to refer to both. It also serves to give women a 'voice' in discussions of language use; some criticisms of accounts such as Austin's and Grice's have focused on their implicit assumption that participants in interaction are, typically, male.
6 Searle in fact uses the term 'preparatory conditions' in place of Austin's 'felicity conditions'.
7 Page references for all of the articles by Grice cited in this chapter are to Grice (1989).
8 This example is used, to illustrate this point, by Stephen Levinson in his book *Pragmatics* (1983).
9 An exclamation mark at the beginning of an example sentence is a conventional way of indicating that, although it may be grammatically correct, it is in some way 'unacceptable' in terms of meaning: for instance (as in this example) that it is logically contradictory.
10 A fairly common reaction to this example is to suggest, as an alternative explanation, that B may be hinting that Smith doesn't have a girlfriend *because* he has been going to New York a lot. In other words the implicature intended may be that he is too busy for much of a social life at the moment. This isn't a possibility which Grice seems to recognise, but it is nevertheless one which can also be explained with reference to the co-operative principle, and particularly the maxim of relevance. The alternative interpretations serve to highlight the way in which particularlised conversational implicatures are not attached to the actual form of words used, but dependent on various factors in the wider context.

5 Language and mind

1 We won't, for instance, be looking at what has been written about how we process and understand language when we encounter it in speech or writing. Issues such as this are, however, highly important in modern linguistics and psycholinguistics, and reference to some introductory work can be found in the 'further reading' section of this chapter.
2 See, for instance, John Carroll's introduction to *Language, Thought and Reality*, 22.
3 Bloomfield himself favours the term *mechanistic,* but *materialistic* is more widely used, especially in contrast to *mentalistic.*
4 Or, according to Quine, 'Lo, a rabbit'. The capital letters here indicate that these utterances are of what Quine calls 'one word sentences', as opposed to simply 'words'. We will observe the notation, but needn't worry too much about the distinction.
5 Chomsky has always maintained that his work on politics and that on linguistics are two completely different interests but, perhaps inevitably, people have tried to find connections between the two. Perhaps the most successful of these attempts is to see them as both dependent on the idea of a 'shared humanity'. In his linguistics this manifests itself in his interest in an innate, human language faculty. In his politics it is evident in his campaigning for equality and human rights.

6 Work in this area has been done by others within the framework Chomsky established. See the 'further reading' section at the end of this chapter for some references to this work.

7 From 'Reply to Putnam' (1969) 302.

8 The innatist account includes a 'critical period for language acquisition', a period in the child's development which naturally ends around the onset of puberty. This, it is claimed, explains the fairly widely accepted fact that the ability to acquire languages deteriorates at about this time.

9 The particular issue of whether language can be said to be unique to humans has been the subject of lengthy and heated debate. For a discussion of the extent to which non-human animals can be said to 'have language', see Chapter 16 of O'Grady *et al.* (1997) *Contemporary Linguistics*. Various attempts have been made to teach animals, particularly apes, to 'use language', and varying degrees of success claimed. For an overview of this debate, and a discussion of its implications, see Jean Aitchison (1989) *The Articulate Mammal*, Chapter 2.

10 Other arguments have been put forward in support of the IH which we have not considered here. For instance, it appears that when, in particular circumstances, two groups of monoglot speakers find that they need a third, common language, a fully complex and rule-governed language, known as a *creole*, appears by the second generation. See Pinker (1995) *The Language Instinct*, Chapter 2, for an outline of the significance of creoles to the IH.

11 Page references are to the article reprinted in Block (1981) 292–9.

12 Chomsky notes that his terms can be likened to Saussure's *langue* and *parole*, but are not identical. Structuralist grammar is a matter of listing, not generating, sentences.

13 Some subsequent discussions of CDS have in fact presented the opposite point of view. Specifically, they have claimed that CDS is specific to certain, Western cultures; it isn't practised at all in many other cultures.

References

Aitchison, Jean (1987) *Words in the Mind*, Oxford: Blackwell.
——(1989) *The Articulate Mammal*, 3rd edn, London: Unwin Hyman [1st edn 1976].
Allwood, Jens, Andersson, Lars-Gunnar and Dahl, Osten (1979) *Logic in Linguistics*, Cambridge: Cambridge University Press.
Austin, John Langshaw (1961) 'Performative utterances', in J. L. Austin (1979) *Philosophical Papers*, 3rd edn, Oxford: Oxford University Press. Reprinted in A. P. Martinich (ed.) (1996) *The Philosophy of Language*, 3rd edn, Oxford: Oxford University Press [1st edn 1985] 120–9.
——(1962) *How to Do Things with Words*, Oxford: Oxford University Press.
Ayer, Alfred (1971) *Language, Truth and Logic*, Harmonsworth: Pelican [1st edn Gollancz 1936].
——(1976) *The Central Questions of Philosophy*, Harmondsworth: Pelican [1st edn Weidenfeld and Nicolson 1973].
Barnes, Jonathan (ed.) (1984) *The Complete Works of Aristotle*, 2 vols, Princeton: Princeton Univesity Press.
Bates, Elizabeth (1976) *Language and Context: The Acquisition of Pragmatics*, New York: Academic Press.
Berkeley, George (1988) *Principles of Human Knowledge*, Harmondsworth: Penguin [1st edn Dublin 1710].
Blakemore, Diane (1994) *Understanding Utterances*, Oxford: Blackwell.
Block, Ned (ed.) (1981) *Readings in the Philosophy of Psychology, Vol. 2*, London: Methuen.
Bloomfield, Leonard (1935) *Language*, London: George Allen & Unwin [1st American edn 1933].
Brown, Penelope and Levinson, Stephen (1978) 'Universals in language useage: politeness phenomena', in E. Goody (ed.) *Questions and Politeness: Strategies in Social Interaction*, Cambridge: Cambridge University Press, 56–311.
Brown, Gillian and Yule, George (1989) *Discourse Analysis*, Cambridge: Cambridge University Press.
Burton-Roberts, Noel (1989) *The Limits to Debate*, Cambridge: Cambridge University Press.
Cann, Ronnie (1993) *Formal Semantics*, Cambridge: Cambridge University Press.
Carnap, Rudolf (1937) *The Logical Syntax of Language*, trans. Amethe Smeaton, London: Kegan Paul [1st German edn 1934].

——(1956) *Meaning and Necessity*, Chicago: University of Chicago Press [1st edn 1947].

Caton, Charles (ed.) (1963) *Philosophy and Ordinary Language*, Urbana: University of Illinois Press.

Chomsky, Noam (1957) *Syntactic Structures*, The Hague: Mouton.

——(1959) 'A review of B. F. Skinner's *Verbal Behavior*', *Language*, 35, 26–58. Reprinted in Jerry Fodor and Jerrold Katz (eds) (1964) *The Structure of Language*, New Jersey: Prentice-Hall, 547–78.

——(1965) *Aspects of the Theory of Syntax*, Cambridge: MIT Press.

——(1966) *Cartesian Linguistics*, New York: Harper & Row.

——(1969) 'Quine's empirical assumptions', in Donald Davidson and Jaakko Hintikka (eds) *Words and Objections*, Dordrecht: Reidel, 53–68.

——(1972) *Studies on Semantics in Generative Grammar*, The Hague: Mouton.

——(1980) *Rules and Representations*, Oxford: Blackwell.

——(1981) 'Reply to Putnam', in N. Block (ed.) (1981) *Readings in Philosophy of Psychology, Vol. 2*, London: Methuen, 300–4.

——(1986) *Knowledge of Language*, New York: Praeger.

Clarke, D. S. Jr (1987) *Principles of Semiotics*, London: Routledge and Kegan Paul.

Davidson, Donald (1967) 'Truth and meaning', *Synthese*, 17, 304–23. Reprinted in Davidson (1984) *Inquiries into Truth and Interpretation*, Oxford: Clarendon Press, 17–36. Reprinted in A. P. Martinich (ed.) (1996) *The Philosophy of Language*, 3rd edn, Oxford: Oxford University Press [1st edn 1985] 92–103.

——(1979) 'Moods and performatives', in Avishai Margalit (ed.) *Meaning and Use*, Dordrecht: Reidel, 9–20.

——(1984) *Inquiries into Truth and Interpretation*, Oxford: Clarendon Press.

Derrida, Jacques (1988) *Limited Inc*, Evanston: Northwestern University Press.

Devitt, Michael and Sterelny, Kim (1987) *Language and Reality*, Oxford: Blackwell.

Donnellan, Keith (1966) 'Reference and definite descriptions', *Philosophical Review*, 75.

Dummett, Michael (1993) *The Seas of Language*, Oxford: Oxford University Press.

Eagleton, Terry (1983) *Literary Theory*, Oxford: Blackwell.

Evans, Gareth (1982) *The Varieties of Reference*, Oxford: Oxford University Press.

Evnine, Simon (1991) *Donald Davidson*, Cambridge: Polity Press.

Fletcher, Paul and Garman, Michael (eds) (1986) *Language Acquisition*, 2nd edn, Cambridge: Cambridge University Press [1st edn 1979].

Fodor, Jerry (1976) *The Language of Thought*, Hassocks: The Harvester Press [1st American edn 1975].

Frawley, William (1992) *Linguistic Semantics*, New Jersey: Lawrence Erlbaum Associates.

Frege, Gottlob (1892) 'On sense and meaning', in Peter Geach and Max Black (eds) (1980) *Translations from the Philosophical Writings of Gottlob Frege*, Oxford: Blackwell [1st edn 1952] 56–78. Reprinted in A. P. Martinich (ed.) (1996) *The Philosophy of Language*, 3rd edn, Oxford: Oxford University Press [1st edn 1985] as 'On sense and nominatum', 186–98.

Gazdar, Gerald (1979) *Pragmatics*, New York: Academic Press.

Geach, Peter and Black, Max (eds) (1980) *Translations from the Philosophical Writings of Gottlob Frege*, Oxford: Blackwell [1st edn 1952].

Gellner, Ernest (1979) *Words and Things: An Examination of, and an Attack on, Linguistic Philosophy*, London: Routledge and Kegan Paul [1st edn 1959].

Glock, Hans-Johann (ed.) (1997) *The Rise of Analytic Philosophy*, Oxford: Blackwell.

Goodluck, Helen (1991) *Language Acquisition*, Oxford: Blackwell.

Goodman, Nelson (1984) *Of Mind and Other Matters*, Cambridge MA: Harvard University Press.

Grice, Paul (1957) 'Meaning', *The Philosophical Review*, 66. Reprinted in Grice (1989) *Studies in the Way of Words*, Cambridge MA: Harvard University Press, 213–23.

——(1958) 'Postwar Oxford philosophy', in Grice (1989) *Studies in the Way of Words*, Cambridge MA: Harvard University Press, 171–180.

——(1975) 'Logic and conversation', in P. Cole and J. L. Morgan (eds) *Syntax and Semantics vol. 9: Pragmatics*, New York: Academic Press. Reprinted in Grice (1989) *Studies in the Way of Words*, Cambridge MA: Harvard University Press, 22–40. Reprinted in A. P. Martinich (ed.) (1996) *The Philosophy of Language*, 3rd edn, Oxford: Oxford University Press [1st edn 1985] 156–67.

——(1978) 'Further notes on logic and conversation', in P. Cole and J. L. Morgan (eds) *Syntax and Semantics vol. 9: Pragmatics*, New York: Academic Press. Reprinted in Grice (1989) *Studies in the Way of Words*, Cambridge MA: Harvard University Press, 41–57.

——(1981) 'Presupposition and conversational implicature', in P. Cole (ed.) *Radical Pragmatics*, New York: Academic Press: 183–99. Reprinted in Grice (1989) *Studies in the Way of Words*, Cambridge MA: Harvard University Press, 269–82.

——(1989) *Studies in the Way of Words*, Cambridge MA: Harvard University Press.

Guttenplan, Samuel (1986) *The Languages of Logic*, Oxford: Blackwell.

Hacking, Ian (1975) *Why Does Language Matter to Philosophy?*, Cambridge: Cambridge University Press.

Haegeman, Liliane (1994) *Introduction to Government and Binding Theory*, 2nd edn, Oxford: Blackwell.

Harris, Roy (1996a) *The Language Connection: Philosophy and Linguistics*, Bristol: Thoemmes.

——(1996b) *Signs, Language and Communication*, London: Routledge.

Hofmann, Thomas (1993) *Realms of Meaning*, London: Longman.

Horn, Laurence (1972) 'On the semantic properties of the logical operators in English', Ph.D. thesis, University of California, Los Angeles.

——(1985) 'Metalinguistic negation and pragmatic ambiguity', *Language*, 61, 121–74.

——(1989) *A Natural History of Negation*, Chicago: University of Chicago Press.

Hurford, James and Heasley, Brendan (1983) *Semantics: A Course Book*, Cambridge: Cambridge University Press.

Jowett, Benjamin (1964) *The Dialogues of Plato*, 4 vols, 4th edn, Oxford: Clarendon Press [1st edn 1871].

Kant, Immanuel (1929) *Critique of Pure Reason*, trans. Norman Kemp Smith, London: Macmillan [1st German edn 1781].

Katz, Jerrold (1972) *Semantic Theory*, New York: Harper and Row.

Kempson, Ruth (1977) *Semantic Theory*, Cambridge: Cambridge University Press.

Kenny, Anthony (ed.) (1994) *The Wittgenstein Reader*, Oxford: Blackwell.

Kripke, Saul (1959) 'A completeness theorem in modal logic', *The Journal of Symbolic Logic*, 24, 1, 1–14.

——(1972) 'Naming and necessity', in D. Davidson and G. Hartmen (eds) *Semantics of Natural Language*, Dordrecht: Reidel. Reprinted in A. P. Martinich (ed.) (1996) *The Philosophy of Language*, 3rd edn, Oxford: Oxford University Press [1st edn 1985] 255–70.

Leech, Geoffrey (1981) *Semantics*, 2nd edn, Harmondsworth: Peguin [1st edn 1974].

——(1983) *Principles of Pragmatics*, New York: Longman.

Leibniz, Gottfried Wilhelm von (1951) *Theodicy*, trans. E. M. Huggard, London: Routledge [1st Latin edn 1710].

——(1981) *New Essays on Human Understanding*, trans. Peter Remnant and Jonathan Bennett, Cambridge: Cambridge University Press [1st French edn 1765].

Levinson, Stephen (1983) *Pragmatics*, Cambridge: Cambridge University Press.

Lewis, David (1973) *Counterfactuals*, Oxford: Blackwell.

Linsky, Leonard (ed.) (1952) *Semantics and the Philosophy of Language*, Illinois: University of Illinois Press.

Locke, John (1993) *An Essay Concerning Human Understanding*, London: Everyman [1st edn 1690].

Lyons, John (1977) *Semantics* (2 vols) Cambridge: Cambridge University Press.

——(1981) *Language, Meaning and Context*, London: Fontana.

——(1995) *Linguistic Semantics*, Cambridge: Cambridge University Press.

Martin, John (1987) *Elements of Formal Semantics*, London: Academic Press.

Martin, Robert (1987) *The Meaning of Language*, Cambridge MA: MIT Press.

Martinich, A. P. (ed.) (1996) *The Philosophy of Language*, 3rd edn, Oxford: Oxford University Press [1st edn 1985].

McEnery, Tony and Wilson, Andrew (1996) *Corpus Linguistics*, Edinburgh: Edinburgh University Press.

McCawley, James (1981) *Everything that Linguists Have Always Wanted to Know about Logic*, Oxford: Blackwell.

Mill, John Stuart (1867) *A System of Logic*, London: Longman.

Montague, Richard (1974) *Formal Philosophy*, New Haven: Yale University Press.

Morris, Charles (1938) 'Foundations of the theory of signs', in O. Neurath, R. Carnap and C. Morris (eds) *International Encyclopaedia of Unified Science*, Chicago: University of Chicago Press: 77–138.

O'Grady, William, Dobrovolsky, Michael and Katamba, Francis (eds) (1997) *Contemporary Linguistics*, 2nd edn, London: Longman [1st edn 1987].

Pinker, Steven (1995) *The Language Instinct*, Harmondsworth: Penguin [1st American edn 1994].

Putnam, Hilary (1967) 'The "Innateness Hypothesis" and explanatory models in linguistics', *Synthesis*, 17, 12–22. Reprinted in N. Block (ed.) (1981) *Readings in the Philosophy of Psychology, Vol. 2*, London: Methuen, 292–9.

Quine, Willard Van Orman (1956) 'Quantifiers and propositional attitudes', *The Journal of Philosophy*, 53, 177–87. Reprinted in A. P. Martinich (ed.) (1996) *The Philosophy of Language*, 3rd edn, Oxford: Oxford University Press [1st edn 1985] 330–6.

——(1960) *Word and Object*, Cambridge MA: MIT Press.

——(1961) *From a Logical Point of View*, Cambridge MA: Harvard University Press [1st edn 1953].

Radford, Andrew (1988) *Transformational Grammar*, Cambridge: Cambridge University Press.

Russell, Bertrand (1905) 'On denoting', *Mind*, 14, 479–99.

——(1919) *Introduction to Mathematical Philosophy*, London: George Allen & Unwin.

——(1940) *An Inquiry into Meaning and Truth*, London: George Allen & Unwin.

——(1957) 'Mr Strawson on referring', *Mind*, 66, 385–9.

——(1978) *Autobiography*, London: George Allen & Unwin [1st edn 1967].

——(1980) *The Problems of Philosophy*, Oxford: Oxford University Press [1st edn 1912].

——(1992) *Human Knowledge*, London: Routledge [1st edn 1948].

Ryle, Gilbert (1953) 'Ordinary language', *The Philosophical Review*, LXII, 167–86. Reprinted in Charles Caton (1963) *Philosophy and Ordinary Language*, Urbana: University of Illinois Press.

——(1957) 'The theory of meaning', in C. A. Mace (ed.) *British Philosophy in the Mid-Century*, London: George Allen & Unwin, 239–64. Reprinted in Charles Caton (ed.) (1963) *Philosophy and Ordinary Language*, Urbana: University of Illinois Press.

Sadock, Jerold (1974) *Towards a Linguistic Theory of Speech Acts*, New York: Academic Press.

Sapir, Edward (1970) *Language*, London: Hart-Davis [1st edn Harcourt, Brace & World 1921].

Saussure, Ferdinand de (1960) *Course in General Linguistics*, trans. Wade Baskin, London: Peter Owen [1st French edn 1915].

Schiffrin, Deborah (1984) *Approaches to Discourse*, Oxford: Blackwell.

Searle, John (1965) 'What is a speech act?', in Max Black (ed.) *Philosophy in America*, London: George Allen & Unwin, 221–39. Reprinted in J. Searle (ed.) (1971) *The Philosophy of Language*, Oxford: Oxford University Press, 39–53. Reprinted in A. P. Martinich (ed.) (1996) *The Philosophy of Language*, 3rd edn, Oxford: Oxford University Press [1st edn 1985] 130–40.

——(1968) 'Austin on locutionary and illocutionary acts', *Philosophical Review*, 57, 405–24.

——(1969) *Speech Acts*, Cambridge: Cambridge University Press.

——(1975) 'Indirect speech acts', in P. Cole and J. L. Morgan (eds) *Syntax and Semantics vol. 9: Pragmatics*, New York: Academic Press, 59–82. Reprinted in John Searle (1979) *Expression and Meaning*, Cambridge: Cambridge University Press, 30–57. Reprinted in A. P. Martinich (ed.) (1996) *The Philosophy of Language*, 3rd edn, Oxford: Oxford University Press [1st edn 1985] 168–81.

——(1977) 'Reiterating the difference: a reply to Derrida', *Glyph*, 1, 198–208.

Seldon, Raman (1989) *Practising Theory and Reading Literature*, London: Harvester Wheatsheaf.

Skinner, Burrhus Frederick (1957) *Verbal Behavior*, New York: Appleton-Century-Crofts.

Smith, Neil and Tsimpli, Ianthi-Maria (1995) *The Mind of a Savant*, Oxford: Blackwell.

Smith, Neil and Wilson, Deirdre (1990) *Modern Linguistics: The Results of Chomsky's Revolution*, Harmondsworth: Penguin [1st edn Pelican 1979].

Sperber, Dan and Wilson, Deirdre (1995) *Relevance*, 2nd edn, Oxford: Blackwell [1st edn 1986].

Stainton, Robert (1996) *Philosophical Perspectives on Language*, Ontario: Broadview.

Stalnaker, Robert (1974) 'Pragmatic presuppositions', in M. Munitz and P. Unger (eds) *Semantics and Philosophy*, New York: New York University Press, 197–213.

Strawson, Peter (1950) 'On referring', *Mind*, 59, 320–44. Reprinted in A. P. Martinich (ed.) (1996) *The Philosophy of Language*, 3rd edn, Oxford: Oxford University Press [1st edn 1985] 215–30.

——(1952) *Introduction to Logical Theory*, London: Methuen.

Tarski, Alfred (1944) 'The semantic conception of truth and the foundations of semantics', *Philosophy and Phenomenological Research*, 4, 341–74. Reprinted in A. P. Martinich (ed.) (1996) *The Philosophy of Language*, 3rd edn, Oxford: Oxford University Press [1st edn 1985] 61–84. Reprinted in L. Linsky (ed.) (1952) *Semantics and the Philosophy of Language*, Illinois: University of Illinois Press, 13–47.

Thomas, Jenny (1995) *Meaning in Interaction*, London: Longman.

van der Sandt, Rob (1988) *Context and Presupposition*, London: Croom Helm.

Vendler, Zeno (1972) *Res Cogitans*, Ithaca: Cornell University Press.

Whorf, Benjamin Lee (1956) *Language, Thought and Reality*, Cambridge MA: MIT Press.

Wilson, Deirdre (1975) *Presuppositions and Non-Truth-Conditional Semantics*, London: Academic Press.

Wittgenstein, Ludwig (1922) *Tractatus Logico-Philosophicus*, trans. C. K. Ogden, London: Routledge and Kegan Paul.

——(1958) *Philosophical Investigations*, trans. G. E. M. Anscombe, Oxford: Blackwell [1st edn 1953].

Index